Critter Costuming

Making Mascots and Fabricating Fursuits

by Adam Riggs

Ibexa Press

Critter Costuming:
Making Mascots and Fabricating Fursuits

Copyright © 2004 Adam Riggs

Executive Editor: Dawn Devine ~Davina.

Assistant Editors: Christine Schoedel, Brian Hagen, Tim Baverstock, Peggy McCloghrie, Brian Underwood.

2011 reformat and cover layout by Jerry Case

Ibexa Press

Find us on the web at www.ibexa.com.

To report errors, please send a note to errata@ibexa.com.

Trademarks

Many of the designations used by manufacturers and sellers to distinguish their products are claimed as trademarks. Ibexa Press has made every effort to include trademark information where relevent. All products named are used in an editorial fashion only and for the benefit of such companies.

Notice of Liability

The information in this book is distributed on an "as is" basis, without warranty. Although every precaution has been taken in the preparation of this book, neither the author nor publisher shall have any liability to any person or entity with respect to any loss or damage caused or alleged to be caused directly or indirectly by the instructions contained in this book.

ISBN-13: 978-0615584232 (Ibexa Press)
ISBN-10: 0615584233

Dedication

This book is dedicated to my wonderful parents who didn't laugh too hard when I announced that I wanted to build giant furry animal costumes.

Special Thanks To

Special thanks to my editor, contributing writer, and co-publisher Dawn Devine ~ Davina, who inspired me to create this book. Special thanks also go to my loving wife Beth for her invaluable support during this undertaking.

This book would not be possible without help from all of the designers, costumers, and professional mascots who contributed their time and talents to the project.

Finally, thanks go out to my photographer and co-publisher Barry Brown; editors and proofreaders Janice Riggs, Brian Underwood, and Beth Riggs; many supportive fellow costumers and supportive friends: Anthony Bianca, Jonathan Decker, Robert Durden, Paul Fritsche, Paul Groulx, Chris Horne, Ashley Kitto, Freddy Praul, Glen Rockhill, Sean Rook, Tony Spangler, Dale Trexel, and Steve Yurk. Finally, thanks to my present and future readers for continuing to support this book.

Costume and Photo Credits

Photos by Barry Brown unless otherwise specified.

Archie, by Gill Wichi.
25, 43, 189 (middle). Photos by Tor.

Blobulous, by Dennis Lancaster.
34 (middle). Photo by Tor.

Blooper, by Tony DeMatio & Jimmy Chin.
9, 19, 42, 102, 106, 107, 117, 189 (top), 193, back cover.

Blue Raccoon, by Adam Riggs.
Appears throughout the book.

Chairo, by Lee Strom.
19, 23, 27, 80, 93, 100, 106, 171, front cover.

Charmichael, by David Cooksey.
15, 172, 199, back cover.

Collie Dog, by Lance Ikegawa
80. Photo courtesy of Lance Ikegawa.

Dangerous Dinos, by Dennis Lancaster.
24 (bottom), 109. Photos courtesy of Dennis Lancaster.

DarkFang, by Mike McKiernan.
59, 104, 107, 134, 141 (top), 144 (detail), 163, front cover.

Davina the Tiger Dancer, by Dawn Devine.
31, 147.

Detail of fursuit, by Lance Ikegawa.
56. Photo courtesy of Lance Ikegawa.

Dizzy, by Chris Trahman.
11, 80, 106, 115, 116, 128, 191, back cover.

Fox, by Lance Ikegawa.
80. Photo courtesy of Lance Ikegawa.

Grandpa Bunny, by Dennis Lancaster.
108. Photo courtesy of Dennis Lancaster.

Hug-E-Bear, by Mark Murillo.
29. Photo by Tor.

Humbolt, by Gill Wichi and Eric Yee.
51. Photo by Tor.

Hyena, by Lance Ikegawa.
127. Courtesy of Lance Ikegawa.

Juggling Mouse, by Adam Riggs.
28, 105 (top), 135, 173.

Kayle the Party Shark, by Dennis Lancaster.
34 (top), 105 (middle). Photos by Tor.

Marrok, by Gary Allen.
140. Photo by Tor.

Narina, Indian Tigress, by Peggy McCloghrie.
33, 145, 147.

Noodles, by Richard Halliday.
45.

Oshin, byLance Ikegawa.
130. Courtesy of Lance Ikegawa.

Paw detail, by Lance Ikegawa.
141 (middle). Courtesy of Lance Ikegawa.

Polka-Dog, by Jimmy Chin.
59, 138, 175, 175, 177, 184, 189, 195, 196, 197, front cover.

Realis – Dog of War, by Lance Ikegawa.
21, 125. Courtesy of Lance Ikegawa.

Safari Tiger, by Beth Riggs.
33, 147, 153.

Shenandoah, by Lance Ikegawa.
107, 126, 131, 157, 190. Courtesy of Lance Ikegawa.

Terra Luna, by Richard Halliday.
77, 80, 142 (detail).

Thomas, by Lee "Chairo" Strom.
80, 106, 107, 174, 189, 100.

Violet, by Brian Hagen.
80, 186, 187. Photos by Tor.

Wild Dog, by Lance Ikegawa.
24 (top), 80. Courtesy of Lance Ikegawa.

Yowly, by Gill Wichi.
34 (bottom). Photo by Tor.

Ysengrin, by Wolf Corlett.
80, 105 (bottom), 142 (detail), 162, 163, 173, back cover.

Table of Contents

Introduction

If you picked up this book, it probably means that you either think you might want to make an animal costume, you know you want to make an animal costume, or you badly misread the title. If you're in the first category, I hope you'll move to the second category as we look at different designs, tools, and techniques for making your own costume. If you're in the third category, well, you're already reading this, so you might as well give it a shot, right? It's time to get in touch with your fuzzier side!

We begin by examining the design process for a costume. The instructions will walk you through generating a unique character idea, adapting it to the realities of costume design, and the artistic decisions involved.

We then examine the wide variety of tools and techniques available to the costumer. There are so many different approaches to different costuming situations that it would be impossible to cover everything in a single book or, even, a shelf of books. So we try to give a broad overview of the possibilities while focusing on some specific techniques that I've found useful and which can be easily learned.

But building a costume isn't merely a technical endeavor. We can't overlook the importance of the performance skills that bring the character to life! The last part of this book provides tips for developing the character after the physical costume is finished.

Why are we interested in making animal costumes? The process of designing and building your own costume from scratch can be a lot of fun. It is a form of artistic expression and can therefore be a great way to engage your creative side. There are also the varied uses for costumes: mascots, performing characters, advertising, charity events, Halloween costumes, theater work, and more.

I can only speak for myself when I say that the best thing is the happiness that costume characters can create. That's something special in this world and something that I hope to share with you through this book.

Part I

Design and Planning

Costuming is an exciting endeavor, especially for new artists. This part covers the genesis of any costume project: the design of the character and planning of the project.

The first step in creating a costume is to design the character. It's important to get a clear vision for the character before beginning construction. It's also important to understand how and where the costume will be used, as this will affect the design.

Your costume might be based on an original character or an interpretation of an existing character. Either way, you need to plan out the project. Once the design is complete, you can determine what techniques are best for your costume and what materials will be required. This will help you estimate the cost of your project and plan your budget.

1 • Your First Costume

Maybe this is your first attempt at making a costume. Perhaps you're looking at this book trying to decide if you can really do this. My advice: "Try it!"

Anyone with the time and inclination can put together a costume. The fact that you're reading this book shows that you already have the interest and motivation. Sure, your first costume might not turn out exactly the way you imagined; but if you don't even try, it's certain that it won't turn out at all. This book can help guide you through the process.

Many of the skills in costuming are best learned by doing them. Books like this one can help by providing information about techniques, materials, tools and safety information. No matter if you are a beginner to a master craftsman in the field, the actual skills of costuming are learned through personal effort and experience. The only way to get this experience is to try it! For your first project, remember that old formula, KISS—Keep it Super Simple! Select a critter with simple shapes, markings, and body proportions to make your first project less difficult. At the beginning, every step of the design and construction process will be a learning experience. As you progress, you'll develop your own preferences for materials, styles, and techniques. Just remember, part of the craft of costuming is improvisation!

Managing Expectations, Managing Time

I won't lie to you: costuming can involve difficult work and long hours. Don't let these be barriers! Although a single costume may take a lot of time, the patience pays off, with an enjoyable and challenging experience. The whole process challenges you to express your creativity in new ways and to develop new skills.

Set aside time to work on your costume, perhaps one day on the weekend or several hours during specific weeknights. I generally don't schedule a time block shorter than two hours for costume work, since some of the processes take a long time; once you're in the groove, it's easier to keep going for a while. Although it may not be quick and easy, making your first costume can be very rewarding.

Starting Simple

When working on your first costume, try to set reasonable project goals. Don't try to create a photorealistic werewolf as your very first foray into the field. Choose a costume project that's not too complicated or overly detailed. Before you begin the design process, evaluate your skills in arts and crafts. Unlike most ordinary costume styles, critter costumes tap a wide variety of talents. If possible, leverage crafting skills that you already have. This will put part of the project in familiar territory. Or, have you done leatherworking? Consider a character wearing a leather outfit or an abstract leather mask. Are you experienced with assembling models? Perhaps a framework head would be better than a carved head.

Chapter 1

Don't expect your first costume to be perfect. In fact, after all these years I've yet to build a perfect costume! There are always some minor mistakes and flaws; usually these are overlooked by other viewers. However minor, flaws always stand out like a sore thumb to the artist who built it! For your first, second and even third costumes, try not to be too hard on yourself. You will probably using new materials, tools and techniques. Expect there to be a learning curve for learning how to build critter costumes. Remember to be flexible! As you work you will make minor mistakes and last-minute changes to your design. This is normal; I've never known anyone whose first costume turned out exactly as planned. This is just part of learning to be a costumer.

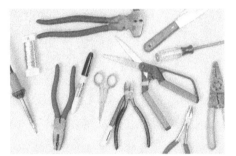

A collection of costuming tools.

Acquiring Good Tools

If you're serious about costuming and plan to make money at it, I urge you to invest in high-quality tools. When you set out to build your first costume you are also beginning the process of equipping your workshop. Purchasing tools is an investment and can be quite expensive. Do not include the cost of buying tools as part of the expense of your first costume. During your first costume project, you'll probably have to purchase quite a few tools.

With tools, it's definitely true that you get what you pay for. Cheap tools will last through only one or two projects before they need replacement. It makes sense to buy durable tools and make your investment last. Higher quality tools are usually easier to use, prevent injury and strain, and improve the quality of your work. If you want to save money during your first project, I would advise you to buy fewer tools rather than inferior tools. That way, should you decide to continue making costumes, the tools you've purchased will have been worthwhile investments. Planning here can quickly pay dividends. See Chapter 5 for more detailed information on the tools you will need and how to set up your workspace.

Estimating Costs

Once you've completed your design for the costume and know what materials you will be using, it's a good idea to estimate the total cost of the project. This is trickier than it sounds. Unless you've built costumes using the same techniques, it's difficult to know how efficiently you can use the materials and what extra supplies may have been forgotten. You can compensate for this with conservative overestimation. I always like to factor this in, even when I think I know what I'm doing. Factoring in a margin of 10% to 25% over the estimated budget will create a cushion in case you need to spend more.

If you're working for a client, estimation skills are critical. They will need a cost estimate up front. This is usually based on a formula that includes the estimated material costs plus a fee for labor. Unless the client agrees to a flexible price, any mistakes in your estimation will translate into lost profits. By the time you are working for others, you will be familiar with your skills and better able to judge what materials will be used in the production of the costume. If you work as part of a theatre group or costume company, estimation is an important skill. Being able to estimate costume costs reliably will be good for your reputation and may forestall some hard questions when budgeting for the next production.

Robert King

Robert King became involved in costuming as an amateur enthusiast. He has since helped to organize fursuit discussion forums and events. He was a founder of Midwest FurFest, a convention for fans of animal characters and costumes.

How did you get started in costuming?

In college, I went to my first sci-fi convention. At the time, I was very inspired by the *Ghostbusters* movie. I looked at the costumes and figured I could fairly easily make one, with overalls and the backpack. So I wore it around and I got terrific feedback! People would applaud sometimes when they saw me! So I was hooked, both on the ego boost of a well-received costume and the fun of making it.

Later, as I became more interested in anthropomorphic characters, I became fascinated with designing character faces that combine human and animal aspects in an aesthetically pleasing fashion. I started working in that direction with my costumes.

Did you originally coin the term "fursuit"?

Yes, as far as I know, that's right. In 1993, I was on a plane back from a fan convention which featured costumes. I was chatting with a friend next to me about the need for an amateur costumers' mailing list -- a place to discuss and share ideas and techniques. There wasn't any informal distribution channel available to hobbyist costumers at the time.

In this discussion about putting an email list together, I needed a name. We were primarily interested in making furry animal costumes, so I attached the words "fur" and "suit" together to make a word that described our costumes; it was also a pun on the word "pursuit", meaning hobby. So originally it was only intended to be the name of a mailing list, but people naturally adopted it as a slang term for the costumes themselves.

What factor is most important to the quality of a costume, however you might define "quality?"

The sculpting and shaping of it. I approach costuming from an art perspective. When I make costumes I try to alter the shape of my body. The blending of animal and human shapes can be very interesting.

I primarily focus on the construction process. I see costumes as a sort of opportunity to create living sculpture. Performance has never been my strong suit and I prefer to focus on the construction. I don't as often perform for kids since I think of my costumes more as artistic works; I don't want peanut butter all over something I put so much time into, if you know what I mean.

What are the biggest costuming challenges you've faced?

Overall, I'd say it's the variety of skills that I've had to master in the process: sculpting, plaster work, fabrics, latex, mold making, metalwork, and so forth. The interdisciplinary aspect of the craft is challenging. I don't want it to sound too scary to beginners; really, part of the fun is developing all of these new talents.

What one piece of advice would you give to a beginning costumer that you wish you had received?

Do it! Don't spend too much time planning and worrying. Many people get caught in "analysis paralysis." It's better to just do it wrong three times and then get it right than to sit around and not do it at all. You learn by trying it.

Also don't worry too much if the costume doesn't look good while you're building it. Many times a costume will look terrible right up until the last moment! Don't get discouraged by this. Sometimes, in the end, it just takes sheer force of will to pull it off!

2 • Creating a Character

Getting Started

You may already know what character you want to create: you've either developed your own idea for a costume or you've been asked to fabricate a representation of an existing character. But what if you don't have a character in mind? You might be planning to make a costume for a specific event, as an artistic experiment, or just to have the ultimate Halloween costume you always wanted! It's possible that you want to create a costume and just don't have a clear idea yet. How do you get started? Where do you begin?

A little inspiration is all you need to begin designing a new character. Look for something that appeals to you or stirs some sort of emotional reaction. Maybe you have a favorite animal? Perhaps you want to create a character that exemplifies some trait? Grab your inspiration and see where it leads; once you've found a starting place, it's just a matter of developing that until you have a complete design.

During the initial brainstorming process, you will probably come up with far too many ideas to fit into one costuming project. Don't be afraid to abandon ideas either. Ideas that initially seem good may fall apart when you start fleshing out a full character. Such is the way of inspiration. The key is to be able to let go of ideas that don't work and to keep looking for the ones that do.

What's in a name?

Most people name their character during the design phase. Either the costume is based upon an existing character or some part of the personality seems to inspire a name. I've never been very good at naming my characters, often waiting until after the costume construction is complete before doing so. Whenever you choose to christen your character, here are some points to consider.

Choosing a Unique Name – If your character is meant to be distinctive and unusual, choose a name which reflects that. Try putting together words and syllables to create an interesting moniker that says something about the personality, species, or history of your character. Do your best to check that your planned name is not already used by another mascot or cartoon character.

When creating an original name, try to keep it pronounceable. Think about it this way: If you hand out business cards at one of your performances, would they recognize it as a name and be able to say it correctly?

Choosing a Generic Name – The opposite approach is to assign a common first name to your character. Maybe your character just seems like a "Tommy" to you. Nothing says you can't choose a simple name! This will be particularly popular if your character is interacting with little kids since the name will be easy and familiar to them.

The common tendency with generic names is to make the first name alliterative with the character's species. I recommend avoiding this just because it is so heavily overused. If you really do want to create a generic mascot name, though, that is how to do it.

Animal: Selecting a Species
Does one of the following critters catch your fancy?

Wolf	Bear	Mouse	Fox	Cat
Cheetah	Tiger	Kangaroo	Dog	Werewolf
Unicorn	Teddy Bear	Rat	Turtle	Cow
Raccoon	Lizard	Skunk	Hawk	Dragon
Koala	Crocodile	Bat	Bumblebee	Moose
Dragonfly	Chicken	Minotaur	Panda	Toad
Rabbit	Otter	Badger	Lion	Gazelle
Zebra	Ibex	Flamingo	Aardvark	Hyena

Attitude: Selecting a Mood
How about a word describing your character's personality?

Friendly	Beguiling	Oblivious	Timid	Cute
Athletic	Speedy	Clever	Mischievous	Sleek
Clumsy	Sneaky	Evil	Intelligent	Sexy
Scary	Spooky	Cool	Intense	Confident
Bashful	Coy	Vain	Proud	Sad
Nervous	Intimidating	Fierce	Grumpy	Silly
Serious	Snooty	Flamboyant	Indignant	Brave

Shape: Selecting Body Characteristics
Does your character fit into a specific physical mold?

Tall	Spiky	Gaunt	Muscular	Slender
Segmented	Rotund	Winged	Lithe	Fluid
Chunky	Insectoid	Fluffy	Compact	Soft
Smooth	Sleek	Bulbous	Voluptuous	Scaly
Wooly	Tufted	Short	Old	Fuzzy
Gangly	Reptilian	Feathery	Chisled	Dumpy
Sinewy	Slippery	Buff	Fit	Stout
Angular	Curvey	Awkward	Small	Squishy

Don't be afraid to mix and match species, attitudes and shapes. Some of the most memorable characters have been created by taking very contrasting characteristics and blending them. Who could forget Mighty Mouse?

Start a Notebook

Get a small notebook or sketchbook and start a costume diary to keep track of your ideas and progress. Take some time to make some simple sketches of your character—not necessarily the whole character, but different parts that you visualize especially clearly. You can focus on assembling these into a cohesive whole. Later, you can develop these bits and pieces into more complete sketches and then ultimately translate these 2-D drawings into the 3-D costume. Try to keep your notebook handy. You never know when inspiration will strike!

Your notebook will become the bible for your costume. It is the best place for keeping track of plans and materials. As you work on the design, make notes about any particular techniques or materials you want to use, either for the costume itself or for props. Record any ideas about presentation or accessories that might add personality to your character. As you experiment with new materials or products, write down their names, how you used them, and their effectiveness. This sort of background information is useful not only for the current project, but also for future works.

"I Can't Draw!"

This is a common cry of costumers when faced with the prospect of making detailed character sketches. Don't worry! You don't need to be an expert artist to make useful sketches. The goal is not to create a masterful rendering of your character, but to produce a simple and practical reference for construction. Even if you feel you can't draw, I encourage you to give it a try. There are many excellent books on drawing that can help you develop your sketching technique.

Instead of a perspective sketch of your character, you may find it easier to draw plan views; in animation. It's called a model sheet. First, draw simple line drawings of the profile and front view of the head. Then try to draw out the whole character, showing a front, back and side view.

Why is it so important to draw your character? For beginning costumers, it can be a great way to focus on the different parts of the character's anatomy. As you draw each part of the character, you can focus on the shape and proportion. How should the feet look? How wide are the hips? These kinds of design questions are naturally answered through the drawing process.

Additionally, a good outline drawing of the character gives you a chance to check your planned color scheme. Include lines for the color boundaries or markings, allowing you to see the overall proportions of different colors on the body of the costume. Experiment with moving the color borders at this stage until you're happy with the marking patterns and the way the dominant and subordinate colors balance. Use markers to color your drawing so that it matches the materials you plan to use.

Keep a notebook of sketches when developing costume ideas. These are some of the early concept drawings for the blue raccoon built in subsequent chapters and shown below.

You might find inspiration in your household pet!

Reference Artwork

Working on animal costumes requires reference materials. Collect photographs, drawings, and artwork featuring your selected animal. If possible, look for artwork that depicts anthropomorphic versions, so that you can get a feel for how the animal's shape might be adapted to a human frame. If you're creating a costume of a specific existing character, finding reference art shouldn't be a problem. If you end up with loose pieces of artwork, paste them into your notebook for safe-keeping. If you are using digital references, keep a folder of images on a machine easily accessible from your workspace.

Developing the Character Concept

Once you have a basic inspiration for the character, it must be developed into a full-fledged character description. The more work you do visualizing the character, the easier it will be to construct and perform it. Consider what your character looks like from all angles. After all, you have to build every side of the costume! What does the back of your character's head look like? How about the sides of its legs? It often takes quite a bit of drawing and reworking to get a concept to actually look right yet still be practical.

What makes your character unique? Suppose that you want a wolf costume. There are lots of wolf costumes already in existence. Numerous companies will happily sell you a generic-looking wolf costume. But you don't want a commonplace wolf suit; that's why you're embarking on this project! Instead, you need to develop a genuine wolf character that will set you apart from the crowd (er, "pack"). Putting work into developing the personality of the character, as well as the physical aspects of a costume, helps to open up artistic possibilities. Investing time now will be rewarded later by easier construction, quicker builds, and characters that are fun to play!

What personalities do each of these drawings suggest to you?

Utilizing Archetypes

Archetypes are the different roles for characters you commonly see. Comics and animation can be an excellent source of inspiration in this area. Representations of prototypical traits through physical aspects have developed as a form of "visual shorthand."

Consider glasses. If you see a cartoon character with glasses, do you form an impression about his or her personality? Generally, glasses have come to represent intelligence, either as the wise elder or the young nerd.

Teeth are often used to imply mental traits. Large flat teeth, especially at the front of the mouth, tend to show lower intelligence. Fangs descending from the upper lip represent a vicious character while such teeth rising from the lower lip represent a witless brute.

Even something as simple as the placement of the eyes relative to the other facial features can vastly change the impressions people form. Sketch out your character idea with some different facial proportions to experiment. Does one seem to better express the personality you're seeking?

These are just a few examples of archetypal features. You can use these to your advantage when designing your character to impart information to the viewer before they even see you act.

If you stretch these too far, they can quickly become stereotypes. This can be good or bad, depending on how you want to portray the character. My advice is to use these traits subtly enough that people won't think it too "obvious."

Questions for Your Character

Here are some questions to help you further develop your character concepts. Visualize yourself as your character as you answer these questions. Put yourself into your character's shoes, metaphorically speaking. (We'll get to the literal aspect of shoes in a later chapter.)

Some questions may have an immediate response. This is fine, as it means that you've got a clear idea of that aspect of your character. Others may be something you'd never considered. Ponder different possibilities before settling on an answer. Once you do have an answer, though, remember it for later.

Are you furry? Is your fur long, short, or varied?

Do you wear glasses? How about sunglasses?

Do you have a long muzzle?

What colors are you? Any unusual coat markings?

Do you wear clothes at all? What do you wear?

How about shoes?

What color are your eyes?

How old are you? Is your age physically apparent?

What color is your nose?

Do you have hair? What color is it?

What sorts of hats would you be likely to wear?

Do you carry a cane? How about an umbrella?

Do you wear a watch?

Do you have a moustache?

Do you carry around sports equipment?

Do you have a tail? Is it carried upright or hanging down?

Are you a fighter? Do you carry a weapon? Is it comical or realistic?

Do you have large ears?

Do you wear a scarf? How about a bandanna? Or a sash?

Do you wear any jewelry? A pendant? Earrings? A bracelet?

How many fingers do you have on each hand?

Are you from an historical time period? Do you wear period clothes?

Do you wear a collar? Does it have a tag on it?

Do you wear a tie? Straight or bow tie?

Do you sport bells, bangles, or some source of noise?

Do you carry a backpack, satchel, or bag?

Are you from a specific culture? What do you wear to reflect that?

Do you have a job? Do you carry any tools of your trade?

Do you wear a uniform?

Are you disabled?

Chairo has many attributes that give his character a unique personality. Not only does he have a charming face, but he wears clothes and uses props to define his character.

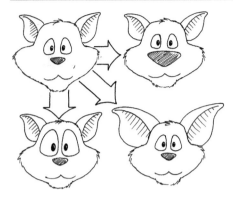

Placing emphasis on a single feature can change the feel of a character. Try sketching different variations of your concept as an experiment.

Balance and Selective Exaggeration

At this point, I hope you have a bunch of great ideas about how to represent your character. Before the design is really finished we need to sort these ideas into a cohesive whole. A collection of traits and descriptions is *almost* a character; we can't call it a finished character until we make some decisions about the relative significance of different features.

A character needs a certain visual balance to be successful. When someone sees your costume for the first time, it needs to be a cohesive whole and not simply a jumble. If we put a lot of character touches together as a collection of equal parts, it turns into visual clutter. If you were to choose too many things from the above lists, it would be a mess. Keep it simple!

When a costume is overdone, people aren't sure what they should look at first! Too many ideas can collide. The mind doesn't know what's significant, which results in confused impressions.

Conquer this problem by exaggerating one important aspect of the character. There needs to be one salient feature that creates a first impression. The rest of the traits you've chosen are then balanced with respect to it.

What you exaggerate should say something about your character, either by utilizing the archetype concepts above or literally accentuating the animal qualities. A large muzzle might emphasize the shape of a wolf's head. Large pink ears are iconic features for mice. Sports paraphernalia and a jersey would be good for a team mascot. Emphasize what you want observers to use when forming their first impression.

An exaggerated aspect doesn't need to be a single feature, either; it could be a design element running throughout the costume. Striking color schemes or unusual flashy outfits can grab attention. Huge teeth and bony spikes might be good features to emphasize for a vicious dragon.

The key is to keep in mind the visual balance of the character. During the design process, occasionally try to step back and see the character as if for the first time. Does it make sense? Does it give a feel for the character? Do the most important qualities of the character jump out at you?

Remove details that aren't contributing to the character if the image seems too busy. Change the shape or location of features that seem lost. You can use color contrast to draw the eyes to important features. Don't be afraid to keep reworking the character if it isn't yet right; it's easier to do it now than once you've started building it!

Color Palette

A final though very important design decision is thecolors to use. This is something that's highly specific to individual characters, so it's difficult to offer design rules suitable for everyone. These are guidelines I use in most of my designs.

Availability – Fur is a difficult material to dye. If you don't want to deal with dyeing, look at the colors of fur available for order. This limits your choices of both unique and subtle colors.

Number of Colors – You want to avoid mixing too many furs and creating a color explosion. On the other hand, using only one color can make the costume's features seem flat. I recommend two contrasting colors, or three colors if one color is black or white. Four-color schemes work in cases where color and contrast are an exaggerated feature.

Blending – Do the different colors blend together or have distinct dividing lines? Blending creates a more natural appearance; sharp boundaries create a cartoon appearance.

Contrast – You can choose colors that are complementary or similar to create different effects. Contrast creates more visual interest and can highlight physical shapes and contours. Similar colors or different shades of a color can create more subtle markings and shadowing.

Finishing the Design

Once you have reached this point, you might figure that you've finished the design for your character and are ready to start building. Unless you're an experienced costumer, though, you might find that you have overlooked some of the practical aspects of design. What you likely have created is an idealized design.

In the next couple of chapters we'll study how to adapt designs for different purposes and environments. After these final considerations, you should have a finished design!

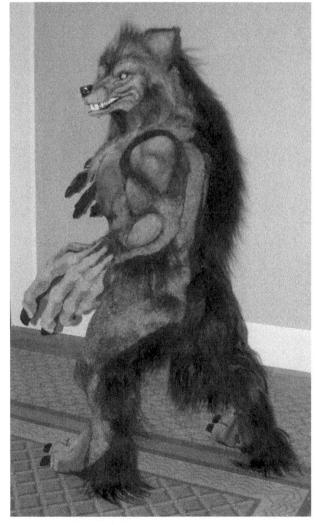

Notice how the definition of the musculature and primary features are emphasized through contrasting color and texture.

3 • Design Considerations

At this point, you should have a solid concept for your design. In developing this, you've been invoking imagination and creativity to create an idealized vision of your character. But the most beautiful and fanciful costume designs are often the least practical to construct and perform. The trick now is to inject a necessary degree of pragmatism into the design without losing the magic you've put into the character.

Part of the design process is planning the materials and construction details necessary to realize your character. Ideally, this won't change the design of the character itself. Experience with costuming and the materials involved will help you in this regard.

Sometimes, unfortunately, concessions must be made. Materials implied by the character design might not be available, durable enough, workable, or affordable. In such cases, it's necessary to alter the design to use materials that meet all of your project requirements.

This chapter focuses specifically on adapting designs for different performance requirements. How you plan to use a costume may force changes in either construction plans or materials. With some creativity, experimentation, and practice you should be able to adapt the design to different project requirements without losing the underlying essence of the character.

Designing for the Venue

There are many different reasons why you might want to build an animal costume. I won't even try to enumerate all of the possible uses for costumes! What is important is that you identify how a suit will be used when planning the project to avoid surprises later.

In your design notebook, write a description of how you think the costume will be used. Try to make the list as broad as possible, thinking of potential performance opportunities that might arise after the costume is completed.

Most costumes are designed to suit a broad range of general performance requirements. In creating your own costume, you have a chance to tailor the design to your specific purposes.

Adapting a character concept to construction considerations often means trading off realism in favor of practicality. By pinning down performance requirements during the design phase, you can know precisely where and how a design may need to be adapted. This extra knowledge allows you to create a costume that is optimized for a specific use. For example, a stage costume is very different from a walkabout mascot. This means that you can create the best realization of the character concept possible for the given circumstances.

Stage Performance

If you are designing a costume specifically for stage use, you can tailor your design to the venue. For example, the audience is at a known distance from the costume. Unlike designing a mascot for close public interaction, this gives

Chapter 3

you some leeway in the details; minor points of seaming and painting are not likely to be visible to the audience.

The fact that details cannot be seen is also a disadvantage. All significant character features must be large enough to be observed from the audience's viewpoint. Shapes and forms need to be exaggerated. Small details need to employ high contrast colors for extra visibility.

A second aspect of stage performance is that the costumes can have more limited vision, if that makes it easier to build. Vision is a perpetual design problem when creating fully-enclosed costume heads. Since stage performances are scripted and all of the actors have predetermined marks, good vision is less important and may be sacrificed to improve the appearance of the costume.

Finally, since performances will be strictly scheduled, the costume can be intricate to put on and take off. Depending on the troupe, it may be acceptable to design a costume that requires assistance to don; extra hands can be arranged to assist the costumed performer(s). Although it might sound counterintuitive at first, it can be easier to build a suit, especially for large creatures, where the performer cannot put it on without help.

Film and Television

Designing animal costumes or makeup effects for film and television is a very specialized trade. The level of detail required for work in this arena is beyond all but the most experienced costumers. Specialized (and often quite expensive) materials are used to create the ultra-realistic costume effects required for close camerawork.

Costume design for film and television work is really part of the special effects industry. However, many of the fundamental design principles presented here still apply. The exotic construction techniques extend beyond what can be covered in this book. Consult the appendix for other literature which may cover the specifics of film effects.

Outdoor Public Venues

Some of the most common places to use costumes are outdoor venues: team mascots at sporting events, characters at parks, mascots at company events, entertainers at children's parties, etc. More than likely you will be designing costumes for at least some outdoor use. Fortunately, this shouldn't place many restrictions on your designs.

The first thing to consider on costumes for outdoor use is the soles of the feet. These need to be tough and durable. Whereas leather pads or slipper feet might be fine for indoor use, vulcanized rubber soles should be used on any outdoor costume feet. The easiest way to incorporate durable soles is to build the costume feet directly on top of old sneakers.

Similarly, be careful with any dangling portions of the costume which might touch the ground. The most common example of this would be a hanging tail. In such cases, use a durable material and expect discoloration as that part of the costume picks up dirt. Avoid elaborate coloration or soluble glues which would prevent frequent washings.

Indoor Public Venues

Malls and trade show floors are common indoor venues where a costumed character might be interacting with the public. Indoor crowds are generally denser than outdoor crowds, so vision is especially important here. Even with handlers to assist, the performer must be able to see the people with whom they are interacting in order to perform effectively.

Since these types of suits are generally designed for personal interaction with the crowd, it's important that the costume look good up close. Figure that people will get within one foot of the face of the costume head; keep this guideline in mind during construction. Make sure that construction details or other flaws which might spoil the illusion are not obvious from one foot away.

In a crowd situation, people will also see the costume from all angles. Don't neglect the back of the head and body in your design!

Private Venues

Ah, Halloween parties! These and other private events can be fun locations for a costume performance. Here you have an advantage in that the crowd is probably friendly towards you. On the other hand, don't expect people to appreciate all of your detail work unless you're at an event with other costumers. The effort that you put into the fine points of your costume will still contribute to the overall impression it makes, though, so the time spent is worthwhile.

Be careful about parties, clubs, or other indoor environments with low lights. Many costume eyes rely on screens or mesh to hide the actor's eyes; this also has the effect of reducing the visible light reaching the inside, similar to putting on a pair of sunglasses. Try to design your head so that it has good vision.

Venues with Children

Creating costumes that appeal to children requires special design skills. Children view and react to costumes differently than adults. Designing your character for a venue with children requires both knowledge of what they would like to see in a costume and how to safely bring such a character to life.

Audience Age Groups

Depending on the age group of the target audience, you can adapt designs in different ways. For younger kids, it's very important that the character appears friendly and non-threatening. Anything scary may frighten them to the point that they don't want to meet the character. (Imagine being approached by an unknown furry thing three times taller than yourself. No wonder they hide!)

Kids between six and ten years old tend to be more receptive to costumes. You can give your characters more expression and detail. Familiar, non-threatening animals are appealing to this age group. You can also design "evil" characters that have a menacing yet unrealistic appearance; study popular cartoon villains for ideas inspiration.

Above age ten, the way in which children react to costumed characters becomes more unpredictable. Boys may begin to resist characters that are too cute or "childish." In their pre-teens, they will usually avoid them since being seen with a cartoony character would be uncool. This behavior emerges mostly in groups, though; one on one, they might really like the character.

Girls still tend to enjoy costumes, though they usually prefer something more than a simple cartoon character. All children at this age begin to look for more sophisticated design in their costumes, moving away from simple children's characters towards the sorts of costumes appreciated by adults.

If you're uncertain about how to tailor a costume design towards a particular age group, examine popular toys. Note the recurring shapes, colors, and elements you see. Extrapolate from these factors to determine what might make a costume appeal to your target age group.

Character Facial Expression

In my experience, the primary factor in how a character is perceived by young kids is the facial expression. A menacing, or even neutral, expression will not encourage interaction. The character absolutely must have a happy or benign expression when working with very young audiences.

The addition of eyelids and eyebrows can create strong expressions.

From a technical standpoint, this can be accomplished by having large and colorful eyes. Cartoon eyes without eyelids will look very active and alert. You can tone down this expression by adding lids, either added as a layer over the eyes or painted onto the eye surface. For a sympathetic character, make the eyelids near the tops of the eyes and slope the lids slightly up towards the center.

If the character has eyebrows, place them well above the eyes. Resting them on top of the eyes allows them to overshadow the eyes and create a glowering expression when the head is low and tilted downwards. Eyebrows that arch and are higher on the inner edge than outer edge will create an inquisitive or alert expression. Eyebrows that are evenly arched and well above the eyes create a startled or surprised expression.

I think that mouths should be smiling on children's characters. Make the smile obvious and exaggerated, lifting the corners of the mouth up and back. Often the smile will extend out onto the front of the cheeks in an impossibly wide grin.

Teeth and Claws

If the character has its mouth open, it would seem natural to give the character teeth. Exposed fangs definitely make the character appear more vicious and threatening. Depending on your target audience, this can be good or bad for your design. Bared teeth can be frightening to very young kids but seem cool to older kids.

This facial sketch shows an exaggerated smile with a "solid grin" design. The teeth can be created as a single piece.

One compromise is to use what I call a solid grin. The teeth are created as a single curved surface; black lines are added to outline the teeth. This can be a good design for slick cartoon characters. The lack of points and canines helps to avoid a menacing appearance for younger kids.

You can build a solid grin from any flexible or moldable plastic. Alternatively, a softer material such as white closed-cell foam could mbe used. Although less durable, this prevents the teeth from being a hard, and possibly painful, surface.

If you decide to add individual teeth to a children's costume, I recommend large and rounded shapes to reduce the scare factor. Including canines and eye teeth can help to define the species and attitude of a character. Some characters virtually require teeth. (Can you picture a sabretooth-less tiger?)

Claws present similar problems. They immediately make a character more intimidating, even if they aren't recognized consciously. I would never recommend putting claws on a costume designed for a young audience.

Colors

Young children generally prefer bright colors; use this bit of knowledge to your advantage! Make your characters bold primary colors even if this makes them appear very unnatural. If you need inspiration, look at some storybooks for young children and note how few realistic animals there are. Follow this model when developing your characters.

Another important technique is high-contrast coloration. Sharp contrast can attract attention and focus the eye on important parts of the character. The choice of contrasting primary and secondary colors will make your character more obvious in a crowd. The bright colors will also make the character seem more energetic.

Good Vision

Good vision for the performer is one of the elements that I feel is often overlooked, so to speak. Costumes designed for stage work or general performance often have very limited visibility from inside as a tradeoff for a more realistic outward appearance. But if you are specifically building costumes for use with children, I feel it would be wiser to enhance the vision in the costume. Small children move quickly through crowds. It's easy for unsupervised kids to run circles around a character. Without appropriate vision design, it's as if the performer is watching a tennis match through a keyhole.

Downward vision is also very useful. Besides simply being able to navigate around stairs and obstacles more readily, it helps when interacting with children. This is because kids have a tendency to run up to characters and stand immediately in front of them. If they're old enough to understand the purpose of costumed characters, they'll dash up and patiently wait for a hug. It's polite behavior from their viewpoint! But if the performer didn't see their approach and doesn't have good vision, he might not even realize that a kid is standing in front of him. I'm sure you can see (ha-ha) where I'm going with this.

Material Limitations

If the costume is going to be interacting directly with children, you should only use completely safe materials on exposed parts of the costume. Although this may seem self-evident, it is easy to lose sight of it when building a costume, since so many materials in the costumer's arsenal are either toxic, breakable, or potentially sharp. Avoid using any decorative elements which might get broken or detached from rough handling; insect antennae and long ears are particularly vulnerable.

If any solid portions of the costume structure are exposed, ensure that they are not a danger. One common example is large noses on cartoon characters: the underskull usually has the nose shape sculpted into it and is merely painted. In such instances, make sure that the nose shape has no corners or edges which might result in injury.

All of these seem like common sense rules, yet I have seen numerous costumes which break them. If you're not used to designing costumes for interacting with children, give some extra consideration to material selection.

Special Movement and Mobility Requirements

Sometimes costumes have special requirements based on what they are supposed to be able to do. In stage performance, an unusual action may be called for in the script. These actions might be a schtick that's part of the character's personality.

For example, I created a mouse jester costume. Since I also happen to be a juggler, I wanted to be able to juggle in costume to emphasize the jester aspect of the character. This made it very challenging to design the head of the costume with enough vision for me to follow the juggling clubs and keep a cautious eye out for anyone that might be wandering too close. A secondary design constraint was that all of the arm joints needed to have a wide range of movement without a lot of resistance.

In these types of cases, it's important to identify all of the activity's implications early in the design process. These may be constraints on patterns, materials, vision, weight, or other factors. As you sketch out revisions of your costume design, check that they consistently meet all of the restraints you've established.

Durability and Lifespan

Depending on where and how often the character will perform, you can estimate the expected lifespan of the costume. If the costume is something that will only be worn at a few events, the durability of materials is less of an issue. You have leeway to cut some corners.

With a costume that is worn more than once a week, it's important to choose materials that are durable and won't wear out. Pay particular attention to surface materials on the feet and paws, which often see disproportionate wear and tear. Purchase high-quality synthetic fur. Choose the strongest adhesives and fasteners that are practical.

There may also be construction implications. When a suit is only worn rarely, there is ample time to repair it during the downtime. With a frequently worn costume, the design and construction must be rugged enough to go without any major repairs for the expected performance life of the suit. If possible, design all major joints and assemblies in the costume with redundancy to minimize the problems that will appear with ongoing use.

Depending on the materials and adhesives, washing a costume can reduce its lifespan. For a longer costume service life, be sure to choose durable and washable materials. Synthetic fur tends to last very well with washing. After a couple of cleanings, the texture is less smooth than it was originally; beyond that, fur can last through hundreds of washings if properly handled.

Packing and Transportation

Consider how you will disassemble, pack, and transport your costume during the design phase. The head of the costume is often the largest piece. It is difficult to design a head that can be disassembled for transportation. If you have existing storage and shipping containers, ensure that your head is small enough to fit in them. If you plan on taking your costume on commercial airlines, check baggage size restrictions with your carrier.

See Chapter 27 for more information on travel and storage.

Mark Murillo

Mark Murillo runs Bay Area Bears, a Northern California branch of the Good Bears of the World charity. He does charity performances as his character, Hugg E. Bear. You can find him online at www.bayareabears.org.

How did you first get involved in costume performance?

It started out as a desire to make the world a better place. I felt a need to give back to the community. When I was growing up, charity was always emphasized as an important virtue. It sounds really corny but I'm proud of that.

So I decided I wanted to get into some charitable work and began looking around. I found the Good Bears of the World, which I thought had a really cool concept. The group is about giving teddy bears to people who need love, solace, and caring in difficult times, such as victims of disasters and domestic violence. The group distributes teddy bears and gift bags. It doesn't sound like much but it means a lot to them.

After joining Good Bears, I eventually decided to start my own chapter. I thought it would be really cool to have a teddy bear as a mascot character for this work; a walking talking teddy bear giving away these gifts to the children. That's where the idea of Hugg E. Bear came from.

What were some of the toughest things to learn about performance and your new role?

Well, one of the hardest things to do, when performing, is to visualize yourself. When you're wearing an oversized suit like I do, you must make your movements completely exaggerated. You must double all your movements or you don't really look like you're moving at all.

That was something that was initially very hard for me to get a grasp on. If it wasn't for people videotaping me and then watching and reviewing myself on tape later, I don't think I'd be half as good performing in a suit as I am now. It takes a lot of practice to get used to moving around.

When performing as a character, you have to become five years old. You have to regress. I'm not talking about being childish but being childlike. That is the key to being a lovable character and being accepted by the audience. Reach out to people, be curious, be open, question with looks and actions, and just be silly.

Part of being a character is doing things which we wouldn't do normally. Wave at everyone! Play with ordinary objects! Hug a stranger! It's all about how you communicate the personality and fun of the character. That's also what makes it genuine and special for the children.

What is most important in defining the "quality" of a costume?

The actual quality of the costume truly comes from the performer in the costume. You can have the cheesiest suit in the world but if you are really a good performer, you can bring that suit to life and it doesn't matter what it looks like. It's really the person inside that makes it happen. I've also seen people in beautiful, gorgeous suits where you might as well have had a mannequin inside. It's what you do not the physical suit itself.

Do you feel that working as a mascot has helped you to promote the charity and increase donations?

Absolutely. I got that tip from several friends of my father who owned their own businesses and had mascots, too. It's important to have a recognizable character that can grab people's attention and bring them in. Seeing a giant teddy bear will really attract people's notice, they ask about it, and that results in donations. I always like to have a handler there who can explain what's going on and hand out business cards for the charity.

When out performing dressed as an enormous teddy bear, do you ever have any trouble with macho attitudes from people?

Almost never. I've had some of the biggest, toughest guys you'd ever want to meet—heavy-set bikers, guys with obvious gang tattoos, and all sorts—actually come up to me and give me hugs! I think it's because the teddy bear is so universally loved; I rarely have people that don't react positively.

4 • Design Techniques

Design is the creative process by which an original concept is developed into a completed costume. While it is possible to build a costume ad hoc, any project is sure to be improved by some planning and attention to detail. Understanding different aspects of design will help you with the development of a costume plan.

Elements of design are the building blocks used by designers to create a work of art. These elements are used in every design project, whether it is a painting, a sculpture, or a costume. The strategies for combining these elements are the principles of design. To help you apply these elements and principles to your own designs, we will cover some of the key elements and principles of design and how they may apply to your costume projects.

Elements of Design

Line is one of the most straightforward concepts in design and is also one of the most complicated elements to fully utilize. Lines are what define the shapes within the costume and also the alignment of different costume pieces. Not only is it an element of design, lines also help to define many other design elements such as shape and form. Lines make up the boundaries between parts of the body.

Lines pull the eye around the costume and create visual movement. Lines may be straight, curved, or branching to encourage different visual transitions. Over the full costume, line has a role in defining shapes and in delineating different portions of the body.

Shape is not only the silhouette and outer edges of the costume. It is present in all of the visible parts of the costume. Shapes can help to define and highlight the individual components of a design. In a critter costume, there are several shapes that play an important role in defining the species. The structure of the head and muzzle, the contours of the outer body, and any fur markings or species coloration are all examples of shape.

Form describes the overall shape of the costume, the space it occupies and the contours that are created by it. One can think of form as the composition of shapes in three dimensions. In costume terms, form is the main element you consider when you are developing the flow of the head, ears, haunches, and tail. Introducing visual elements that extend beyond the principle body shape can help dramatically define the form of the final costume.

Texture is present in the materials from which the costume is made. When working on animal costumes, the length and density of the fur are likely to be the primary textural elements. There is also some variation in sheen between different furs; matching or contrasting this element can diminish or emphasize boundary lines.

It is also important to consider the sheen of the material chosen for the eyes, nose, mouth, or other trim elements. Every visible element of the costume adds to the overall palette of textures and should be deliberately selected. The texture of materials can even be altered through the application of coatings such as gloss lacquer.

Design inspirations can come from anywhere!

Tracing different contour lines on an animal emphasize different elements of the form.

Color is one of the most obvious traits of a costume. It is also one of the most fundamental elements of design. Color can dictate a costume's realism, intended audience, attitude, and even species. When working with fur, color selection is often limited; when designing, determine what colors would be ideal and only then adjust it for the pragmatic considerations of availability.

Hue is the term for the spectral shade of color. Hue is what people commonly mean when they use the term "color." In costuming, employing complementary, neighboring, and contrasting hues contributes to the visual impact of the piece.

Value is a description of the saturation and intensity of the color. Value will affect the quality of the color and, ultimately, the emotional impression of the costume. Most solid-color furs commonly available have relatively intense values.

Principles of design

Balance is found in the relationship between the various costume components. Most costumes seek a relatively even balance since this imparts a certain visual harmony, but the deliberate inclusion of imbalance in the design can be used to draw the focus to specific parts of the costume. If the balance is skewed without a single strong element to capture the focus, it can lead to a disordered impression.

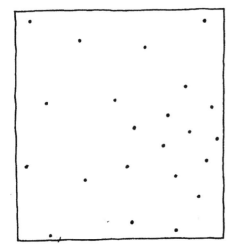

To better visualize this, consider the unbalanced distribution of a dozen dots on an otherwise blank box. The eye moves between the dots in no particular order, understanding that there is an imbalance but without a distinct destination for this movement. When a single larger dot is added, it can anchor the pattern and create a visual anchor. This is a dramatic use of imbalance.

In costumes, we most often want this anchor to be centered in order to achieve balance. When designing the head, the nose or eyes can be good focus points. Emphasizing these elements can pull the attention to the center of the face, making your character more engaging.

Movement – The gaze of the viewer moves around the costume, exploring the different components of the overall creature. Lines, shapes, forms and textures work together to guide the eye of the viewer; here, we are not necessarily concerned with leading the eye to a particular focal point but instead influencing the flow of the viewer's gaze.

Direction of movement is created through the use of strong lines. Lines lead the eye along their length. Most costumes are both bilaterally symmetrical and taller than they are wide. The use of belly patches, arm and leg markings, and other vertical elements can pull the eye up and down the costume, emphasizing the height.

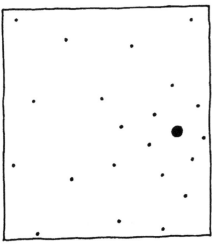

A simple experiment in visual balance. The large spot on the right offsets the small spots on the left.

The placement of a prominent (e.g. contrasting) nose in the center of the face creates radial symmetry. This specific balance introduces visual movement that first draws the eye in; focus then has a tendency to shift out and away, along radial lines, to other parts of the face and costume. The use of balance when placing other facial features—such as the eyes, the mouth, a mane, or fur markings—can enhance the perceived radial symmetry.

Repetition and Rhythm – This principle refers to the repetition of distinct design elements or patterns to create visual interest throughout the costume. Stripes in fur coloration are a good example of this principle. Many species have contrasting stripes that are repeated over the body. Repetition of this stripe pattern, especially in outer areas of the costume such as the arms and legs, can serve to unify the design.

Repeating given shapes, colors, or textures over a costume can create a visual rhythm. This can be varied by changing the spacing, density, or intensity of the markings.

Scale and Proportion – Scale is the absolute size of a part of the costume; proportion describes the relationship between the scaling of different parts or components of the costume. Proportion is a particularly important principle to consider when designing fursuits. Since these costumes are designed to disguise the shape of the human body, the costume needs to introduce new proportions to reflect an animal's form.

A giraffe, for example, has very recognizable neck and head proportions; if the costume does not at least approximate that, the illusion will not be convincing. Proportions can also play a part in defining the age of the character. A puppy costume would have oversized paws and a larger, rounder head in order to emphasize the creature's immature status; an older dog character would have smaller paws and a more defined, sculpted head.

Scale is a consideration when we start looking at proportions that stray significantly from the human body. A costume of fixed proportions must be scaled up until a human can fit inside the most constricted area. Always remember to keep the scale manageable from a performance perspective.

Scale and proportion are most important when adapting an existing character. In this situation, the character has already been clearly defined. The costume needs to recreate the feel of the original character while also making necessary concessions to reality. Try to preserve the proportions of major elements while adjusting the scale of intervening minor pieces.

Contrast and Emphasis – Whenever two disparate items are put in proximity it creates contrast. Essentially, this is the interaction of different textures, colors and shapes. Contrast is a fundamental tool for creating visual elements, such as lines. It is also a useful principle for creating areas of high and low visual interest by varying the contrast of elements.

Emphasis refers specifically to the creation of a focal point or multiple areas of interest. Emphasis may be created by contrast or any combination of other principles. For example, create emphasis through exaggeration, a specific manipulation of balance and proportion. For a mascot style costume, facial features are often the target of emphasis.

Unity – In general, a costume design should form a cohesive whole; all of the elements should seem to belong together. This more abstract quality is the principle of unity. If you feel that some portion of the costume doesn't match, consider it from the point of view of each of the principles presented here.

Each animal is unique, from the shape of her head to the coloring of her nose. The above photos demonstrate how markings create an individual look, while still letting you know that these are indeed tigers!

Animal Markings

The fur's marking and coloration is an important part of an animal's identity. Special attention should be given to markings when adapting a species for a costume project. Once the animal has been anthropomorphized to fit on top of human proportions, markings may be essential in helping people identify it.

Unless your goal is an absolutely realistic costume, it may not be best to directly copy the markings of the animal. Instead, try to generalize the patterns in the animal's coat and then reapply these patterns to your costume's form.

This intermediate abstraction may help you to simplify the markings, making is more practical from a costuming standpoint.

As an example, consider a tiger's stripes. A real tiger may have twenty or so stripes crossing its back. While we could recreate this on a costume, it would be more practical to construct only half that many stripes. By structuring each of the stripes with the same overall character as the original animal's, we create the impression of tiger stripes. We also reduce the contrast emphasis on the back while allowing us to put that visual focus somewhere more significant.

Animal Shapes

When designing a costume of a particular species, there are a wide variety of ways in which the animal's shape can be adapted. The animal may be interpreted or stylized yet still be recognizable for what it is. The trick here is understanding what shapes and forms are visual keys to the animal's identity.

In order to experiment with this, I like to trace lines on top of reference photos of the animal. Starting each time with a blank piece of paper, try to add the fewest number of lines that will clearly define the animal. Experimentation will quickly reveal which shapes and contours are distinctive elements and which can be excluded. Different combinations can even create different moods and impressions based on how they distribute emphasis.

Using this knowledge, you can determine what shapes and contours are essential to the animal's form. When designing the costume, pay attention to these shapes and their proportion; they become the core of your critter's visual identity. Distinctive stylization of the original animal is possible by emphasizing and exaggerating these shapes and their relative scales.

Notice how padding can change the distribution of weight and body proportions to emphasize different animal aspects.

Part II

Tools and Materials

Before you start creating costumes, it's important to understand the tools of the trade. Costuming, particularly for mascots and animal characters, requires many tools and materials beyond common sewing implements. In the upcoming chapters, we review both familiar sewing and craft tools as well as more esoteric supplies.

It's important to have a workshop space for costuming projects. For the home enthusiast, this may be a desk or table in a back room. For the professional costumer, this may be an open studio space with worktables. Chapter 5 addresses not only which tools to buy, but how to store your supplies and set up your workspace. Chapter 6 presents vital information for selecting and working with synthetic fur. Following that are chapters that address some of the more unusual supplies such as glues and foam.

Safety First!

Always consider safety first when working with all materials and tools. I've attempted to include relevant warnings in sections discussing hazardous chemicals or dangerous tools. However, it's important that you take the time to familiarize yourself with and review the warnings for the materials you select for your project. Always use good sense when working. Safety first!

5 • Sewing Supplies

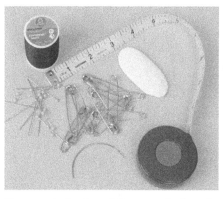

These are just a few of the many tools and supplies used in mascot costume construction.

Setting Up a Workspace

It's important to set up a good workspace before undertaking any costume project. Having a work area established will simplify your life and allow you to work more efficiently.

If you don't have a separate space to dedicate to costuming, try to assemble a portable set of costuming tools. You should realize that it takes a fair amount of space to store materials and tools, let alone the area needed when actively working on a project.

Work Surface

Regardless of where you set up shop, a good workspace centers around a good work surface. You'll need a sturdy work table on which to lay out fabric pieces and assemble parts of the costume. It's best if the surface of the table is fairly durable and will resist the inevitable cuts and gouges. The table should be of a height such that you can sit in a chair with your legs under it; while it's easier to work from a standing position, it's often more comfortable to work while sitting.

Six-foot banquet tables have served me well as work surfaces. These are the rectangular tables with folding legs and, most commonly, a brown laminate surface. They can be found at office stores for high prices or bulk/club stores for more reasonable prices. Occasionally you can find used ones at thrift stores or repo sales; as long as the legs appear to be in solid condition, grab it.

If you want a better work surface than the raw tabletop, find a local plastic store. Pick up a quarter-inch sheet of high-density polyethylene (HDPE), the same stuff used in common plastic kitchen cutting boards. It will also make a great cutting board in your work room! You can glue it to the table or leave it separate (a portable work surface).

Storage

As you work on different costumes, you will acquire an inventory of tools and materials. It's important to plan ahead for storage requirements in your workspace. Tools need to be stored safely, yet be easily accessible.

If costuming is something that you're likely to do infrequently or as a hobby, you're not as likely to accumulate a large catalog of materials. Storage containers that can be packed into closets or stacked in a corner of a back room are good choices. Office stores often sell inexpensive plastic drawer sets that can be stacked on top of each other. This can be a good way to organize sewing materials and small tools.

If you are setting up a serious workshop, I would recommend installing drawer sets wherever possible. Create a filing area with oversized folders for storing custom patterns. Metal utility racks should be available for stacking bolts of fabric.

A toolbox is an excellent way to store your sewing gear. Not only will it keep your tools and notions secure, it's easy to grab for sewing on the go.

Lighting

Lighting is another basic workspace consideration. It's important to have enough overhead light to be able to clearly see what you're working on. It's also useful to have access to one or two bright desk lamps, so that you can direct light onto specific areas or the underside of a project.

I like halogen lamps because they produce a good "white" light and are reasonably priced. The type of light source does play a big role in our perception of color, so it is important when working with colored materials, paints, or dyes. Under the presumption that our costumes will be seen outdoors, we need to design them to look best in natural light. The easiest solution is to have windows in your workspace; the flaw in this plan quickly becomes apparent on that first late night session, though…

These days, there are a number of bulbs designed to produce a bright light with a good spectral distribution. They are often sold as "natural" or "full-spectrum" bulbs; they are even available for fluorescent fixtures. Regular incandescent bulbs with high wattages are a decent choice if the other options aren't possible. Avoid generic industrial fluorescent tubes at all costs!

If you want to learn more about light fixture options and spectral qualities, find a local lighting store manager or theater tech. After an hour you will either be passionate about the subject yourself or you'll remember an important dental appointment.

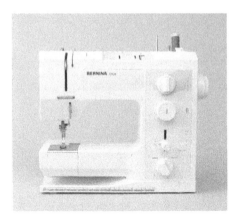

Your most expensive piece of equipment may be your sewing machine.

Sewing Machines

The sewing machine is the workhorse of the costume shop. I recommend that you machine sew wherever possible. Modern sewing machines, correctly used, produce a very reliable stitch and are much faster than hand stitching.

You can set up your sewing machine on one end of your work table (see previous section). Alternatively, you can have a separate table or desk set aside for the sewing machine. Some machines (usually older ones) come built into desks, which settles the matter. Sewing tables, specially designed for the task, can sometimes be found in fabric shops or department stores.

When shopping for a sewing machine to use in costuming, it is particularly important to find one that is advertised as heavy-duty. Fur is just about the worst thing that you can force through a sewing machine, short of motorcycle leather. It's important that the sewing machine you choose be built to handle the challenge. Look for one with sales material bragging about the ability to handle leather and denim. If you can, try to find one that has metal (as opposed to nylon) gears and internals.

You don't need a machine that has a lot of fancy stitching features in order to create mascot costumes. Don't be wowed by the electronic machine that can sew a line of ducks onto a quilt. It won't help you. All that's required is a straight stitch and a zigzag stitch, moves so basic that every machine built in the last half-century should be able to do them.

If you just want to buy a machine for creating furry costumes, a used machine may be a good option. Check your local yellow pages for sewing machine repair shops (which seem to be inexplicably intertwined with vacuum cleaner repair). Such shops often sell used sewing machines at very reasonable prices. This can be a great way to pick up a first sewing machine or one that you won't mind running into the ground.

Familiarize yourself with any new sewing machine before getting into the middle of a project. Run some tests on cheap fabric to get a feel for how it operates; each sewing machine is slightly different. Experiment with different thread tensions and stitches.

It's also important to maintain your sewing machine. Remember that fur will clog up a machine much more quickly than any other fabric. Clean your machine after each project. Read and follow the maintenance instructions in the manual. Periodically, take it to a sewing machine shop to have it thoroughly cleaned. (For extra fun, watch the staff try to guess what you were sewing as they pull brightly-colored fluffs of fur from inside your machine.)

Sergers (Overlock Machines)

Sergers are not the same as sewing machines, despite the family resemblance. Sergers handle between three and five threads at a time, creating a finished seam in a single pass. They utilize an overlock stitch to join fabrics at their edges and they trim the fabric edges for you as you are stitching.

A serger isn't a substitute for a sewing machine. There are specific situations where a serger is preferred, but it does not have the same versatility as a regular sewing machine. Buying a serger for costuming is definitely desirable but normally not necessary. When working with fur, both a serger and a sewing machine can work about equally well, depending on your personal sewing skills.

The big advantage of a serger is that the resulting overlock stitch can stretch. A straight (locking) stitch has almost no stretch in it. A zigzag stitch has a bit of movement, but it's still quite limited. A serged seam, however, can take quite a bit of stretching without undue tension on the individual threads. This makes the serger ideally suited for spandex materials.

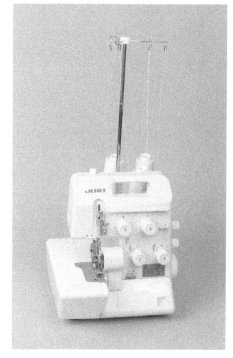

If you plan on making spandex bodysuits, a serger gets the job done!

Needles

Having a sewing machine does not obviate the need for hand stitching. Some detail work and joints will always need to be done manually. Always keep a selection of needles on hand.

There are myriad needles available to bewilder a beginner. Even someone who has been sewing for years may not be entirely sure what type of needle is best for a certain job. For the purposes of costuming, however, we can identify a small subset of needles that are especially useful. A set of these needles should stand you in good stead for any animal costume challenge.

Ballpoint Needle – This general-purpose needle is the best choice when working with fur, due to fur's knit backing layer. The ballpoint needle is good with all knit or loose-weave fabrics, where the rounded tip can slide through the knit without tearing apart the fibers.

Short Embroidery Needle – A small sharp needle is useful for detail work and maneuvering in tight spaces. An embroidery needle has a larger eye than most needles for easier threading. The point is sharp, so this needle can be used on fabrics other than fur.

Upholstery Needle – This unusual curved needle is useful when you are limited to working on a seam from only one side. They are harder to find and sometimes referred to as carpet needles.

Leather Needles – If your project involves working with leather, seek out the specialized tools for it. Leather needles, also called glovers, have points designed to penetrate lightweight leather without any tearing. These needles also work well for rubberized materials.

Thread

For costuming, I always recommend using synthetic thread. Costumes tend to be very heavy, unlike regular clothes. They also undergo a lot of strain during their use, so choose a heavy thread to create seams that will last under the stress.

Cotton thread is the most common type of thread, but it's insufficient for costuming. Look for polyester thread at minimum. Polyester thread is available in a wide range of colors and works well for machine sewing.

Heavier nylon monofilament thread is even better. It's usually sold as "upholstery thread" in stores and comes in only a small selection of colors. Some sewing machines will balk at the stiffer nylon thread, so test it with your machine. At the very least, it's a good thread for hand stitching.

You'll rarely find a thread that exactly matches the color you're working with. Choose the color closest to the base material of your project. If it's a light-colored material, tend towards a thread that is lighter than the material. If you're using a dark-colored material, tend towards a thread that is darker.

I recommend picking up a thread rack at your local sewing store. These racks are basically an array of wooden pegs on which you can store your spools. It's much more convenient than a drawer because you can browse the colors easily. Additionally, you can mount the rack on the wall to make better use of space.

For hardened do-it-yourselfers, you can create a custom wall-mounted thread rack with ¼" wooden dowel and a backboard. The size and shape of the board can be chosen to fit your workspace and thread collection. Plywood or thin board lumber will work. Drill ¼" holes into the backboard, angling them slightly downward (relative to mounting orientation). A drill press is useful for consistency. Cut the dowel into small pegs that will extend about 3" out from the backboard when inserted into the holes. Use wood glue to secure the pegs.

Pins

It's good to have a large box of quilting pins nearby when working with fur. Unlike other materials, cut pieces of fur will not want to lie together for a nice easy seam. The pile of the fur will try to force the pieces apart and make them shift. I recommend heavily pinning all fur seams to be sewn, spacing your pins about 1½" inches apart. (On a bodysuit, this means several hundred pins at a time.) I also insert pins at opposing angles to prevent shifting in any direction at the fur pieces try to push themselves apart.

Look for long straight pins with spherical heads. These are easiest to keep track of in dense fur. Avoid the T-headed pins, as they can snag loose fibers and get tangled in your project.

Scissors

Your choice of scissors is surprisingly important. You will use them frequently and a bad pair of scissors can tire or injure your hands. Quality scissors are more expensive but well worth the investment. You can find a range of scissors at local fabric, craft, and office supply stores.

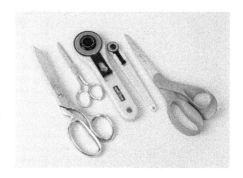

Basic Scissors – A basic pair of bent handle dressmaker scissors is a good choice for cutting fabric. These work particularly well on lightweight fabrics, such as cotton or spandex. The offset handle design allows you to cut the fabric while it is lying on your work surface, by sliding the lower blade beneath the material.

Be sure to find a pair that can be disassembled (i.e. the center pivot is a screw and not a rivet). This allows them to be cleaned and sharpened.

Fiskars™ – I specifically recommend the Fiskars brand of scissors for costuming work. I've been impressed with their quality and design.

The handles have large padded pressure areas to minimize hand problems from extended sessions at the cutting table. They are spring-loaded so that they reopen after each cut, making them easier to use. The blades maintain a good edge, even after use on heavy materials such as fur. For fabric and fur work, look for the Fiskars with the drop handle design shown (model #9911).

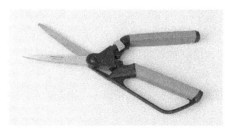

Fiskars model 9911.

Thread Scissors – It's useful to have a compact pair of scissors. The small blades can easily snip threads. The pointed tips are useful for poking into seams when they need to be taken apart.

For easy storage, buy a small adhesive-backed plastic storage hook from a hardware store. Apply this to an unobtrusive part of your sewing machine and hang your thread scissors there so that they'll always be handy when you sew.

Fiskars model 9888.

Knives

Knives and razor blade tools are useful for cutting materials that can't be handled by scissors. Whenever working with tools with exposed blades, pay careful attention and handle them safely.

Penknives – Penknives, also called hobby knives, are very useful tools to have around. They are sometimes referred to simply as "X-Acto™ knives," though this is actually the trademark of one of the leading brands.

Penknives will find many uses as part of your tool kit. They can score or cut through sheets of plastic and rubber. Their sharp point fits into tight areas, such as inside masks. Use them to tidy edges and remove excess glue.

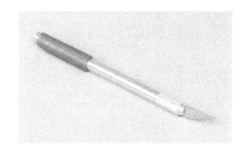

The addition of an anti-roll pencil grommet can make a penknife safer.

When choosing a knife, I recommend getting one with a small barrel handle, like the one shown (an X-Acto No.1 knife with Type A handle). The tubular metal handles are easy to work with, but these knives suffer from an annoying tendency to roll off work tables onto the floor, where they're a real hazard. The solution is to buy some of the angular rubber grommets sold to prevent pencils and pens from rolling. This way, the knife will stay put when you put it down.

Disposable Razor Knives – These small plastic knives have a segmented razor blade about four inches long which can be extended from the handle. As the tip of the blade gets dull, you're supposed to break off the segments of the razor blade along small score marks. The design provides a small razor tip that is always sharp. Some people also use the knives with the blade fully extended to provide a larger cutting surface.

I think that these types of knives are unnecessarily dangerous and I do not recommend them. If used with the blade extended, the knife is wobbly and it is difficult to apply pressure evenly. The cheap assembly of the disposable handle is flimsy and subject to shattering.

Even if only the tip of the knife blade is used, it's difficult to apply pressure to any resilient material. The sliding handle, used to control the blade, moves easily, and the blade will retract into the plastic housing. To keep the blade extended, you need to apply considerable thumb pressure, making it difficult to cut along a straight line and also making it more likely that your grip will slip.

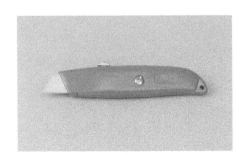

Utility Knives – These rugged cousins of craft knives can be found in home and hardware stores everywhere. They have an adjustable heavy-duty razor blade which can typically extend up to about an inch. Utility knives are good for cutting tough materials, such as vulcanized rubber and vinyl.

When buying a utility knife, spend a little time shopping around, as quality varies widely. The large molded handle should fit comfortably in your hand to provide a secure grip. Some models are designed for replaceable blades while others are simply disposable.

The most important thing to examine is the ratcheting action of the slider that controls the blade extension. Be sure that it requires you to push down in order to shift the blade. When you apply pressure to the blade, the upward motion should lock the slider in position. This is the feature that I find most impacts the safety and ease of use of a utility knife.

A yardstick and a French curve are essential for doing pattern alteration work. If you are planning on doing production work or developing your own pattern making skills, you should invest in the right tools for the job.

Gill Wichi

Gill Wichi creates and performs his own original costume characters. He does charity work including parades and children's hospital visits. He's also known as Brokken, the name of one of his characters. You can learn more about Gill at his website, www.timberwolf.org.

Tell a little about how you got started in costuming?

I have to say I've had an interest in costumes for as long as I can remember. I started sketching costumes out when I was nine but I hid all the plans from my family because I didn't know how they'd react! I grew up in El Salvador in Central America. There wasn't much in terms of costume supplies so I had to make do with what was available. The very first animal costume that I wore was when I was in kindergarten. I played the Cowardly Lion in our school production of *The Wizard of Oz*.

As far as creating costumes professionally, I didn't start that until I moved here to the San Francisco bay area. Sometime after '94 I joined the fursuiters community. For a while, I considered myself a performer, but I later became interested in building suits myself.

As a costumer starting out, what were some of the biggest challenges you faced?

The very first thing that I had to manage was putting together my workshop. When I was making Domino, my first character, I bought supplies and started using them without paying heed to the idea that I would be making more costumes later on. I thought, "Who needs more than one?" I didn't know how addictive it would be!

When I was done, I just put leftover supplies away into boxes or I threw them away. For my second costume, I turned out that I was buying everything all over again. By my third costume, I started really keeping track of things and keeping my costume-related stuff organized.

One of my goals was also to assemble a material library of fur. So I started buying furs if they looked interesting, whether I had a project in mind or not. There are certain staples that you should always keep around, such as white, black, and gray, that a lot of critters can use.

So I think that establishing your workshop and getting it stocked with materials is really one of the biggest hurdles. Once you have it all set up, it's just a matter of picking and choosing what tools you need from your library.

You started out performing before transitioning to costume construction. At this point, do you consider yourself more of a performer or a builder?

I would say I enjoy both aspects of costuming. I do like to build stuff and I derive a great deal of enjoyment from that process. Whenever I'm in a costume that I've made myself, there is a certain pride that goes with that: knowing that it's entirely your creation.

What factor is most important to the quality of a costume, however you might define "quality"?

My own belief about costumes is that it's like beauty: it's skin deep. So my own concern is how to make things look good. I'm not the type that engineers everything to last for years under constant wear. I have to say that my costumes are more hall or stage costumes; they're not like mascot costumes. They require some attention. They're not shoddy, obviously, but neither are they designed to take abuse.

A costume is meant to present an exterior appearance. It's not meant as a utilitarian commodity, such as a car. In a car, function is much more important; it can have a scratch as long as it runs. Whereas a costume is more skin-deep... or fur-deep, I guess.

6 • Synthetic Fur

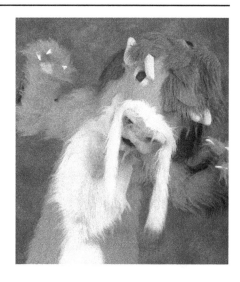

Throughout this book, where I refer to "fur," I do, in fact, mean fake fur. Apart from the obvious ethical problems associated with using real animal pelts, fur is not suited to costume work. Real fur is expensive, difficult to work with, tedious to maintain, and less durable. Throughout this book we'll be dealing exclusively with synthetic fur materials. These are sometimes referred to as "deep pile fabrics" or "plush fabrics." They're available in fabric stores and other sources.

We should examine the anatomy of these materials. I think that it's important to fully understand the things you use from the ground up to be able to utilize them most effectively.

Fur materials are built on top of a knit synthetic backing material. When fur fabric is sewn together, it's the backing layers that are sewn to each other. On one side of the backing, individual fibers extend a roughly uniform length to form the pile of the fur. The fibers will tend to fall naturally in one direction, known as the nap. You can find the nap of a piece of fur by brushing across it with your hand. If the fibers lie down smoothly, you are running in the direction of the nap; if the fur stands upright and feathered, you are running against the nap of the fabric.

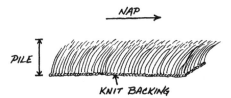

Diagram of fur construction.

Other variable qualities of synthetic fur are density and texture, which affect the hand (weight, body, and feel) of the fabric. Density is a measurement of the number of fibers per square unit of material. The fibers of the fur can be made from a number of different materials, and these affect their texture and sheen; there can be quite a variance among the fabrics from different manufacturers. These are both things that you need to determine by examining and feeling the fabric directly.

What sort of fur is appropriate for your project will depend upon the particulars of the design and your personal preferences. Most projects will require more than one type of fur. In these cases, it's also important to consider how the different fur materials look when adjacent to each other. Differences in color and pile are good for creating contrast between different areas of a character, whereas differences in texture and density are more often distracting to the eye.

Synthetic fur is usually made from acrylic or modacrylic. These are plastic polymers that can be spun into durable fibers. Both the fur pile and backing are formed from the same fibers. The ends of the loose fibers are what create the pile of the fur. Should you come across fur where the pile is actually loops of fiber (as in terry cloth) I'd suggest you avoid it—this is a cheaper method of manufacture and indicates an inferior product.

The backing of fake fur is usually a double knit (as opposed to woven) fabric. A double knit is a complex pattern of interlocking loops. Unlike weaves, where single threads stretch the breadth of the fabric, knits have more localized construction. This helps provide knits with a little bit of stretch, though the heavy synthetic fibers used in fur prevent the material from having much dynamic movement.

Fur materials will stretch by 6-12% lengthwise and 10-20% crosswise, in my experience. Stretch on the bias falls somewhere between these amounts. The

Synthetic fur comes in a wide variety of textures, colors, and fabrications.

Fabric Terminology

Selvage is the term for the finished edges of the fabric. The selvage in fur is usually a double thickness of backing and should not be included in any pattern cuts.

Lengthwise refers to the grain of the fabric parallel to the selvage edge.

Crosswise is the grain of the fabric running perpendicular to the selvage edge.

Bias is a fancy fabric term for "diagonal." A "true" bias is a diagonal direction 45° from both the lengthwise and crosswise grains.

Yard is the unit traditionally used to measure fabric quantities. It represents one linear yard cut from the fabric bolt; the width of the bolt varies, but is usually 58"-60" for furs.

Bolts are large rolls of fabric, as they come from the manufacturer. A bolt of fur is usually at least 12 yards, while regular fabric bolts may be much larger.

percentage of stretch is measured as the increase in length versus the original "relaxed" measurement. As always, be sure to check the exact material you plan to use before figuring any stretch into a pattern. In general, I assume that the material is fairly static when designing a pattern.

Also be aware that stretching the fur reduces the density of the pile. This thinning effect is sometimes visible in very short pile plush fur. It won't be seen in longer shag fur.

Fur based on a stretch backing material is available, but it is quite expensive and usually manufactured on a custom-order basis. In such materials, the backing exhibits an enormous degree of stretch along one or both directions. This means that joints may be patterned more tightly to prevent sagging.

The only company I'm aware of that takes such orders is National Fiber Technology—see the Resources section for contact information.

Finding the Right Fur

The most obvious place to check for fur is at your local fabric shops. Local stores will often have a few bolts of fake fur tucked away next to the fleeces and felts. For a serious costumer, however, it's insufficient. When we design a project, we often have a clear idea of exactly what colors and lengths we need. Sure, the local fabric store may be able to offer some plain white or black furs, but they're unlikely to have all of the other colors you need.

A lot of fabric stores also stock cheaper furs. This is not, by any means, a universal truth. Check out the shops in your area and examine the fur closely. The pile should be dense and even, without prominent ridges when brushed down. Ridges in the fur can indicate a poor weave in the backing material. The texture should be smooth and resilient, never spiky. A spiky or rough texture can be a sign of larger and cheaper fibers used in the pile construction to visually compensate for low density.

If local fabric stores don't have what you need, the next option is to go with online or mail-order stores. There are a number of companies that will sell cut yardage (i.e. less than a complete bolt) through the mail. See the References section for specific suppliers.

Mail-order suppliers offer a better selection of colors and styles; but the disadvantage is that you can't inspect the fur before you buy it. Different retailers will carry different varieties and qualities of fur; the only way to be able to judge is to purchase a small order from a supplier. Mail-order is usually cheaper than local stores, but you can end up paying for the difference in shipping costs.

If you're working on a large project or series of projects, it may make sense to purchase fabric from a manufacturer. Most manufacturers will sell full bolts directly to customers. Buying fur this way is much cheaper, sometimes only half as expensive as through a retailer. Buying several colors from one manufacturer is also a way to guarantee that the quality and texture of the fur match when assembled.

Monterey Mills

One fur manufacturer I've had good experiences with is Monterey Mills. They will sell 15-yard rolls of fur directly to individuals. They have a sample kit available for a small fee. See the Resources section for contact information.

Should you need less than a full bolt, ask your local fabric stores if they order fur from Monterey Mills. Some companies will do special orders for customers, if you know to ask. The store orders the bolt of fur and then sells you just the cut yardage you need (with markup, naturally). The advantage of knowing what mill the retailer purchases the fur from is that you can get a sample set directly from the fur manufacturer to gauge the quality and color of the product before you order it.

If you're just working on a single costume, this may be the best way to get the fur for your project.

National Fiber Technologies

Another option worth mentioning is custom fur manufacturing. To the best of my knowledge, this is only done (in the U.S.) by National Fiber Technologies (NFT). This company is well known in the film effects industry for being able to handle any order; their fur comes in every color and length you could want. They can even handle color gradients and mixed colors, such as you might see on guard hairs.

Their fur is available on their standard semi-stretch or special full-stretch backing. Their knit backing can stretch by about 75%, allowing a lot of flexibility to be designed into a costume. If you're working on a serious project requiring tight furring around the joints or unusual mobility, this is the best choice.

The only downside of NFT is the price tag. Their custom-made fur, though absolutely superb, is expensive enough to be outside the budget of most costume hobbyists and even some small theater groups. To help make their fur more affordable, they've introduced a selection of stock fur fabrics which have no setup fees and reduced prices. They have an excellent stock "white fursuiter fur" made from rayon and nylon with a soft texture. Contact them for details or a sample kit.

Note when ordering that their prices are measured per square foot instead of per linear yard, as with fabrics.

Cutting and Marking Techniques

Cutting fur is a little more challenging than cutting regular fabrics, but it can be quickly mastered using a few simple techniques.

If we cut straight across the fur with scissors, the nap of the fur will be cut, too. This shortens the pile on one side, resulting in an odd appearance when brushed out—not to mention a shower of fluff and fibers as the cut tips of the fur fall away.

Instead, cut just the backing and the pile of the fur will pull cleanly apart. You can cut through the backing with a rotary wheel, penknife, seam ripper, or scissors. Use whichever tool you find easiest for the job.

If you're using a penknife or seam ripper, flip the fur over so that it's right-side down, with the pile pressed against your cutting surface. Using gentle pressure, trace along your cut lines with just enough force to cut through the backing. Note that this technique is more difficult with long shaggy fur, since the thick pile creates a springy effect that makes it tricky to apply even pressure with the knife. Don't press too hard or you'll end up cutting the pile fibers along with the backing.

Monterey Mills sample card

Fur samples from National Fiber Technologies allow you to chose the color and texture that is right for you.

The two main ways of cutting synthetic fur: using a seam ripper (above) and scissors (below).

Chapter 6

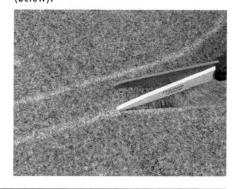

Small soap bars can be carved down and used to mark cutting lines.

If you're using scissors, hold the fur right-side down so that you can see the backing. With your scissors open, slide the lower blade close along the under (furry) side of the fabric; the blade of the scissors can support the fabric as you work. Moving along the cut, push the lower blade of the scissors through the pile of the fur, so that only the backing is left in the jaws of the scissors.

Even using these methods, cutting fur will release a lot of loose fibers. Be prepared to vacuum! To avoid inhaling the fibers, don't lean over the fur while you work. While I've not seen any medical studies specific to this subject, I'll wager that inhaling tiny plastic fibers is not good for your lungs. If you're cutting a lot of fur or working without ventilation, consider wearing a dust mask. Take special precautions if you suffer from asthma or other respiratory problems.

Finally, some tips on marking fur for cutting. Before cutting pattern pieces, mark out where you plan to cut on the reverse side (the exposed backing). Do not use pens for this purpose, as the ink may migrate through the fur. Since the fur is made from plastics, the ink doesn't dry quickly or thoroughly. If you're dealing with a light-colored fur, the ink may transfer through the backing to the pile, where it will be visible. Instead, use a soft lead pencil to make light marks. The graphite from the pencil won't flow through the material, though it may rub off the insides of seams during the first few wearings of the costume.

If you are working with a darker color of fur, I recommend you use soap to mark the cut lines. It follows the same idea as the chips of tailoring chalk sold in fabric stores. Keep old bars of hand soap as they start to wear down to slivers. Dry them out and use these soap chips to rub white lines onto the fur backing.

You can sharpen your soap using a penknife. Create a chisel edge that can be rubbed across the fabric to indicate cut lines.

Sewing Fur

Fur can be machine sewn, like other fabrics, as long as appropriate care is taken. Fur is a much heavier material than most machines are designed to handle. Be careful when putting more than two pieces of fur through the machine at once; it can be very easy to snap a needle when going across seam intersections. Fur can also be sewn using a serger, although this requires more sewing experience in order to achieve good results.

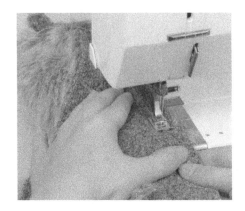

Fur pieces should always be sewn with their nap sides together and the knit backing sides out. If fur is fed through the machine with the pile exposed on the top side, the fibers will be trapped in the stitches; this is unsightly but can be corrected by hand-picking out the captured fibers. Fur should never be fed through a sewing machine with exposed pile on the underside; the fibers in the fur can snag the feeder and bobbin mechanisms of the sewing machine.

Pin fur pieces together before sewing. Given the springy nature of pile fabrics, the pieces will tend to shift out of alignment if not firmly pinned. Although it is not necessarily good sewing form, I often leave the pins in place while sewing fur. This results in some extra broken needles from pin strikes but prevents any shifting as the thick fur sandwich is forced under the sewing machine's foot.

Once all of the sewing on the suit has been completed, including fitting adjustments, it is good practice to "pick" the seams. The pile of the fur can fold over and get caught in the stitching of the seam. Many of these fibers can be freed by slipping a pin under them and pulling them upwards, helping to restore the fur's pile and hide the seam.

You can minimize the amount of fur caught in seams by carefully brushing the pile away from the seam location prior to pinning. Running a finger between the fur pieces as they are being pressed together for pinning is another method for keeping seams clear.

Shaving Effects

When working with a deep pile fur, you can sometimes create interesting effects by shaving down portions of the fur. There is even more apparent if the fur has guard hairs, where one color of fiber is longer than the primary color of the fur.

Shaving can be used to create a number of different effects. Shaving just the tips of an uneven pile fur can create the look of a combed or smooth-coated area. Shaving closer to the backing can create a short-napped appearance and more even color.

A shorter area of fur also makes it easier to see details of shape and form. If you're using a shag fur on a costume head, consider shaving down the fur to half-length around the eyes and mouth lines to help prevent character details from being lost in a big ball of fluff.

Fur can be shaved using a common beard trimmer; check your local drug stores and hair salons. Try to find a model with a wide (more than one inch) head, as used in barbershops. Before shaving, brush the fur against the nap so that it stands upright. A slow pass with the beard trimmer should result in an evenly shorn fabric.

It is commonly recommended that you trim down the edges of fur pattern pieces before sewing them together. This has the advantage of creating a flatter and tighter seam, since the deep pile of the fabric normally creates a springy sandwich between the thread stitches. It also prevents the tips of the fur from getting caught, pulling a section of the pile into the seam.

Shaving seam allowances does work, given a few caveats. Make sure that the pattern has been fully adjusted as you want it, since you won't be able to adjust seams once you've trimmed down the pile of the fur. Also make sure you sew the seams exactly on your pattern line. Too far to the outside, and a narrow strip in the center of the seam will appear bald; too far to the inside, and the seam will become bulky and the benefit of shaving is lost.

I normally sew costumes without shaving down the fur. It saves a lot of time and the small improvement in seaming barely makes a noticeable difference in the finished product. Instead, I just try to brush the fur inwards from the cut edge of the pattern pieces while I'm pinning. After sewing, I use a pin to pull loose any fur that gets matted into a seam; loop the pin under a small group of fibers and pull upwards, pulling their tips from the seam.

Washing and Drying Fur

Fur is a fairly hard-wearing material due to its synthetic fiber content and construction. It does eventually require washing and cleaning, though.

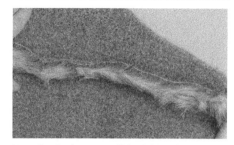

Your finished seam will look like this on the inside (above). When you examine the outside, a well-sewn seam will be nearly invisible (below).

Chapter 6

Simple Drying Racks

No drying racks in your workshop? Here's a quick and easy solution:

At a hardware store, buy some of the grid inserts made for the industrial fluorescent light boxes in drop ceilings. These are the silver or gray plastic grids commonly used in office building overhead lights when they don't use the faceted plastic diffuser sheets. Your corner hardware store might not carry them, but most larger stores with an industrial section should have them.

Buy three of these grids and two lengths of two-by-four lumber (or other supports of your choice) per full body suit being dried. Find an open area and lay down the two-by-fours parallel to each other, about two feet apart; they will suspend the plastic grids above the floor to allow air to circulate underneath. Place the grids across the two wooden supports, edge to edge.

This rig should be large enough to allow a full fursuit to be spread out for drying. Place a box fan on the floor near the head of the suit to provide airflow above and beneath the plastic grids.

For more information on cleaning products and supplies, take a peek at Chapter 27, "Travel & Storage."

The exact procedure for washing a costume depends on its construction. Parts of costumes, particularly heads, may not be washable at all; they can only be surface cleaned. To generalize, the following information applies only to fur, whether loose or sewn. For washing precautions for different types of foam, see Chapter 9.

Fur should be hand-washed, if possible. A bathtub is a convenient place to do this, since you have a ready source of heated water. If it's not practical to hand-wash the costume, machine washing with light agitation will work. If you're washing a bodysuit or sewn piece, turn it inside out before washing.

Wash fur with a mild detergent. I've had good luck using Woolite. Avoid heavily scented soaps; remember that you'll be trapped inside a closed space with that scent when you put the costume back on!

For fursuits with no dye or paint effects, you can add a mild bleach solution to help remove particularly tenacious stains as well as thoroughly disinfect the costume. As always, when working with bleach, test for color fastness on a small sample of fur. I've never found a synthetic fur that's affected by bleach, though.

Once the fur has been washed, it needs to be left to air dry. Never put fur in a clothes dryer. Even on a low setting, a dryer gets hot enough to partially melt the plastic fibers used to make fur, causing them to curl around themselves. The result can vary from the fur losing its texture and flowing movement to the nap completely contracting until the fur resembles a plastic Brillo pad!

To air dry your costume, arrange a raised rack or poles that can support the suit while it dries. After washing, hand wring as much water as possible from the fur. Then spread it as flat as possible on your drying rig. If you washed the costume inside out, return it to right-side out at this point. A box or window fan to direct air flow across the fur will speed up evaporation.

Allow at least 48 hours for the costume to dry; heavy shag costumes with no forced ventilation can easily take twice that long. Rearrange the fur every 12 hours or so to ensure all surfaces are open to the air.

I do not recommend drying a fursuit on a hanger. The weight of the waterlogged fur can distort the shoulders of the costume, since all of the weight is borne on a small area of the fabric. The knit backing of the fur will stretch and never quite return to its normal shape. The weight of wet fur requires that it be spread flat.

In fact, tests at the Riggs Hydraulics Laboratory[1] show that fake fur can absorb up to twenty times its own weight in water! This means that the weight of a wet costume, even after wringing out most of the water, is enough to cleanly snap a plastic clothes hanger. Have a sturdy drying rack ready before you have a heavy pile of sodden fur on your hands.

[1] Okay, fine, it's my kitchen… but I have a scientific-looking scale!

7 • Dyes & Paints

All costuming relies heavily on the use of color to convey visual concepts. When creating animal costumes, color is essential for characterizing both the species and the individual. Dyes and paints are used to modify the color of material surfaces in costuming.

This chapter contains information about selecting dyes or paints to achieve different effects. Which coloring technique is best depends on the desired visual effect, the materials being colored, and the resources available. This chapter does not cover the dye process in detail, since it varies by product; consult the instructions provided by the dye manufacturer for specifics.

Natural and Synthetic Fibers

All fabrics are fabricated from fibers. (Say that three times fast!) The composition of the fibers determines how a fabric will react to dyes, paints, and other liquids. We can broadly divide all fibers into two groups: natural and synthetic.

Natural fibers, as the name implies, are naturally occurring materials which can be used to make fabric. Natural fibers are normally water absorbent, which means that they will soak up water. If we use a water-based dye, the fibers will absorb the dye along with the water. The dye is then free to chemically bond with the fiber.

Natural fibers also tend to have a rough texture unless sizing surface treatments have been applied to them. Thus they are a good receptacle for paint, which can easily cling to the fibers. But we find that the absorbency of natural fibers is also a weakness: they stain more easily. Fabrics made from synthetic fibers will wear better and require less washing.

Synthetic fibers are manmade plastic[1] polymers. Like other plastics, these fibers tend to shed liquids rather than absorb them. It's difficult to dye these materials; the fibers are not receptive to most dyes. Coloring agents are usually added to synthetic fibers during their manufacture, while they are still in liquid form, to give the fabric its final color.

Dyes have been developed for every type of fiber. Whether the dye is practical for small-scale use, however, is another question. I've tried to keep these sections more practical for the home costumer.

Keep in mind that the art of dyeing has been around since ancient times. There are many ways to dye and many different tricks to employ – far more than can be included in this chapter. Always read the instructions specific to your dyes and consult other references if you plan to use dyes heavily in your projects. Check the bibliography for books on dye techniques.

Common Fibers

Natural Fibers
- Cotton
- Linen
- Rayon*
- Wool
- Silk

Synthetic Fibers
- Acrylic
- Modacrylic
- Nylon
- Polyester
- Spandex

* Alhough Rayon is manufactured, it's derived from wood pulp and has mostly natural fiber characteristics.

---

[1] Technically, spandex may be classified as an "elastomer," but let's not go there. We'll just label all synthetic fibers as "plastic" for our purposes.

Chapter 7

continued on next page...

Dye Terminology

Bleach – A chemical used to "whiten" fabrics by removing unwanted colors. We commonly think of chlorine bleach (*sodium hypochlorite*), though many household "color-safe" bleaches no longer contain chlorine. Dyes will react differently to bleach based on how they've bonded with the fiber; pigments, by contrast, are rarely affected. Excessive bleaching may damage natural fibers.

Bleeding – If color is lost into a water bath when finished material is rinsed, it is said to "bleed." Rinses during the dye process itself do not constitute bleeding. Compare **migration**.

Colorfastness – A measure of how well a color treatment endures over time. Colorfastness is often separated into *lightfastness*, resistance to fading in sunlight, and *washfastness*, resistance to loss of color due to washing.

Diluent – An inert solid substance used to dilute dye powders. Diluents are used to compensate for differences in dye efficiency so that different colors of dye can be equivalent by weight.

Dye – A coloring agent that bonds to fibers. Dyes work by absorbing light in part(s) of the spectrum, meaning the underlying fabric reflects only other portions of the spectrum. Since dyes are *subtracting* color from white light, you cannot dye something to a lighter shade. Compare **pigment**.

Dye Bath – The large volume of water and chemicals in which dyeing occurs.

Fixative – A chemical used to improve **colorfastness** that is applied *after* dyeing is completed. Compare **mordant**.

Migration – The spread of colors to adjacent pieces of fabric is color

Coloring Fur Fabrics

In the upcoming sections, we'll examine several different methods for coloring materials. Each technique has notes on how well it works for both natural and synthetic fibers. Choose your dye technique based on the fiber content in your project.

Since we're focusing on animal costumes we'll be putting a special emphasis on fake fur. Because fur is mass-produced in a limited range of colors, costumers often want to dye it. In addition, animals are never a flat color. They have species markings and unique coat patterns that can only be achieved by custom dying your fur.

Most synthetic fur is made from acrylic and modacrylic fibers, though you may also find some nylon or rayon. (If you have a fur of unknown provenance, assume that it's modacrylic.) The resistant chemical composition of these plastics makes it hard for common dyes to bond to the fibers. The dye has a tendency to rinse right out of the fur. This doesn't mean it's impossible to dye fur, it's just more of a challenge.

Occasionally, you may deal with high quality furs created from natural fibers (e.g., mohair). You might also deal with tufts of natural hair (e.g., horse hair) for specific effects or accents. Items such as these may be dyed as you would other natural protein fibers, such as silk or wool. Always dye natural fibers separately from any synthetics you may be using in the same costume.

In general, to create a new solid color it's best to start with a fur close to the desired color or a solid white. For markings, start with a fur of the correct base color. If you need to create several contrasting colors on one piece of material, start with white fur. Iif you're working from a sewing pattern, cut out all of the pattern pieces first before dyeing.

Always color as much material as you could possibly need in a single dye lot, since the color will be virtually impossible to match later on. Be wary of doing this with multiple passes through the same dye bath. Since the fabric absorbs the chemicals from the bath, the dye concentration will be weaker on the second batch of fabric done in the same bath. It's generally safer to use a larger dye bath and one dyeing session.

Mixed Materials and Mixed Dyes

Sometimes you will be working with a material made from several types of fibers. This is common when dealing with stretch fabrics, materials that are often spandex and cotton blends.

In these cases, dyes may not be able to create strong colors in the fabric because the dye is only bonding to a portion of the fibers, while the rest stay the original color. The result is that the original color persists and contributes to the overall color of the fabric, giving a slightly "washed out" appearance. If this color effect is acceptable (or even desirable) for your project, then dyeing mixed materials may work well. Be sure to use a stronger color dye than your chosen final color to compensate for the lightening effect of the undyed fibers. As always, experimentation is key.

Mixing different dyes can result in a similar problem. Dyes, especially synthetic dyes, undergo different chemical processes in order to bond with the fibers in the material. Different dyes will be absorbed at different rates. Dyes that bond very effectively may even displace weaker dyes.

The net result of all this is that the material will not be the color you see in the dye bath. The dye colors may look good in solution, but their uptake into the material happens at different speeds.

If you need to blend dye colors, be sure to shop for dyes specifically designed to allow mixing. Some families of dye products are designed to act at the same rate, so that they will reproduce blended colors in a dye bath correctly. Check product literature or containers to be sure that all of the dye colors you're using are designed to be mixed. Black is a notoriously difficult dye color and often doesn't work well in mixes.

General Dye Tips

Most dyes, regardless of their chemical base, follow the same basic process. The principle is to create a water bath with the dye dissolved in it. The bath should be large enough to accommodate all of the fabric with some room to spare. Make sure your fabric is clean before you dye it. A quick wash with a light detergent will remove sizing and finishing products that interfere with the dye process. Wetting the material will enhance dye uptake. Some dyes require a room temperature dye bath, while others must be kept simmering. Be sure you have a stove or heating element large enough.

Fabric should be lowered into the dye bath unfolded. Allow it to naturally settle in the bath. Ideally the fabric will be heavier than water and stay below the surface. If you're working with a fabric that tends to rise, you can force it down with a wire screen or vigilant stirring. Exposed fabric at the top of the bath is fabric that's not absorbing dye! Stir frequently, refolding the fabric in the dye bath if necessary, to ensure even coloring.

Remove the material from the dye bath after the specified time or when the color is satisfactory. To test the color, lift a corner of material out of the bath and rinse it with a little bit of fresh water. This will approximate the final color after rinsing out the excess dye. Once the material is out of the dye bath, rinse it until the water runs clear. Some dyes benefit from a light detergent at this stage (soaping). The goal is to remove excess dye that hasn't bonded to the fabric. If you leave this loose dye in place, the color may rub off and smear.

migration. Usually this happens as a result of an improperly bonded dye or pigment seeping within a material. Compare **bleeding**.

Mordant – Some dyes, especially natural dyes, do not create strong bonds with fibers. A mordant is added during the dyeing process to help the dye bond more effectively, increasing **colorfastness**. Most mordants are metallic salts (chromium is commonly used in the form of *potassium dichromate*) and can be quite toxic. Fortunately, very few modern dyes require separate mordants. Compare **fixative**.

Pigment – A colored particulate substance that is water insoluble. Pigments do not bond directly to fibers; instead, they must be adhered by another agent. Paints are examples of pigment systems. Synthetic fibers are often colored by adding pigments during the fiber's manufacture, trapping pigment within an otherwise clear fiber. Compare **dye**.

Soaping – Immediately after dyeing and rinsing, fabrics should be washed with a mild detergent and then rinsed again. This process, **soaping**, helps to remove unbonded dye from the material and thus prevent **bleeding** and **migration** of colors.

Comparison Chart

This chart provides a quick comparison of the different techniques covered in the upcoming sections. This information is based on my personal experience, information from manufacturers, and dyeing manuals.

Coloring Method	Works On	Sample Brands	Ease of Use	Washfastness	Bleach-safe
Union Dye	Natural Fibers	Rit, Deka	★★★	★	★
Reactive Dye	Natural Fibers	Dylon, Procion	★★★	★★★★	★
Disperse Dye	Synthetics	Dylon	★	★★★	★★★
Basic (Alkaline) Dye	Acrylics	Aljo	★★	★★★★	★
Acrylic Ink	Any Fibers	Higgins, FW	★★★★	★★★	★★★★
Leather Spirit Dye	Any Fibers	Fiebing's	★★★	★★	★★
Permanent Marker	Synthetics	Sharpie	★★★★	★★	★★★★

Union ("All-Purpose") Dyes

These are the ubiquitous consumer dyes found in all fabric, craft, and grocery stores. They are designed for use with cotton and other natural fibers. Their advantages are that they're inexpensive and easy to use… and that's about it. All you need is a large pot, water, and a mordant (such as table salt).

Union dyes are actually a combination of several different dye chemicals designed to work on a variety of natural fibers. Union dyes sometimes also contain a disperse dye to provide some color to synthetics. All of the dyes weakly bond with the host fibers. The weak affinity between the dyes and the fabric means that union dyes are not very colorfast. Many people are discouraged when they first try dyeing since they use union dyes and the colors bleed even after a dozen washes.

I recommend you skip union dyes for any serious costuming work. You'll have much better luck if you choose a dye (or other coloring method) specific to your material rather than try to use this catch-all household product.

Reactive Dyes

These dyes are commonly found at fabric and craft stores, sometimes labeled as "cold water dye." (Cold compared to some other dye processes, I suppose.) These dyes are designed primarily for natural fibers and work particularly well on cotton and silk. They also have a limited capability to dye synthetics, which includes most fur; they are more likely to impart only a tint.

Reactive dyes are applied in a dye bath of warm water along with a fixative to improve fastness. A heated dye bath can obtain a more intense color with some dye formulations by encouraging the dye to react with the material. Soak the fabric in the bath for the time indicated on the dye instructions, stirring to ensure even distribution of the colorants.

The fur can be simmered in the dye while being continually stirred. Control the temperature carefully and keep an eye on the fur fibers to make sure they aren't being affected by the heat. When working with acrylics, keep in mind that most of the color will rinse out (when in the bath, the fur holds a lot of water with dissolved dye that is not bonded to the fibers). To get an idea of the expected color, lift a corner of a fur piece above the dye bath and rinse it with a little clear water. Dyeing fur this way takes some practice, experience, and skill. Some luck doesn't hurt, either.

Disperse Dyes

This special category of dyes is about the only thing that will work with polyester fibers; although tailored for use with polyester, disperse dyes can be successfully applied to a wide range of synthetic fibers. Disperse dyes actually use microscopic particles that are insoluble in water. They precipitate onto the surface of the polyester fiber; a finishing process, either a special chemical carrier or high-temperature high-pressure treatment, forces the dye particles into the fiber.

Given the complex process involved in applying these dyes, I generally do not recommend them. If you're stuck working with polyester, this might be the solution.

Basic (Alkaline) Dyes

Basic dyes are ideal for acrylic and modacrylic fibers, where a portion of the dye chemically bonds to the ends of the acrylic polymers. There are special modified nylons and polyesters which can also accept these dyes. Basic dyes also work very well on silk and are sometimes used in decorative scarf painting. Results with other materials vary widely.

By chemically bonding with the acrylic, basic dyes have excellent washfastness. Their strong affinity for the fiber means that a lot of dye can be absorbed, resulting in intense colors. The only downside is that the chemical bond can be disrupted by bleaches and some alcohol-based solvents; as long as the material is washed with mild laundry detergent, there should be no degradation of color. These dyes will fade over time when exposed to sunlight (ultra-violet light can break down the dye compounds). If stored away from light when not worn, this shouldn't be a problem for the useful lifetime of a costume.

Basic dyes are a little more complex to use than regular dyes. They can very effectively stain a variety of materials, including buckets, gloves, tabletops, etc. So I recommend using disposable materials in a disposable room.

Follow any instructions provided with the dye. Also be sure to follow all listed safety precautions, since basic dyes tend to be toxic. Most basic dyes require a heated dye bath. Ensure that you have an appropriate heating setup available. Monitor the heat carefully to prevent damage to the fibers; overheating the fur can cause the fibers of the pile to curl and shrivel, ruining the fur's appearance and texture. For best results use an accurate thermometer and adjustable heat source. Test the process on a fur sample before risking all of your yardage.

Basic dyes can sometimes be difficult to locate, since there isn't a large consumer demand for them. (As hard as it is to believe, most of the public doesn't dye fake fur very often!) Try the Aljo Manufacturing Company listed in the Resources section.

Acrylic Paints and Inks

Acrylic does a good job of adhering to itself, which makes acrylic paints a good choice for coloring synthetic (acrylic) fur. However, acrylic paint is quite viscous and will attempt to glue fur fibers together into one big plastic lump. Instead of attempting to dye the fur in a bath, thinly apply the coloring by hand. This is a much more labor-intensive process than dyeing, but the results can be well worth the effort.

I recommend using acrylic artists' ink, since it has an almost water-thin consistency. You could also use acrylic paint formulated for airbrushing. Regular acrylic paint, however, is simply too thick to be worked into the fur without matting.

Apply the ink to the fur using a disposable acid brush. Use a scrubbing motion to work it down into the pile of the fur, all the way to the backing. This coats the individual fibers in the fur with a thin coat of acrylic. After applying the acrylic to a small patch of fur, use a metal comb or brush to keep the fur fibers from matting together. Brush the fur you're working on every minute or so to prevent matting and preserve the texture. Brushing the fur can also transfer some paint to surrounding fur, making color edges smoother and more natural.

Alternatively, acrylic paints can be airbrushed directly onto fur or other fabrics. Be sure to clean all parts of your airbrush thoroughly after use to prevent clogging.

Either of these techniques is great for applying spots or markings to animal costumes. If applied without working the ink all the way down into long fur, it can even provide the effect of "tipped" colors in a coat. It can be difficult to apply color evenly over large areas. Due to the application technique, a mottled appearance results. This can work well for an animal costume by giving the coat an organic appearance.

Craft stores sometimes sell products for creating imitation stained glass decorations labeled as "plastic dyes." In reality, these are usually regular acrylic paints that are applied to the surface, creating a coating layer. Since they're made with transparent colorants, the "plastic dye" looks as if it has imparted a colorful tint to the plastic surface. For most costuming work, it's easier to simply use regular acrylic inks.

The vivid coat markings in this costume were created by airbrushing spirit dyes.

Leather Spirit Dyes

There are several different brands of alcohol-based ("spirit") dyes available for leatherworking. These dyes consist of a colorant suspended in a fast-evaporating alcohol medium. They are intended to be used as stains or tints on leather, but they can also be applied to fur and other materials with great results.

The principle is the same as with acrylic ink: the dye coats fibers in the fur to change their apparent color. Spirit dyes don't present as much trouble with sticking fur together due to the alcoholic medium. Spirit dyes are fairly washfast..

Spirit dyes can be applied with a hand brush or airbrush, as described above for paints. Airbrushing with a very low pressure seems to produce the best effects.

Permanent Markers

Permanent markers can be a quick and inexpensive way to apply small pattern elements to fur. I like to use the Sharpie™ brand of markers for this. You can use the tip of the marker directly in the fur pile to rub color onto the fibers. This can be a good way to add finishing touches to a costume's patterns. Be aware that this is a very tedious method to create a reasonably solid color. Only use it for smaller markings and accents.

One downside is that it can take a long time for the ink to "set" on the fur. This is because the carrier fluid of the ink is not being absorbed by a porous material (such as paper), so it is still liquid until the alcohol can completely evaporate. The ink clings to the fibers by surface tension. Given a long period of air drying, though, the ink is fairly colorfast. To test whether the ink is dry, gently poke a finger into a colored area of the fur and see if any ink transfers to your skin.

Over time, the ink may migrate around the fur. The black ink is actually composed of several different pigments that have different fastness with fabrics. A yellow component appears to transfer more easily and, over time, will create a yellow halo effect. It's unusual to be able to notice this in fur, but it is definitely apparent in cotton fabrics.

The ink will not stand up to heavy washing, since it can loosen the pigment to the point where it gets rubbed off in the wash. Gentle hand washing would probably not remove the ink markings. Bleach has little to no effect on Sharpie™ ink. One advantage of permanent markers, however, is that the coloration can easily be reapplied should it begin to fade.

Containers and Equipment

When working with paints, dyes, and other colorants, it's important to have the right equipment on hand. Always make sure you have enough containers and the right equipment before you get started with a complex procedure.

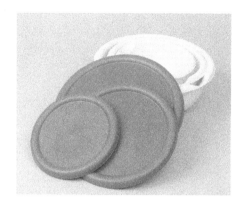

It should go without saying: always wear gloves when working with dyes. Given the wide variety of synthetic dyes in use today, be sure to read any instructions or safety information. If a chemical is potentially dangerous, the company should be able to provide a Material Safety Data Sheet (MSDS) upon request. (A sample MSDS can be found on page 201.)

The most elusive piece of equipment for dyeing can be the dye bath container. A suitable vessel should be large enough to hold the amount of material to be dyed (loosely folded) with a minimum of six inches of air space on all sides; you need enough volume to be able to fully submerse the fabric and stir it.

Dye vessels must be a material that will not react with the dye; you want the color of the dye to be absorbed by the fabric, not your container! Porcelain can be microscopically porous and absorb some dyes (so skip the sink). Fiberglass reacts with some dyes and can be permanently stained (so skip the bathtub).

I like to use large Rubbermaid™ storage bins for cold bath dyeing. Most large plastic containers are made from polyethylene or polypropylene plastics (see sidebar) which are chemically resistant. Unfortunately, these products cannot be used on a stove, so dyes requiring heating while the fabric is in the bath are impractical. In those cases, look for a large stainless steel basting pan. Although expensive, stainless stands up well to dyes. Alternatively, most dyes will work in an aluminum pot; run a test first to be sure that the metal doesn't interfere with the dye.

Keep several additional containers around for mixing, clear water rinses, and storage of extra dye. Some dyes are light sensitive and must be kept in opaque storage containers.

Paints have fewer container considerations than dyes. Most paints come in a container that can also be used for storage. If you need to store premixed colors of paint, look for small plastic containers with airtight lids.

8 • Glues & Adhesives

Glues and adhesives serve a wide variety of roles in costuming, from temporarily securing a fabric piece to holding together structural elements. The variety of glues available to consumers today is staggering. In this chapter, I focus on several representative products and compare their applicability to costuming problems. There are certainly many other glues you could use and I encourage you to explore the options; these glues were selected because I think they're broadly applicable to costuming situations.

The terms **glue** and **adhesive** are generally used synonymously today. Originally, glue specifically referred to animal-derived products. One technical distinction that some people like to make is that a glue is a type of liquid adhesive that fully dries (i.e. loses its stickiness). Some adhesives remain tacky almost indefinitely (yellow sticky notes). In general, the terms are used interchangeably.

Hot glue is useful for making emergency repairs.

What adhesive is right for a situation depends on several factors. First, consider what sorts of stresses will be placed on the joint. Use a stronger glue in areas of the costume which support other parts. For surface pieces or decorative items, you might select a weaker or cheaper glue. Second, consider the materials being glued together, called **substrates** or **adherents**. Some glues simply will not adhere well to certain materials; other glues will actually damage inappropriate materials.

Another consideration is the method of application. Some glues are sprayed on, some are brushed on, and a few have unique application requirements. Use a technique which makes you comfortable and is practical for your workspace and the costume.

Last but not least is the toxicity of the adhesive. Some glues are relatively non-toxic while others require goggles, gloves, and respirators for safe use. Electing to work with dangerous materials is a personal choice; some costumers are wary of toxic products while others embrace their superior results.

The key is awareness. Always be aware of the safety provisions for the products you're using in your workspace. In this chapter, I've tried to include relevant information about the safe handling of the different adhesives so that you can take this into account when choosing what to use yourself.

Technical information about risks, precautions, and emergency response can be found on Material Safety Data Sheets (**MSDS**), available from the manufacturers. Retailers sometimes keep MSDS copies for products that they sell, although this isn't required by law. For more information about interpreting these forms and their recommendations, see the MSDS samples. See page 201 for a sample MSDS.

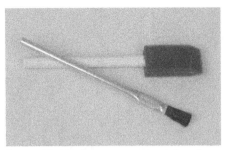

Disposable brushes are an essential tool when working with adhesive products.

Drying, Curing, and Setting

Most glues are a liquid which hardens into a solid. The liquid can be applied to a substrate, covering the surface. As it solidifies, the glue physically locks into the texture of the surface. This creates a physical bond based on the tensile strength of the dried glue.

Some adhesives also work by chemical action, bonding to materials. These are usually specialized glues for working with particular materials. For example, they make a special acrylic plastic cement which uses chemical action to "weld" pieces together.

Different glues use different mechanisms to bring about the change from liquid to solid state. They may rely on temperature changes (either heating or cooling), evaporative action, or chemical catalysts.

During the transition from liquid to solid, many glues pass through a **gel** state. At this time, the glue is partially solidified and will resist further spreading or brushing; working the glue too much while it's in the gel state can greatly weaken the final bond. If you're still trying to work with the glue when it gels, consider removing and reapplying the glue for better results.

The time between first mixing or applying the glue and when it begins to gel is referred to as the **pot life** of the glue. The term comes from measuring how long you can work with an open pot of glue before it becomes unusable.

Curing is the term for the change in physical properties of the glue based on chemical action. A glue is fully cured once it has hardened to its maximum strength. The term **drying** is also used when the hardening process involves evaporative action. **Setting** is the process of the glue is becoming more viscous. When the glue has become stiff, after the end of the pot life, it has **set**.

Safety Equipment

One of the most important things to be aware of is that glues and adhesive products can be dangerous chemicals. Precautions should be taken when working with many of these products to stay safe and healthy. Wearing the proper safety equipment and using the product in an area with proper ventilation are essential to stay safe. Make sure to read all manufacturer's guidelines and packaging before using any glue product. These are only guidelines, if in doubt, play it safe.

The best time to get your safety equipment together is before you begin your project. I like to keep a kit of safety supplies gathered together in a bucket so that I can find them easily and use them when I need them. These are the essential items in my collection.

Disposable dust mask

Cartridge respirator

Thick rubber gloves
Thin latex protective gloves
Dust mask
Respirator
First-aid kit
Towels for quick cleanups

Comparison Chart

This chart is based on my experiences with different glues. All of the adhesives listed will be discussed in the following sections (except "sewing", which is listed as a glue alternative for comparison purposes). These are just some of my favorite products from the myriad adhesives available. Experimentation and experience are always your best guide, so feel free to forge your own path!

		Sewing	Hot Glue	White Glue	CA (Superglue)	Super 74/77/80	Fastbond 100/2000	Epoxy	J-B Weld	Barge Cement	Goop	E6000	Silicone
Cellulose	Wood			●	○		○	●	○	○	●	●	○
	Cardboard			●			○			○	○	○	
	Paper			●		○							
Casting	Fiberglass				○	○		●	●	○	○	●	●
	Alginate				●								
Metal	Wire *							●	●	●	●	●	○
	Sheet Metal *							○	●	●	●	○	○
Fabric	Felt	●		●		●	○					○	○
	Fur	●	●	○		●	○			●	●	●	●
	Synthetic Fiber	●	●	○		●	○			●	○	●	●
	Natural Fiber	●	●	○		●	○			○	○	●	○
Rubber	Vulcanized Sheet *	○								●	●	○	○
	Foam, Closed-Cell		●			●	●			○	○	○	
	Foam, Open-Cell		○			●	●			○	○		
Plastic	Plastic Canvas	●	●					○		●	●	○	○
	HDPE, PP, Plastics							○				●	●
	Acrylic Sheet *		○		●			●	○	●	●	●	●

○ Results vary or glue adheres to less than full potential
● Glue works well on this substrate and is recommended

* Score or abrade the surface before gluing for best results

Chapter 8

Hot Glue

Name: Hot glue

Work Time: 30 seconds

Full Set Time: 2 minutes

Bond Strength: moderate

Bond Flexibility: stiff

Dangers: can easily burn skin

Safety Precautions: normal ventilation, first-aid burn kit

Hot glue gun and glue sticks

One of the most common and versatile tools used in costuming is hot glue or "hot melt glue". This fast and easy adhesive solves a whole host of problems! I always recommend carrying a glue gun and some glue sticks when travelling for last-minute emergency repairs.

Another advantage of hot glue is that it's relatively inexpensive. You can pick up handfuls of glue sticks and a glue gun at a local crafts store without denting your budget. I'd advise against getting any glue gun that doesn't use standard large-diameter glue sticks; it's an attempt to force you to buy specialty (read: overpriced) glue refills.

When using a glue gun, keep track of where the metal tip is at all times, since this is the hottest part of the gun. If your gun comes with a stand, use it; if not, a makeshift stand can be created from some heavy-gauge galvanized wire. Most glue guns don't have temperature regulators, so their electric coils keep heating the glue even after it's nicely melted. If your glue gun has a tendency to overheat, I recommend plugging it into a power strip with a separate power switch. If the power strip is on the floor under your work table, you can flip the power on and off with your foot in order to regulate the temperature of the glue gun. If you want to undertake a more advanced electrical project, a dimmer switch can be used to create an adjustable outlet for the gun.

The glue itself is composed of thermoplastic. At low temperatures, it's a solid waxy plastic; at higher temperatures, typically around 180-200°F, it melts into a thick liquid. Once the glue is applied, it cools naturally and solidifies. Since hot glue is fairly thick, it needs good opportunities to establish a physical purchase. This means that the surface should have a texture which the glue can grip. It works very well with fabrics, where the glue can flow into the weave of the material. A hot glue bond is only as strong as the glue itself. If the glue gets a good grip on the adherent, it can hold fairly well, but hot glue is not a high-strength solution unless you use a lot.

Should you get any glue on yourself, don't panic! Using a rolling motion, peel it off as quickly as possible to prevent skin burns. Remember: if you use hot glue, you *can* burn yourself and you *will* get blisters. It is a ubiquitous, ignoble costuming tradition.

The good news is that the glue itself isn't very dangerous. Hot glue is a fairly inert, nontoxic plastic. Since it releases minimal fumes (from plasticizer additives), unless it starts burning from getting too hot, you need only normal air circulation. Better ventilation is always recommended, however. Wait until we get to the dangerous glues later – you'll start to appreciate this simplicity!

I find hot glue is best for tacking down the backsides of fur pieces to foam understructures. It flows into the weave of materials, making it able to form a strong bond with almost any type of fabric. Just be careful not to drip any glue on the outside of the fur!

White Glue

There is a variety of common white glues available. The Elmer's company produces a line of these adhesives, including the white glue we all used in grade school. Although generally not very strong, these glues are still useful in some costume situations.

This family of glues is known as **emulsion adhesives**. Emulsion adhesives use a water dispersion to deliver tiny glue particles. The substrate needs to be able to absorb the water in the glue to promote fast setting. As the water is removed, the glue particles leave the suspension and aggregate on the substrate surfaces, where they bond together into a single mass. The result is a type of soft plastic. The primary component of most modern emulsion adhesives is a synthetic chemical such as polyvinyl acetate (PVA).

These glues can form light to medium strength bonds, depending on brand and formulation. They work especially well if they're used to join two flat opposing surfaces. PVA glue is also good for attaching small or lightweight decorative items, such as felt cutouts and baubles. The glue is generally non-reactive with other materials, so it's safe to use on almost anything. The only caveat is that at least one of the substrates needs to be able to absorb water, or the bond will have trouble attaining full strength.

Names: White Glue, PVA Glue

Work Time: 2–20 minutes

Full Set Time: 30–120 minutes

Bond Strength: light to medium

Bond Flexibility: moderate

Dangers: none (unless specific to product)

Safety Precautions: normal ventilation

Cyanoacrylate (CA) Glue - Superglue

Though you may not be familiar with the technical name for this adhesive, you're almost certainly familiar with one of the brand names: Krazy Glue™. Cyanoacrylate superglue is available in a variety of other brands, including Zap-A-Gap™, Loctite™, and Insta-Jet™.

For the money, the best place to find CA is at hobby shops. Model builders use it frequently to adhere plastic parts together. Hobby stores tend to have much better prices than craft or fabric stores, as well as a better selection of brands. Each formulation is only slightly different, with assorted thickeners and inhibitors to tweak the behavior of the glue.

Some varieties of CA with retarders to slow the reaction have separate **kicker** sprays; these can be anything which encourages the curing to speed up. I exclusively use regular "instant" superglue, since it's one less chemical bottle to worry about and it makes a slightly more durable bond.

Pure cyanoacrylate monomer is runny, similar to alcohol, and reacts almost instantly. Some brands have thickeners added to keep the glue from being too thin. The catalyst for CA glue is actually water. Even trace amounts of moisture lingering on a surface are enough to allow the cyanoacrylate monomers to polymerize and chemically bond together. Within seconds, this produces acrylic, a strong and rigid plastic locking together the two items.

Superglue can be used on many materials, including acrylic plastic itself. It is one of the only things that can be used to bond alginate. It's also useful because it needs only a small area to get a good grip. It does have negative reactions to some materials, including almost all natural fabrics, styrofoam (polystyrene), and paper products (cellulose). It can release highly noxious fumes and chemicals, including unreacted cyanoacrylate monomer, hydroquinone, and a host of other nasties. Some people are allergic to these chemicals, so take precautions. Even if you're not sensitive to it, always use this glue in a well-ventilated area. There is some anecdotal evidence that exposure to these chemicals over time can cause your body to become *more* sensitive to them,

Names: Krazy Glue™, CA Glue

Work Time: 1 second

Full Set Time: 5–30 seconds

Bond Strength: medium

Bond Flexibility: rigid, brittle

Dangers: noxious fumes, bonds skin

Safety Precautions: good ventilation, glasses

QuickTite™ Super Glue

as they slowly accumulate to toxic levels because your body can't effectively process them.

Be aware that superglue can bond to human skin in a matter of seconds. (My most common mistake is letting a drop roll down the nozzle, bonding my hand to the superglue bottle while my attention's focused on the costume piece.) If the glue dries, the key is not to panic and yank the areas apart. Use a peeling action to loosen the glue from your skin. Acetone-based nail polish remover can help to loosen the bond.

Should you accidentally get CA in your eye, it will likely bond your eyelids together as you have a natural blinking reflex. Do not force the eyelids apart! Seek medical attention to ensure there's no damage to the eye. The glue will naturally separate from the skin, in three or four days, allowing your eye to open by itself.

One curious point is that safety information is not available about the effects of swallowing liquid superglue because it is physically impossible! The moisture in your mouth hardens the glue instantly, making it impossible to ingest. Should a drop of glue flip into your mouth, wait for it to harden, spit it out, and rinse your mouth thoroughly with water.

FoamFast Super 74™ Aerosol Adhesive

Name: 3M Super 74™

Work Time: 1 minute

Full Set Time: 1 hour

Bond Strength: light

Bond Flexibility: very flexible

Dangers: vapors

Safety Precautions: good ventilation

This variant of Super 77 is a thicker formulation designed for use with foam rubber. The adhesive is essentially the same, so the same usage guidelines apply. The thicker non-misting spray makes it easier to apply to open-cell foam without having the glue soak in too fast; instead, the glue remains on the surface so that it can bond with the other adherent.

I find that it's easier to use Super 74 when working with thin fabrics. Super 77 has a tendency to soak through quite quickly, impregnating the fabric with glue but leaving less at the surface. The Super 74 formulation solves this problem with a more viscous flow that's still able to grip the fabric. If you're gluing down fur, Super 74 won't soak into the backing and mat down the fibers of the fur. It's also useful if you're applying foam or fur to a bodysuit; thinner glues will soak through the spandex of the suit and reach the skin (a painful experience, I am told).

Super 77™ Aerosol Adhesive

Name: 3M Super 77™

Work Time: 30 seconds

Full Set Time: 1 hour

Bond Strength: light

Bond Flexibility: very flexible

Dangers: flammable and toxic mist

Safety Precautions: good ventilation, dust mask, goggles

3M Super 77™ is a good general-purpose aerosol (spray) adhesive available in most fabric and craft stores. Like most aerosol products, Super 77 provides a relatively low-strength bond. It's designed primarily for use with fabrics and foam. Using it over a large area can make up for its weak bonding ability, but I would still recommend that it never be used as the sole method of attaching important costume pieces, given the rough working conditions of mascot costumes.

Super 77 does work very well for positioning pieces of fabric or keeping a lining material from sliding around. Use it to tack large areas of fabric or foam together and then sew or glue down the edges to reinforce it.

To apply it, spray a light coating of glue onto both surfaces, moving continuously to get even coverage. Wait for a few seconds to allow the glue to soak into the substrates before bringing the two pieces together. Be sure you align the pieces carefully, since this glue loses strength if you separate and reposition it. If you're working with fabric, always begin at the center of the piece and work outwards, smoothing as you go to avoid any wrinkles.

Although Super 77 isn't too dangerous compared to other adhesives, you should still observe safety precautions when employing it. Since it's an aerosol, it generates a fine mist of glue droplets that tend to hang in the air. *Always* use it in a well-ventilated area. A dust mask will provide a surface to allow any stray glue mist to settle before it gets into your nose or mouth. Goggles are a good idea to prevent overspray from finding its way into your eyes. Should you get Super 77 in your eyes, immediately flush with plenty of water and seek medical attention.

Never use this glue around an open flame or source of ignition, as the vapor and spray are highly flammable.

Gloves are not required when working with this product. Some people have skin irritation after getting the adhesive on their hands, but this appears to be rare. As always, it's good to avoid prolonged skin contact and to wash your hands thoroughly after working with this glue.

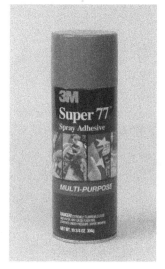

Super 77™ – Multi-Purpose Spray Adhesive

Super 80™ Aerosol Adhesive

This is yet another 3M variety of spray adhesive. Super 80 is not the same formulation as Super 77 and behaves somewhat differently. Super 80 uses neoprene-based adhesives to create a stronger rubberized bond. It is designed for plastic, vinyl, and rubber materials but can also do a good job gluing leather, wood, and laminates. If you're working with fabric, consider Super 74 as an alternative. If you're working with foam, consider Fastbond 100, discussed below.

The strength of Super 80 is fairly good. Used over a decent contact area, it can support a moderate amount of stress. It takes about twice as long as Super 77 to cure to full strength, however, so plan to let pieces sit and dry for a couple of hours.

Super 80 can be a difficult product to locate since there isn't a great public demand for specialized glues. Check your phone book for industrial supply companies if local hobby shops don't carry it. You can also call 3M customer support or go to their website to get the location of the nearest retailer for any 3M product.

Name: 3M Super 80™

Work time: 1 minute

Full Set Time: 2–3 hours

Bond Strength: medium

Bond Flexibility: very flexible

Dangers: vapors

Safety Precautions: good ventilation

Fastbond 100™

This is another 3M neoprene glue, though in a liquid rather than aerosol form. Fastbond 100™ is a water-based solution of neoprene reactant (**poly-chloroprene**) that can be applied directly to urethane foam rubber and other materials. This glue is the ideal product for foam-to-foam bonds. I highly recommend it if you plan on building structural foam.

Fastbond is designed to be used with industrial pneumatic sprayers. I've found that it works perfectly well when applied directly with a disposable brush or foam applicator. I like to put the glue into a paper cup and then apply it with a disposable acid brush. Since costuming usually involves working with smaller areas, this is much more convenient than spray application. The pot life of this glue is very long since it sets only through water evaporation.

Name: Fastbond 100™

Work time: 30 seconds

Full Set Time: 15–30 minutes

Bond Strength: strong

Bond Flexibility: very flexible

Dangers: vapors

Safety Precautions: good ventilation

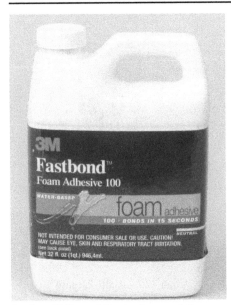

Fastbond™ Foam Adhesive is one of the most essential products in the arsenal of the animal costumer.

As a glue, Fastbond is fairly impressive. It develops a firm set after only 30 seconds so you can hold the foam together while the glue dries. (If it takes any longer than that, you're applying it too thickly.) After it's fully cured, the glue is stronger than the foam itself! Since the glue line is essentially soft neoprene rubber, it doesn't limit the movement of the foam. You can also cut through the dried glue without difficulties. These properties make it an excellent choice for foam padding and shaping in costumes.

Fastbond is also a fairly safe glue. It can be used in a well-ventilated area without safety equipment. When curing, it can release some carbon monoxide and unreacted polychloroprene. With directional ventilation, you can avoid the vapors without the need of a mask or respirator. The adhesive and its vapors are not flammable. It shouldn't affect your skin unless you have an allergy to the rubber itself; avoid excessive exposure, though, just to be on the safe side.

Fastbond 100™ is related to another 3M product, Fastbond 2000™. This is a two-part glue (adhesive and accelerant) which requires a dual-nozzle sprayer. It can be applied by hand but it is more difficult to use than Fastbond 100. Since the glue formulation is almost identical, there's no real advantage to using Fastbond 2000 unless you already have the sprayer equipment available or you need a particularly long drying time.

Fastbond 100 is an industrial product so it can be difficult to locate. Check your phone book for industrial supplies and equipment vendors. As mentioned above, you can call 3M customer support or go to their website to get the location of the nearest retailer for any 3M product.

Epoxy Resins

The term **epoxy** refers to a broad class of two-part chemical resins. One part is the eponymous epoxy (actually a "diepoxy," a molecule with two exposed epoxy tails) while the other is a diamine capable of linking several epoxies together. Traditionally, the epoxy resin is Part A (clear) and the diamine hardener is Part B (yellowish). When combined, the diamine bonds with the exposed epoxy tails, hooking all of the molecules together into a large cross-linked collection of molecules. These powerful chemical bonds are what give epoxy its incredible strength. Since they aren't water-based glues, epoxies can be used around water without adverse effects.

The cure times for epoxy products vary, so examine the labels when you're shopping. For consumer epoxies, the times usually range from 3 minutes to 30 minutes of pot life. Hobby and model shops have the best selection of epoxy products, in my experience. I don't recommend the dual syringe of epoxy you find in most craft stores; it's easier (and cheaper) to work with products provided in two separate squeeze bottles.

Paper cups handy for mixing epoxy. Plastic party cups aren't as good because they can deform, and occasionally even melt from the heat of the epoxy curing. Avoid Styrofoam cups since some epoxies will react with and decompose them. A pack of bamboo skewers make good disposable mixing sticks.

Always mix the two parts together *thoroughly* before applying the epoxy to surfaces. Undermixing epoxy is the biggest reason bonds fail to reach full strength. Apply the glue with disposable applicators (a fancy term for "scraps of cardboard").

Epoxy bonds very well with wood, metal, fiberglass, and hard plastics. It can handle fabric, too, although it's usually not the best choice for the job. Epoxy

Name: Epoxy

Work time: 3–30 minutes

Full Set Time: 1–2 days

Bond Strength: very strong

Bond Flexibility: rigid, brittle

Dangers: toxic vapors

Safety Precautions: good ventilation, glasses

Five Minute Epoxy

forms a very durable, stable, and rigid joint once cured. It is not a good glue to use on rubber or other materials that flex; the flexing action of rubber will dislodge and crack the epoxy, causing the bond to fail.

Although it's not likely to be a problem for most costuming applications, it is worth noting that most consumer epoxies lose strength and/or become more brittle when exposed to below-freezing temperatures. Just in case you're making an ice skating costume… Hey, it might happen!

Epoxy needs careful handling. Always use it in a well-ventilated place, as the fumes are unpleasant. The chemical components in epoxy cannot be readily absorbed through the skin, so gloves aren't required, but given the sticky nature of mixed epoxy, many costumers opt for gloves anyway to make cleanup easier. Because each company uses different additives in its products which may introduce extra handling precautions, check the MSDS sheets for the particular brand of epoxy that you choose.

I recommend wearing safety glasses, even though that might seem a bit excessive. It's unlikely that any epoxy will find its way into your eyes since it's a thick liquid. However, it is very painful and dangerous to eyes, so I think a little extra precaution is in order.

JB Weld™

The JB Weld Company produces a line of specialty metal epoxies under a variety of names (Adhesiveweld™, Autoweld™, Marineweld™, etc.). These are all fundamentally the same adhesive: a modified epoxy resin containing metallic particles. The adhesive is designed to harden without becoming too brittle. The epoxy has a great affinity for the metal particles, which adds to the strength of the compound.

One advantage of this epoxy is that it can be drilled and sanded. If you need to join metal pieces anywhere on your costume, whether exposed to view or internal, it's a good choice. Otherwise, it's used in many of the same ways as ordinary epoxy. Since it is more expensive and slightly harder to work with. I would reserve it for cases where at least one of the adherents is metallic.

In addition to the precautions cited for epoxy, gloves are recommended when working with JB Weld in order to avoid possible skin irritation.

Name: JB Weld
Work time: 20 minutes
Full Set Time: 1 day
Bond Strength: very strong
Bond Flexibility: rigid
Dangers: toxic vapors, skin irritant
Safety Precautions: good ventilation, glasses, gloves

Barge™ Cement

Barge Cement is a glue produced by Korkers, Inc. It's usually called "Barge Cement" because it is a modern replacement for rubber cement adhesives. This product is specially designed for shoe repairs and can be found at footwear stores.

A tenacious and durable glue, it's one of the few that will grip **vulcanized** rubber. It can also bond well with plastics, metal (rough surfaced), and heavy fabrics. The glue itself is a thick gel which can be applied directly from the tube; use a disposable applicator to spread it, if necessary.

Barge is based on toluene *(methyl benzene)*, a highly toxic chemical produced from petroleum refinement (and naturally found in the tolu tree, for which the chemical is named). Toluene is a powerful solvent, used here as a carrier for the glue components. When you apply Barge, toluene and other volatile byproducts evaporate. Because of this, always work in a very well ventilated area. Some of the vapors are heavier than air and flammable. An organic

Name: Barge Cement
Work time: 30–45 minutes
Full Set Time: 2 days
Bond Strength: strong
Bond Flexibility: moderate
Dangers: very toxic vapors
Safety Precautions: forced ventilation or respirator, gloves

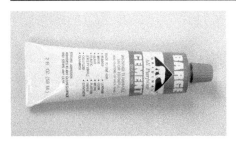

Barge™ Cement

cartridge vapor respirator is recommended if you plan to work with this glue for any extended period. Repeated exposure to the vapors can cause long-term respiratory damage.

Since the toxicity of this glue is so strong, I recommend you do not use it on costume heads. The outgassing from a single glue joint can persist for weeks. You don't want to be trapped inside a costume head with these vapors!

Personally, I tend to avoid Barge because of its toxicity and noisome odor. But there are occasional situations, such as attaching soles to feet, where it is simply the best tool for the job. It's a powerful glue, but you have to treat it with care.

Goop™

Name: Goop™

Work time: 15–30 minutes

Full Set Time: 1–2 days

Strength: strong

Flexibility: moderate

Dangers: very toxic vapors

Safety Precautions: forced ventilation or respirator, gloves

Goop™ is made by Eclectic Products, Inc. (These people have a flair for naming things!) It is similar to Barge in that it uses toluene and naphtha as primary ingredients. The composition is slightly different from Barge and I find that this makes Goop easier to work with.

Goop works very well on a variety of materials. It forms fairly strong bonds, varying significantly by substrate and surface texture. It takes 30 minutes to set to the point that pieces can be safely handled. The bond continues to increase in strength over the next two days.

An advantage of Goop is that it remains semi-flexible when it is fully cured. It is a good adhesive for joints experiencing a lot of flexing motions, since the glue can absorb some of that energy without cracking. Goop tends to be very thick and viscous. When applied to fabrics, it doesn't soak in very heavily.

When working with larger surface areas, squeeze out a line of glue and then spread it with a disposable applicator, such as a disposable plastic butter knife. This allows you to create a smooth, thin layer of glue across a surface, resulting in a very strong bond. This same technique can also serve as a way to seal costume pieces against water, oil, and other liquids. You apply Goop to the outside of a piece and then spread it until it is only a thin surface coating. This effectively laminates the piece in a protective layer of resilient clear rubber.

Goop™ Contact Adhesive

Since it is based on toluene, all of the warnings provided for Barge Cement also apply here. The odor is less intense but Goop should still be used only in a well-ventilated area. There is some risk of skin absorption from extended handling, so wear gloves. Remember to wash your hands thoroughly when you're done and to avoid prolonged exposure. Use a respirator or directional ventilation system to deal with fumes.

Although each costumer must decide what level of product toxicity they are comfortable with, Goop can be very useful with a number of different materials. I have found it to be a very effective adhesive in my costuming toolkit. The key is to always remember safety when using it.

E6000™

E6000™ is another glue from Eclectic Products. This is geared towards the industrial market, so it may be harder to locate at craft stores. The upside is that it's available in dispensing tubes for use with caulking guns, making it very cost-effective to buy in bulk.

E6000 is primarily *tetrachloroethylene*, a synthetic polymer adhesive. It sets relatively quickly, but continues to gain bond strength for the next two days. For best results, apply E6000 to both substrates separately and allow them to sit for five minutes before joining them. This allows it to develop better adhesion with each substrate. E6000 bonds very well with a number of materials, including some tricky synthetics such as neoprene rubber.

It's worth noting that E6000 is a strong insulator and is regarded as safe around low-voltage electrical components. If your project has exposed electronics, this may be a safe way to encapsulate them and protect them from moisture or skin contact.

E6000 can be used without protective eyewear. Goggles may be useful if you are leaning close to the work area, since some people have reactions to the adhesive's vapors. If any your eyes become irritated, flush with water for 15 minutes; if they are still irritated, see a doctor immediately.

Always use it in a well-ventilated space or wear a respirator. Wash your hands thoroughly with soap and water after working with this glue. Gloves are not necessary if your exposure to the glue is limited.

Name: E6000™

Work time: 10–15 minutes

Full Set Time: 1–2 days

Bond Strength: strong

Bond Flexibility: moderate

Dangers: toxic vapors

Safety Precautions: good ventilation or respirator, gloves

E6000™

Silicone Adhesives

There is a variety of silicone adhesives on the consumer market today. I recommend GE Silicone II™ adhesive, though the following information should be applicable to all silicone products. Note that silicone adhesive is *not* the same as silicone caulk!

Silicone is a synthetic polymer made from silicon. Taken alone, silicone doesn't have strong adhesive capabilities except with itself. Special ("trade secret") adhesion promoters are added to give the silicone an affinity for other substrates. Other catalysts, fillers, and plasticizers (to adjust viscosity) are added to the product. Each silicone product is different since there are many variables. Experiment until you find one that works to your satisfaction.

Silicone tends to be fairly stable and durable, a definite plus for costuming. It bonds well with a variety of substrates, including most plastic and rubber materials. When dry, it forms a semiflexible bond of decent strength. Silicone is also available in large dispensing tubes for caulking guns, which cuts down on packaging costs, giving you a better retail price.

Silicone can even be cast in molds (carefully coated in a release agent, such as petroleum jelly or plastic wrap) to create small rubberized items. Special casting silicone is available which will produce superior results for larger cast items. Silicone adhesive can be useful if casting detail is not essential and the cast shape needs to be adhered to some other material, such as a backing.

Although silicone glues are very useful, some of these products also contain very dangerous chemicals. Be sure to take all safety precautions recommended by your product's manufacturer, including ventilation, respirator, goggles (the vapors are strong eye irritants), or gloves.

Name: Silicones

Work time: 10–60 minutes

Full Set Time: 1 day

Bond Strength: moderate

Bond Flexibility: moderate

Dangers: toxic vapors, skin irritant

Safety Precautions: good ventilation or respirator, gloves

Silicone Adhesive

Professional Profile

Bob Duncan

Bob Duncan has managed a foam distribution business for over two decades. His shop provides a variety of foam formulations and shapes. You can find out more at www.bobsfoam.com.

How did you get involved in foam manufacturing?

I got a job working for a foam manufacturer in 1968. I liked the work and I've been doing it ever since. I opened my own business in Fremont, California in 1979 and I've been here ever since.

What about your work is most interesting?

The most interesting thing is everybody that calls or walks in the door. Everybody wants a different product for a different purpose. It's not repetitive, like some industrial jobs. Even the shop changes, day to day.

How do you gauge the quality of foam?

Usually, the heavier the foam, the better it is. That means you're getting more chemical structure and less air. That's a sign of a more solid foam that will last longer. Though there are times, such as some costume work, where you might prefer a lighter product.

Are there any hazards associated with foam?

Foam can burn. These days, most foam manufactured is fire-retardant, since it's used for mattresses and cushions. Even then, the foam will burn if exposed to a flame; remove

the heat source, though, and it will self-extinguish.

The smoke given off when foam burns is very toxic. We don't use hot wires for cutting at all, since they partially burn the foam and release smoke. We cut foam in the shop with band saws and die cutting.

Most foams are polyurethane. What advantages do you get from other chemicals, such as polyethylene?

Polyethylene is very light. It's light but semi-rigid. It's easy to work with a carving knife. In addition to the polyethylene, you've got crosslink foams, neoprene, reticulated.. so there's a lot of different foams you can choose from. It all depends on what you need to make with it.

What are some of the more interesting uses of your foam that you've seen?

Oh, all kinds of packaging people come up with. Lots of requests for beds; people want a mattress that's soft, firm, and medium all at the same time. I suppose we've made some pretty weird things over the years. We made a 26 foot tennis shoe for the Bay to Breakers race. We've also sold special foam to Lawrence Livermore Labs, so some of my foam is circling the Earth in a satellite somewhere.

Foam has a definite lifespan. What are the factors involved and what sort of time span are we talking about?

That can vary from foam to foam. UV light is the worst thing for foam. You want to protect it by covering it somehow. You'll get three to four times the lifespan from covered foam versus exposed foam. Most foams will start deteriorating within a couple days if left outside unprotected.

Foam will often change color based on light exposure. That's not a problem by itself. It's just the nature of foam; it will change colors. But if it's covered or somewhat protected, foam should last for years.

I've always wanted to ask... When you ship foam, do you pack it in foam?

Sometimes we do, yeah. Usually everything is just wrapped in plastic, though, to keep it clean during shipping.

Any comments you would like to add for costumers?

All you've got to do it use imagination and you can make anything you want to! Don't use my imagination, though, use your own. It'll work out better.

9 • Foam Rubber

Foam rubber has numerous purposes for costumes. Most animal costumes will use foam in some way, so it's a material with which you should become familiar. This chapter presents information about many of the types of foam ("There's more than one?") and how they can be used most effectively.

Where to Buy Foam

Some common items, such as batting and open-cell polyurethane foam, can be found at your local fabric stores. These are materials commonly used in cushions and home décor. Other foams may be available either from upholstery stores or theater supply houses.

More unusual foams can be obtained only from a foam distributor. I recommend this option since it will offer the greatest selection and best prices. Check your local phone listings under "foam," "rubber, foam," "packaging, foam" and "industrial supply, foam."

Selecting the right foam for the job can be confusing. The chart below compares various types, characteristics, and uses.

Foam	Composition	Stiffness	Cost	Durability	Waterproof	Common Uses
Open-cell, cushion	Polyurethane	Varies	$$	★★★		Padding, carving
Closed-cell	Polyurethane	Stiff	$$$	★★★★	✓	Structural
Crosslink	Polyethylene	Stiff	$$$$	★★★★	✓	Teeth, structural
Ethafoam	Polyethylene	Stiff	$$$	★★★	✓	Stiffener (rare)
Reticulated	Polyurethane	Medium	$$$$	★★★	✓	Eyes, ventilation
Latex foam, natural	Latex rubber	Soft	$$	★		Prosthetics
Styrofoam	Polystyrene	Stiff	$	★	✓	Structural (rare)
Neoprene	Polychloroprene	Varies	$$$	★★★	✓	Padding (rare)
Nu-foam	Polyester	Soft	$$	★★	✓	Filler, padding
Batting, Fiberfill	Polyester	Soft	$	★★		Filler
Rebonded, carpet	Polyurethane	Varies	$	★		Padding (rare)

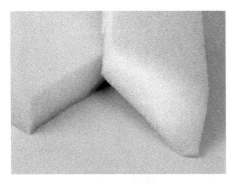

Open-cell polyurethane foam

Open-Cell Polyurethane Foams

This is, by far, the most common variety of foam rubber. This is the stuff that's ubiquitous in cushions and upholstered furniture. When people simply refer to "foam," this is probably what they are talking about.

Polyurethane foams come in a wide variety of densities and textures. Fabric stores usually carry sheets of this foam. Better selection and prices can be had by tracking down a foam supplier in your area.

The term "open-cell" refers to the fact that the bubbles creating the foam are not closed. There are holes and passages running through the foam. This is one of the reasons that the foam compresses so well; it is able to expel the air normally held in the foam's bubbles. If you completely seal this foam over its whole surface (e.g., with a rubberized skin coating), it will become less compressible.

This foam is very useful in costuming. It's soft, fairly durable, and easy to work with. The moderate to stiff varieties carve easily, making it a perfect material for sculpted padding and carved structure (like heads). Sheets of this foam can be cut according to patterns and glued edge-to-edge to create tailored shapes.

Avoid some of the stiffer varieties of this foam if it will be in a place where it contacts the skin. The stiffer polyurethane foams can have an abrasive texture and make the costume uncomfortable. Foam treated with anti-static chemicals seems to have the same problems.

Hot glue can be used to adhere this type of foam. You may need to apply the glue several times, however, as it tends to soak into and impregnate the foam structure on first application. This can lead to undesirable stiffness in the area of the joint. A better alternative is a foam-specific glue such as Fastbond 100™. (See Chapter 8 for more information.)

Lifespan Issues – Like all foams, polyurethane will break down over time. Open-cell polyurethane is a bit more vulnerable to aging than many other foams. Ultra-violet light and high-moisture environments are the major enemies of polyurethane. Solid exposure to ultra-violet light can begin to break down polyurethane in a matter of days. Moisture is a threat mainly because it encourages mildew.

As it breaks down, the foam becomes less resilient and acquires a dark yellow cast. It begins to crumble, releasing a fine powdery dust. Do not use foam that has begun to show these symptoms.

The breakdown of foam is not reversible or preventable, it can only be delayed. With proper care, though, polyurethane foam can remain in good condition for a decade or more. In an actively used costume, these foams should have a lifespan of several years.

Colors – These foams are usually available only in their natural cream color, which varies between white and pale yellow. Anti-static and packaging foams are often colored a neutral gray. Other colors are possible, but they are rarely available to the individual consumer.

Industry Names – Open-cell polyurethane foam is common enough that it often does not have an attached brand name. You will sometimes hear foam varieties referred to by their pores per inch (PPI) or weight per unit volume.

Closed-Cell Polyurethane Foams

This is the same as open-cell polyurethane foam except for the structural formation of the bubbles. The bubbles are denser and fully sealed. This foam is less compressible and tends to maintain a constant volume when manipulated. The surface of this foam appears much more solid than the porous open-cell variety.

Closed-cell polyurethane foam

Because of their denser structure, these foams are stiff and resilient. This can make them useful for creating larger rigid structural portions of a costume. They are also very lightweight for their size, thereby minimizing the encumbrance to the performer. Do not use this foam for padding which must be able to flex. Also bear in mind that, since it has a solid structure, it does not permit airflow.

The surface of closed-cell foam can suffer from abrasion, showing scratches and nicks. I don't recommend that it be used on an exposed part of a costume.

Closed-cell foam usually responds well to simple hot glue. Other adhesives can be used if a stronger bond is required.

Lifespan Issues – Closed-cell foams tend to be very water resistant. Older foam which has developed cracks or holes may be subject to some mold risk, but this is the exception. Since it is waterproof and lightweight, closed-cell foam is quite buoyant.

Closed-cell foam has a good working lifespan. Like other urethane products, exposure to UV radiation (e.g., sunlight) will break it down chemically. The foam will slowly discolor, become stiffer, and release a powdery dust as it breaks down. If protected, closed-cell foam should be fine for the working life of a costume.

Colors – Closed-cell foam is usually produced in white, black, and (less commonly) gray.

Industry Names – Closed-cell foam is sometimes called "L-200" in costuming circles, referring to a specific variety of Minicel™ foam. Airex™ is a trade name for a soft closed-cell foam using polyvinyl chloride (PVC) by Alusuisse Airex. Airex™ is subtly different from other closed-cell foams because of its different chemical composition.

Crosslink Foams

The term "crosslink" describes part of the chemical process by which this foam is created. Crosslink foams can be made from a variety of polymers, though polyethylene is the most prevalent.

Crosslink foam

Crosslink foam is resilient and predominantly closed-cell. When cut with a razor it has an almost smooth surface.

I like to use thin (¼") sheets of this foam in a number of ways. It can be bent and formed into sculptural shapes very easily; hot glue affixes it very well. (More secure bonds can be created with Goop™ or other synthetic cement adhesives.) Such foam inserts can be an easy way to add definition and stiffness inside an ear, for example. Sheets of crosslink foam are easily cut with scissors.

It's easy to create cartoon teethe by carving small pieces of the foam. The teeth use the color and texture of the foam itself. They're also soft enough that they can't injure anyone.

Lifespan Issues – Polyethylene foams are fairly durable. They are less susceptible to UV deterioration, slowly losing resiliency over time. Crosslinked polyethylene tends not to discolor much with age. This foam should not degrade within the working lifespan of a costume.

Colors – Crosslink foams are usually available in black and white.

Industry Names – Softlon™ and Plastazote™ are the trade names of two crosslinked polyethylene foams. Craft stores sell a product called FunFoam™. This is page-sized ⅛" sheets of crosslink foam available in about a dozen colors. It can be a great item for quickly assembling costume details or props; I highly recommend it.

Closed-Cell Polyethylene Foam

This foam is lightweight, durable, and waterproof. The downside is that it's not especially flexible. When it does bend, it can make a telltale crackle. Depending on where you plan to use it, this might eliminate it from consideration.

Ethylene foams are commonly available in the form of long extruded rods used for pool toys and pipe insulation. It is also available in sheets of varying thickness. Thin sheets are often used to wrap electronic components for shipping.

Lifespan Issues – Ethylene foams are quite durable. They tend to deteriorate very slowly from exposure to UV light; regular ethylene foams are less UV resistant than crosslinked varieties. As they degrade, these foams will yellow slightly and lose their resiliency.

Colors – Ethylene foams are available in white, black, blue, and pink. Most ethylene foams have a translucent quality.

Industry Names – Ethafoam™ is the trade name for the foam produced by the Dow Chemical Co. It is the most common brand and the name Ethafoam is often (incorrectly) used as a generic term. Other brands include PolyPlank™, Microfoam™, and Stratocell™.

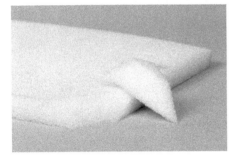

Closed-cell polyethylene foam

Reticulated Foam

This is a highly porous breathable foam often used in air filters. It has large visible pores without any solid bubbles. It's so open, in fact, that you can see through thin sheets of it. This makes it valuable as a material for constructing eyes (see Chapter 13).

This is a very flexible and resilient foam. It is durable, but tears under strain more easily than other foams. Reticulated foam works very well for creating padding and patterned foam shapes. Additionally, due to its open structure, it allows some airflow which improves costume ventilation.

Due to the complex manufacturing process required to produce it, reticulated foam is much more expensive than common polyurethane foam. For small items, such as pupils, this isn't an issue. However, if you're using this foam for larger padding, it may be worthwhile to develop a pattern using inexpensive foam as a test.

Another advantage of its open structure is that this foam is not harmed by water. It's washable and the water can be removed by wringing. This may be important if you're constructing a bodysuit with built-in padding that you want to be washable.

Reticulated foam

Reticulated foam is available in a variety of densities. It is usually measured by the number of pores per inch (PPI). I recommend something between 20 and 35 PPI for most costuming applications.

Lifespan Issues – Reticulated foam has an excellent lifespan. It still suffers from exposure to UV light, but the chemical breakdown is less noticeable because of the structure of the foam. Reticulated foam should easily last for the working life of a costume without any special care.

Colors – Reticulated foam is commonly black. A "white" version, which is more of a cream color, is sometimes available. Other colors are rarely available to individual consumers.

Industry Names – Reticulated foam is sometimes called "Scott Foam" because one of the major manufacturers is Scott Foam Technologies, Inc. This is really a misnomer, since Scott produces a variety of high-quality foam products and does not associate the name "Scott Foam" with their reticulated product.

Batting

Although not a foam, batting is included in this list because it's sometimes used to add body to costumes. Batting is a loose collection of polyester fibers and is commonly used as a filling for stuffed animals. (A sheet of batting between fabric layers, another common padding agent, is correctly termed "quilted batting.")

Batting

By itself, batting doesn't have any internal structure. It should be used only to fill parts of a costume that have been patterned or shaped. Unless sewn into pockets, the batting will sag and migrate over time. Even in pockets, batting will become more compressed over time, losing perhaps 20% of its original volume. This can be remedied by simply adding some additional batting to any areas where it is required.

Batting can technically be washed and packages will always list this fact. In practice, it can be difficult to dry the batting properly. After washing, the batting has a tendency to mat, reducing its volume. Once it's been sewn into a costume, it is difficult to wash and dry the batting without losing some of its body.

Lifespan Issues – Batting will last a remarkably long time. Apart from the compression issue mentioned, batting should easily last for the working lifetime of a costume.

Colors – Batting is usually available only in plain white. You might find black batting at specialty quilting stores. Most batting can be dyed, should white be unacceptable for some reason.

Industry Names – Fiberfill™ is one of the most common trade names for batting. It's made by DuPont from their Dacron™ polyester fibers. I personally recommend Fiberfill, as I've been disappointed with some of the off-brand batting products.

Other Foams and Products

Latex – Foam can be made from natural latex rubber. Although soft and flexible, this foam is not very durable. It has a short lifespan, breaking down rapidly from wear, UV, and moisture. Latex foam is most commonly used in makeup prosthetics. I would not particularly recommend it for other costuming uses.

Styrofoam™ – Generically, this is **polystyrene** foam; Styrofoam is actually a trade name owned by Dow Chemical. Styrofoam is rigid and can crack, making it a poor choice for costuming. Styrofoam pellets are sometimes sold as filling; these are not desirable either, since they produce a distinct rustling sound.

Neoprene – This is usually manufactured as sheets of closed-cell foam. It's flexible, waterproof, insulating, and comfortable, which is why it makes good wetsuits. As far as costuming, it may be useful in odd circumstances. Its insulating abilities usually aren't desirable in a full-body costume.

Nu-Foam™ – This is a new polyester product from Fairfield Processing Corp. It's meant to be an alternative cushion filling or batting. It's durable and washable, but has less structure than traditional foam. If you're looking for a lightweight filling material with some shape retention, it might be a good choice.

Rebonded Foam – Also known as "those foam pads that go under carpeting," these are the multicolor conglomerate sheets of recycled polyurethane foam scraps. Because of the added adhesive, it's stiffer and more brittle when flexed. I normally wouldn't recommend this foam, though I could perhaps see it being useful for costumes made on the cheap and to be used for a short period of time.

10 • Getting Creative

I'm sometimes surprised when people ask me, "What's the best way to build a costume?" There is no single ideal process for making all costumes. If that were the case, this book could be reduced to a shopping list and numbered instructions!

But, of course, costume design and construction are not that simple. Each costuming project presents new challenges. Different techniques and materials may work well in one place and fail elsewhere. The good costumer will gather knowledge of an array of processes, materials, and techniques and then select the best ones for each circumstance that comes along.

This is what makes costuming a craft and an art!

As you work on your costumes, remember that you can use materials other than those found in fabric stores and theatrical supply houses. Whenever you see new or novel materials, make mental (or physical) notes. Try to identify what it's made of, how expensive it is, and what it might be made to look like. You never know when it might be useful.

In this chapter, I present some of my favorite "found" materials for costumes as inspiration.

At the Hardware Store: Zip Ties

Zip ties are small nylon straps with a unidirectional catch, so they will not come loose once tightened. They are stronger than either thread or fabric and are useful for hundreds of applications.

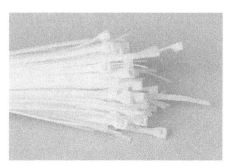

Nylon zip ties. Also called wire ties. Available in large quantities from a hardware store.

Zip ties are an invaluable item in my toolbox. I always carry a couple dozen as part of my travel repair kit.

I also use zip ties when constructing some costumes. When building a framework head, I often use zip ties to secure pieces until they are glued. I simply leave the zip ties in place after gluing.

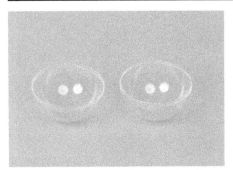

Chapter 10

Two halves of a plastic ornament ball

At the Craft Store: Ornament Balls

Craft stores stock clear acrylic spheres. These are intended for making Christmas ornaments. These plastic ornament balls are available in sizes about 2–6" in diameter. Each ornament sphere snaps apart in half. They are a bit tricky to find in the larger sizes outside of the holiday season. These transparent hemispheres can be very useful as costume eyes.

Some animals, such as rodents, have black spherical eyes. Painting the inside of the hemisphere a solid black creates a convincing reflective eye surface which can be mounted on the costume. With careful use of tinting material, it's even possible to give the illusion of opaque black eyes while still allowing vision through them. (See notes in Chapter 13 about solid eyes.)

Curved cartoony eyes can also be created by painting on the inside surface of the plastic. The outer surface makes the eye look smooth and glossy. Eyes of various curvature can be created by starting with larger spheres and only using a portion of the surface.

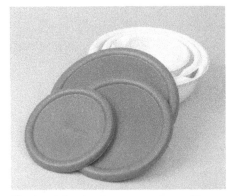

Plastic mixing bowls are great for making eyes and ears.

At the Discount Store: Plastic Mixing Bowls

This is a set of cheap plastic mixing bowls that I found in a local store's housewares section. It's a set of four white bowls nested together. They are made of a soft plastic which can be cut with tin snips.

Think abstractly about these bowls. They are a source of plastic that curves on two axes. I've found two different uses for them so far.

First, they can be used to create large cartoony eyes. The white plastic of the bowl is great for creating the eye surface. All that needs to be done to finish the eye is to cut out a pupil and replace it with black material. If reticulated foam is used, then the performer can see through the eyes.

Plastic bowls are also useful for creating curved internal structure. Their shape is ideal for making mouse ears. The plastic is slightly flexible and not prone to cracking, so the ears won't be damaged if they catch on something.

Using a mixing bowl for this is much faster than sculpting or casting eyes. It's a great time saver.

At the Automotive Store: Window Tint Film

Auto supply stores sell rolls of plastic film for tinting car windows. It's not adhesive backed; it adheres through static cling alone.

Tinted film can be used to create costume components that appear black but are actually transparent. If it's darker on the inside of the surface, the tinted film can be easily seen through. From the outside, the higher light levels create a reflective black surface.

Window tint film

This material is excellent for the construction of solid reflective eyes. Some cartoony costumes benefit from eyes with a glassy surface. This effect is created using clear plastic as the surface of the eyes. Paint the back side of the plastic to create the whites and irises of the eyes. Apply the tinted film to the plastic to create the pupil. From the outside, the surface of the eye is continuous and smooth; from the inside, the pupil is transparent. (Read more about solid eyes in Chapter 13.)

Use tinted film to create prop sunglasses. To look proportionally correct, glasses for character costumes need to be oversized. Fabricate lenses from clear plastic and back them with tinted film.

At the Sports Store: Nylon Webbing

Nylon webbing is the flat, rope-like material used by rock climbers and used in sports equipment to make straps and restraints. Look for it in the camping section of a sporting goods store.

It can be very useful in costuming because it is light, durable, and strong. Webbing comes in test strengths between 200 and 1000 pounds.

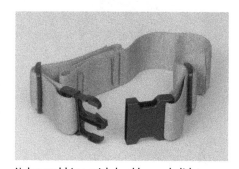

Nylon webbing with buckles and slide

If a costume has a large structural component which must securely mount to the performer's body, I recommend creating a webbing harness to be worn under the suit. Even something as small as a tail will benefit from the support of a webbing belt.

An advantage of webbing is that it's easy to sew. A few seams of zigzag stitching will create a secure joint.

When you cut webbing, use a lighter to seal the edge. The heat melts the plastic and prevents fraying.

Plastic clasps or buckles will hold everything together.

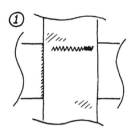 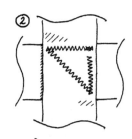 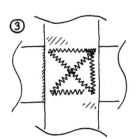 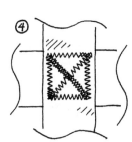

Left: sewing a strong joint between two pieces of webbing can be done with a single run through the sewing machine.

  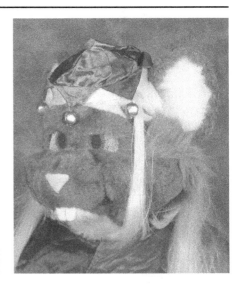

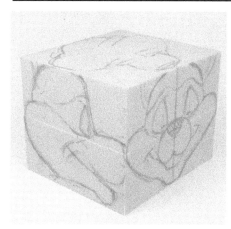

Part III

Head Construction

"The head of a costume is 90% of the character"

There is truth to this aphorism heard frequenly among mascot costume designers. The expression and structure of the head shape the emotional impact of the character. The details of the head are the ones most closely examined. Subtle angles in the head guide the attitude of the whole character.

Given the importance of the head, special attention should be paid to its construction. There are many ways to approach the problem of head construction, each with different strengths and weaknesses. Part of the craft of costuming is learning these different techniques and when to apply them.

In this chapter we review several methods for constructing a head using foam, plastic, rubber, and a variety of other materials. Read through the different ideas presented here to find out what might be the best solution for your character design.

11 • Foam Heads

Foam is a versatile, lightweight, and safe material. It is no wonder that it's a popular material for constructing costume heads! In this chapter we'll look at two different approaches to using foam: carving blocks of foam and patterning sheets of foam.

Selecting Foam

When carving a head, begin with a large block of foam larger than the minimal dimensions of the desired head. Use a medium to firm polyurethane open-cell foam. When choosing the foam, look for one that is firm and dense enough to hold its shape well under pressure. A foam that is too soft will not carve well, as the rubbery material yields too much under the knife blade. Stiffer foams are better, but tend to be more scratchy and abrasive. The head will be sitting on your (or the performer's) shoulders, so find something that is comfortable.

If you're making a patterned head, you'll need thin sheets of fairly durable foam. Look for ½" to 1" sheets of medium firmness foam. While polyurethane is the most common foam used for this application, try reticulated foam for extra durability and air circulation. Keep in mind that it should *not* be applied where it will contact the skin since it can be quite uncomfortable.

Refer to Chapter 9 for more information about these foams and their durability.

Portrait in Foam. This cute cuddly raccoon is made using the foam carving technique. The step-by-step process of how this head was carved begins on page 85.

Comparison Chart

Select your materials based on your construction technique. The chart below compares the advantages and disadvantages of each method.

Carved Foam	Patterned Foam
Advantages • Inexpensive • Easy to make • Very quick to make	**Advantages** • Inexpensive • Easy to make • Sometimes quick to make
Disadvantages • Difficult to make tight-fitting • Limited shear strength	**Disadvantages** • Limited shear strength
Durability • Good durability • Foam has a limited lifespan	**Durability** • Good durability • Foam has a limited lifespan
Primary Materials • Large block of polyurethane foam	**Primary Materials** • ¾"-inch sheets of polyurethane or reticulated foam
Special Tools • Electric carving knife	**Special Tools** • None

The two essential items for making a carved foam head are a large block of foam and an electric carving knife.

Here are a few key tips to help keep your head carving on-track and your design moving in the proper direction.

- Redraw your features onto the foam as often as needed.

- Consult your reference drawings often, keeping them readily visible as you work.

- Keep in mind that fur adds bulk to the head. Have a sample of your fur nearby to lay on the head to test your work.

- Don't be afraid to cut too deeply. Additional foam pieces can be glued to the head if too much material has inadvertently been removed.

- Be careful! Electric carving knives can cut flesh. Practice on a spare piece of foam to get a feel for the tool before you begin.

Carved Foam Heads

This is probably one of the fastest and easiest ways to create a costume head! I highly recommend it for anyone attempting their first mascot-style costume. Another great advantage is that it's relatively inexpensive. It's not a disaster or huge financial loss if your first attempt fails! You can get another block of foam and try again.

I recommend using an electric carving knife to cut foam. Although they aren't very expensive, they will wear out pretty quickly. I usually get two heads done before my knife burns out. If you manage to buy a brand with a manufacturer's warranty, hang onto the receipt.

You'll also need a table at a comfortable working height. Cover the floor with a large tarp or dropcloth to aid in cleanup later. Use the largest dropcloth possible. Trust me, this is a messy project.

As you carve the head, you will inevitably notice that it's not perfectly symmetrical. This is normal. Nature isn't perfectly symmetrical, either. *Don't fret about exact symmetry.* As long as the head appears balanced and is approximately symmetrical, everything should turn out okay.

The carved foam piece serves as the understructure of the finished head. This style of head is snug, fitting down tightly around the wearer's head. While this means it may be less comfortable than some other heads, it also means that subtle movements translate directly through the costume. Fur, eyes, and other details are then glued directly to the foam to create the head's exterior.

Although somewhat difficult, it is possible to install fans in foam heads. Channels can be cut through the foam to serve as air ducts. Fans should be mounted at the surface of the foam below the fur outer covering. See Chapter 15 for ventilation and cooling details.

Mending Mistakes

One of the advantages of using the foam carving method is that it's easy to repair mistakes.

If you cut too aggressively, you may remove more foam than you intended. You also might only realize that you've trimmed something too far when the proportions of the head look a bit skewed. If the area that was trimmed too much has not had additional cuts made, then the chunk of foam which was cut off should fit back into place like a piece of a puzzle. A little aerosol or foam glue will bond it in place and you can pretend that the erroneous cut never happened.

It's important to use the right type of glue for these repairs. You can cut through an aerosol or Fastbond glue line without difficulty. This means that crossing the glue line won't push your blade around and throw off your carving. Heavier glues, such as hot glue, are very difficult to cut and will cause problems.

On the other hand, not cutting deeply enough isn't a cause for worry, either. Make as many passes as necessary to whittle down the foam to the correct shape. In fact, I strongly recommend against carving too aggressively on the first pass. Rough out the shape of the entire head, then revisit sections to carve the final contours. This will allow you to more easily see the proportions of the emerging head as you work.

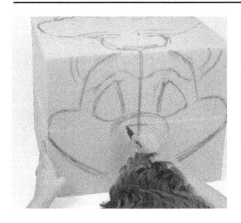

1. Begin with a Block of Foam

Your block of foam should be as large, in each dimension, as the finished costume head. You can exclude the ears in this measurement unless they are integral to the shape of the head. Ears are usually carved separately and attached later.

2. Draw Front and Profile Views

Draw plan views of your character's head on the block of foam using a marker. Details are not important, proportions are. Make sure the eyes are positioned where you want them.

3. Create a Head Hole

Carve directly up from the bottom of the foam block. Cut a head-sized oval, keeping the knife blade perpendicular to the bottom surface. *The knife angle is the most common mistake here. Watch it carefully!* The cut should go far enough into the head that it gets above the level of the character's eyes.

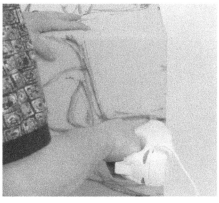

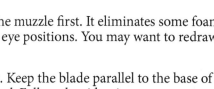

4. Clear the Hole

Reach up into the cut and remove the foam, leaving a large hole for your head. Removing the foam can be tricky, since it hasn't been cut horizontally at the top. I recommend either using a small knife or tearing it manually. Continue working to develop a smooth-sided cavity that fits comfortably around the head.

5. Carve the Top Profile of the Muzzle

I like to carve the forehead and top of the muzzle first. It eliminates some foam weight and makes it easier to gauge the eye positions. You may want to redraw the front view after this primary cut.

As you cut, watch the angle of the knife. Keep the blade parallel to the base of the head to ensure that the muzzle is level. Follow the side-view contours to establish the proper curve moving from the eyes to the nose.

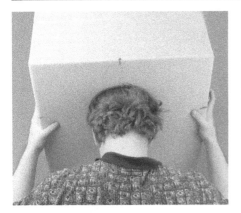

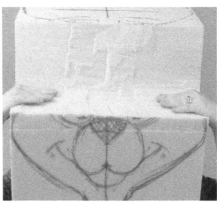

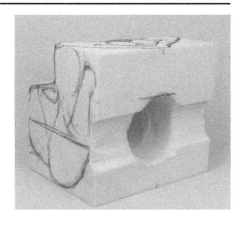

6. Test Fit the Head

Put the foam block on your head. Yes, it looks silly. Expect some "block-head" jokes if anyone is watching. The head should fit snugly. Create a cavity in front of the mouth to allow for breathing. Later, connect it to the outside via the mouth or neck.

7. Determine Eye Level

While wearing the head, hold your hand in front of your face, palm parallel to the floor. Determine the height of your eyes by intuition. Bring your hand towards the foam block until you hit it. Mark that point on the foam (either with a pen or pin). This will help you line up the wearer's vision line with the character's head structure.

8. Raise Eye Level As Needed

Take off the foam and see how your eye level lines up with where the vision should be on the character's head. (In this example, I'm aligning my vision with the area around the character's eyes.) Deepen the head hole by the amount just determined. This adjustment might also be made around the shoulders depending on how low the character's head will sit.

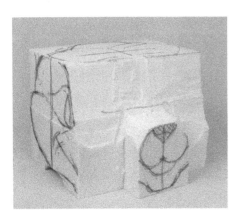

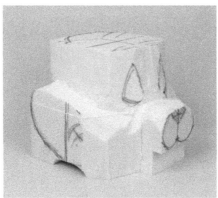

9. Carve the Muzzle Projection

Use the knife to carve the top, bottom, left, and right contours of the muzzle. You've already done the top of the muzzle although it might need further refinement. Don't work on the front of the muzzle or details yet. At this point we're just making major cuts to remove large pieces of excess foam.

10. Carve the Cheek Contours

Make more bold sweeps to shape the tops of the cheeks and the back of the head. Keep the blade parallel to the sides of the foam block. If the cheeks are especially high, you can also carve away under the cheek ridges.

11. Shape the Muzzle and Cheeks

Working down from the eyes, shape the top of the muzzle. Blend it into the cheeks, smoothing and rounding them. I like to cut in a little where the muzzle meets the cheeks to add a bit of character and improve the downwards vision around the muzzle. Keep in mind the desired expression of the character as you're shaping the muzzle.

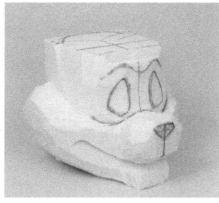

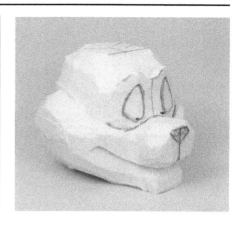

12. Carve the Nose Area

Move to the front of the muzzle, carving the nose area. Include the area under the nose in this step, adding the cleft present in most animal muzzles. Be sure to refer to your designs or reference materials to get the correct proportions and tapering on the muzzle. At this point you may want to draw more quick lines.

13. Carve the Lower Jaw

Finish up any shaping on the muzzle and jawline. Begin to add the expression. Try to capture the basic shape of the muzzle. If your character has a closed mouth, carve an overhang and then the jawline. If your character has an open mouth, carve the split where the cheeks of the muzzle join below the nose. To help visualize proportions, redraw on the foam between steps to help stick to your design.

14. Carve the Eye Ridge

Now return your attention to the eyes and begin working upwards. Establish a brow ridge by carving in above the eyebrows. Pay attention to the thickness of the foam. You don't want to accidentally carve into your head hole! To retain its structural strength, the foam should be *at least* a half inch thick. Depending on your character's personality, you might have an overhanging eye ridge or a recessed area.

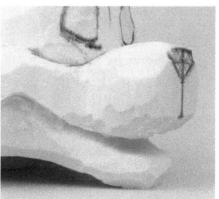

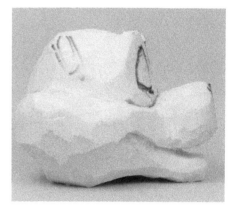

15. Shape the Top of the Head

Round the top of the head so the upward slope from the brows transitions nicely into the top of the head. Shape the areas above the line of the cheeks, keeping in mind placement of the ears. Taper the back of the head into the cheek areas.

16. Develop Detail in the Expression

Depending on the facial structure and the complexity of the expression, this step might involve some significant carving. Carve out any mouth details required. Keep in mind that fur will add visual "inflation" to the sculpture. The depth of the fur will enlarge and smooth all of the curves. In general, any depressions or undercuts should be at least as deep as the fur's pile to be visible.

17. Finish Carving the Cheeks

Finish and smooth the lines of the cheeks. Also focus on the back and undersides of the cheeks, noting how the cheeks will tuck into the neck. It's a good idea to mark the mounting locations for the ears if they aren't attached to the head to ensure they will properly transition into the cheeks.

18. Shape the Back of the Head

Blend all of these curves into the back face of the head. I like the cheek ridges to be almost flush with the back of the head. Some prefer to tuck them inwards, creating a cartioid shape when viewed from above. Others continue the shelf of the cheek around the back of the head, creating a saucer shape. Choose a style that fits the proportion and personality you're seeking for your character

19. Finish the Eye Area

Return to the eye areas. Using scissors, add details to the eye and brow areas. Make sure the eyebrow ridges convey the right emotion. Make all indentations and concave cuts deeper and wider than you think they need to be. Remember: fur adds bulk. Details less than the depth of the pile will be difficult to distinguish on the final head.

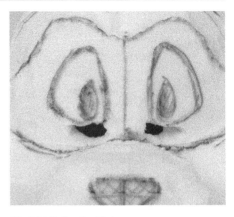

20. Add Holes for Vision

Put on the head and mark (by feel) where your eyes line up with the outside of the sculpture. Cut holes from the outside into the center hollow space. Test the head and ensure that the vision is adequate. In this head, I have lined up the vision just *below* the character's eyes; the wearer will actually be looking out through the black raccoon mask.

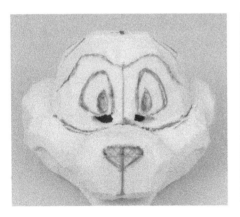

21. Finish the Muzzle

With the eye area completed, finalize the shape of the muzzle. Use scissors to smooth the nose area. Add any details needed around the mouth and lips. If you plan on adding details inside the mouth, carve the floor of the jaw into an even surface to which you can later apply the teeth, tongue, etc.

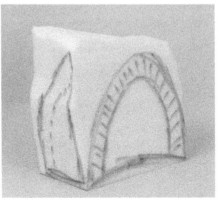

22. Carve and Blend the Ears

If the ears were not carved as part of the head, carving them is the next step. The ears can probably be made from some of the larger pieces of scrap foam (as shown). If you prefer, they can also be made from sheet foam with a simple triangular pattern. Adjust the shape and size of the ears to fit the head and the species. Unusually large ears, such as rabbit ears, may require extra structural support.

Place the ears on the head. You can glue them in place now or just temporarily pin them. Using scissors, make sure the head shape transitions nicely into the ears. What this transition should look like varies a lot by critter and costume style, so use your own aesthetic judgement.

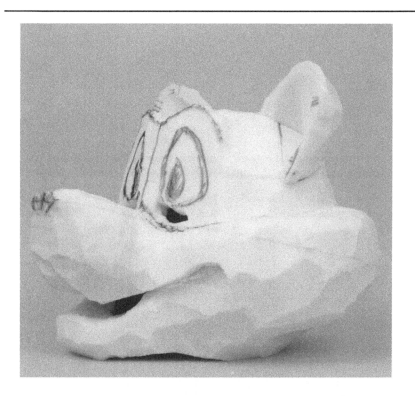

When you are at the finishing stages of your head carving, pause and take a good look at your head from every angle. Now is the time to make any last minute changes to your design. After this stage, you will begin covering the head with fur, and changes to the overall shape become more difficult.

23. Finish the Inside

Now use your scissors to smooth the inside of the head hole. Be sure not to change the depth of the hole, as this will throw off the alignment of the eye holes. Just smooth the sides. In front of your mouth, carve out a hollow area to allow you to breath more easily. If you plan on a fan or hidden ducting, carve these out as well.

24. Final Test Fitting

Put the head on one last time. Double check all of the shaping and expression in a mirror. Then check the clearance between the bottom of the foam and your shoulders. The head should ride just above your shoulders *while shrugging*. If the head extends down too far, shoulder and arm movement may dislodge the head, pushing it upwards. Using the results of your test, create an appropriate bottom contour for the head.

25. Final Adjustments

Take a step back from your project. Close your eyes for a moment and take a deep breath. Then open them and try to see your character as if for the first time. Does it look correct? Does the head convey the right feeling? Will the shape still look correct once fur is added? Does it match your character concept? Make any last minute corrections or adjustments. Then you're finished and ready to fur!

Patterned Foam Heads

I use this term to describe heads assembled from cut pieces of sheet foam. In reality, these may be created from patterns or improvised as a freehand assembly. Both strategies work equally well for this construction method.

The construction follows the same general method. Pieces of foam are cut from a sheet. These are glued edge-to-edge to create the shape of the character head. This is more challenging than a simple carved head since you need a good visualization of the head shape before you begin. You also need to be able to translate two-dimensional patterns into three-dimensional shapes.

It's not possible to give a step-by-step guide for this process, since the pattern will be different for each costume head. You'll need to develop the pattern based on experimentation and experience. Focus on key shapes and features in your head design. Attempt to create these by cutting out small-scale paper patterns. Keep altering and experimenting until you're confident that you understand the general curves and shapes you'll need to construct in foam.

If the pieces of foam are cut according to patterns, there are several advantages. First, the head should turn out symmetrical, assuming identical gluing and assembly on both sides. Second, the head can be replicated once a pattern is created. This means that the same underskull can be recreated and used to make a duplicate head or an entirely different costume head with the same shape.

By using the patterned technique consistently, you can develop a pattern library for different head shapes. This can drastically reduce the time it takes to create future costume heads.

Furring Foam Heads

Once you have the basic structure of the head, apply an outer layer of fur. If your creature is not furry, you might need to apply feathers, scaly fabric, or some other outer skin.

Before beginning to apply the fur, finalize the size and position of the eyes. Depending on how the eyes are mounted in the head, they may need to be inserted before furring. Some eye assemblies are best applied on top of the fur. If the eyes are to be applied after furring, I like to keep cardboard mockups pinned to the foam head while I work to more easily visualize the character's expression.

If you have multiple colors of fur on the head, use a marker to draw the boundary lines directly onto the foam. This will help you line up color edges evenly. Draw a map on the surface of the head.

Nap Direction

A good rule of thumb: The nap flows away from the nose. On most animals, the nap of the fur spreads outwards from the nostrils and lips. The direction of the fur leads down the muzzle, up the bridge of the nose, across the top of the head, and down the back. It parts around the eyes, usually flowing generally sideways in that region; fur spreads up and away or down and away from the top and bottom of the eye, respectively. This is not a universal truth but if you don't have the detailed reference material on hand for the creature you're building this can be a useful fallback. Consult your reference material for details on the fur flow for your critter.

It is important to keep the nap roughly consistent across adjacent pieces to prevent unsightly seams. If the nap needs to shift alignment around curves in the head, use darts in the fur or smaller inserted pieces to transition the direction of the fur. I don't recommend abutting pieces of fur with their nap more than 45 degrees out of alignment, if the fur is supposed to flow smoothly in that region.

I tend to fur heads freehand; I don't use a pattern for the fur pieces. Instead, I cut each one to fit the shape of the head. I begin gluing at one edge, where the piece abuts fur already glued in place.

Start in the center of a piece. Spread it outwards to find where the fur encounters a natural break in the shape of the head. Use scissors to trim the fur back at this point to fit the line of the head.

Gluing Fur

Gluing the fur to the foam understructure isn't difficult. Use regular hot glue. It adheres fairly well to both fur and foam. It also hardens quickly, which allows continuous work. Use a fair amount of hot glue over the entire area covered by a fur piece. If the glue soaks through the fur backing and glues together the fibers of the nap, you're being too generous with the glue. Apply hot glue out to the very edges of each fur piece to prevent seams from separating. (In problem areas, it's possible to go back and hand sew the edges together.)

Super 74™ also does a good job adhering fur to foam. It can be a good alternative to hot glue, especially if you want something lighter and more flexible. However, it lacks the hold strength of hot glue. If you use Super 74™, then you must go back and stitch together the edges of the fur pieces. Otherwise, they will peel and create visible gaps over time.

When you've finished furring the head, I suggest reinforcing seam that might experience strain by stitching them together with thread. Everywhere you've had to cut pieces of fur, there are now potential gaps. Should the foam stretch as the head flexes, the abutting edges of the fur might pull apart enough for the seam to become visible. While chances of this can be minimized by a heavy application of hot glue near the seam edges, it is better to stitch the seam closed.

In the lower photo, the fur has been trimmed to fit around the base of the ear.

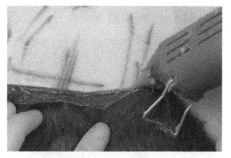  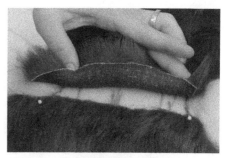

Apply hot glue along all the edges of your fur pieces to prevent the edges from curling up or peeling away. Use pins to hold the fur in place while the glue sets.

Joining Fur Edges

The key to hiding seams in the fur is to make sure that the edges line up precisely. Begin with a piece of fur already on the head. Lay down your next piece and pin it in the center so that it doesn't shift while you're working with it. Spread it outwards and trim the edge of the second piece so that it aligns with the fur already attached to the head.

Apply hot glue to the very edge of the fur piece. Carefully fold down this new piece and use the palm of your hand to smooth it against the original fur. Dextrous handling is required to prevent the hot glue from getting into the fur's nap.

If you cross curved portions of the surface, it will be necessary to dart the piece of fur in order to make it conform to the foam surface. You'll find the fur forming wrinkles around convex parts of the head. Don't compress and force the foam to fit the flat piece of fur! Nip and tuck the fur so that it conforms to the foam.

When you cut the fur, be careful to only cut the backing. This leaves the full length of the nap overhanging the cut edges. Make a second cut to remove the triangle of overlapped fur. The next piece of fur can be cut and tucked under the overhang of the nap to hide the seam. Smooth the joined edge in the same way as described above.

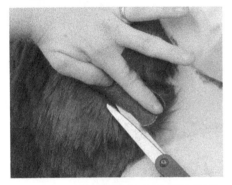

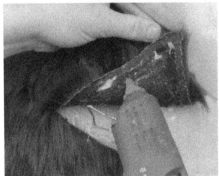

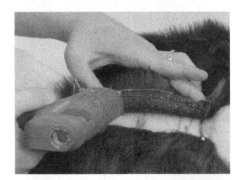

Left, top to bottom: Create darts where fur forms folds. Carefully clip a triangle from the fold and trim the edges so that they lie flush. Then glue the edges in place.

Right: The transition between fur pieces will be invisible if the edges are carefully aligned and glued, as shown.

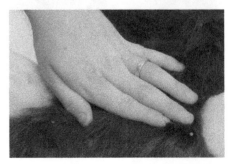

12 • Framework Heads

Costume heads can be built upon rigid assembled structures or frameworks. This structural underskull can be made from any number of different materials, including wire and plastic. Fur and other materials are then attached to this structure to complete the exterior of the head.

In this chapter, I will demonstrate two materials from which I like to build framework heads: heavy wire and plastic cross-stitch canvas. Many other materials could be used, and I encourage readers to experiment. Although the materials may vary, the construction process will be similar for all framework heads.

Internal Harnesses

A framework head is a structure assembled on an internal harness. The harness is whatever item is being worn on the performer's head to translate the motions to the costume head. The framework is built outwards from this harness to create the general shape of the character head. On top of this understructure, the surface is added which receives fur, paint, or whatever other exterior finishing is appropriate for the design.

An effective harness must fit snugly to prevent wobbling of the costume head. A chin strap should be used on any head that is especially large, as the cantilever forces will cause the head to tip easily.

The harness must also be comfortable. In most cases, the weight of the costume head is supported entirely by the performer's head and neck. The reasoning for this is simply that the neck originates most of the movements for the head; if the costume head is not supported primarily by the performer's neck, this range of expression is lost. Since the performer's head is possibly supporting a ten-pound structure for extended periods, it's imperative that the harness be comfortable.

It is possible to build a harness from scratch. Depending on the material being used in the framework of the head, it may be expedient to simply design the harness into the structure of the head itself. If so, be sure to cover a large enough area of the head to distribute the weight of the costume piece.

A lifecast of the performer's head is a good starting point for a scratch-built harness. Thermoplastics and resins can be used on a sealed lifecast to create a helmet for a tailored harness. Some thin sheet foam glued to the inside can make it more comfortable.

Finding Harnesses – Although they are not advertised as "head harnesses," there are a number of commercially available items that can be adapted to our cause. They are already tailored to fit snugly on people's heads, saving us the trouble of engineering something. The downside is that they often add bulk, making it harder to construct close-fitting costume heads.

Hardhats – Your local hardware store sells inexpensive hardhats which are great to use as a harness for costume heads. Hardhats usually feature an internal adjustable harness of plastic straps. The plastic harness is suspended from the dome of the hat, allowing air to circulate. This air space makes the costume head seem cooler when worn.

Depending on the shape and style of your head, cut the bill from the hardhat with a hacksaw. The dome of the hardhat is a good mounting base. It may be drilled with holes for bolts, and the plastic is receptive to epoxy glues.

The disadvantage of hardhats is that they add a lot of bulk to the inside of the costume head. If you plan on constructing a large mascot-style costume, this isn't be a problem. However, if you are trying to make a smaller-scaled head, a hardhat may be unworkable.

Baseball Caps – A baseball cap which fits comfortably and snugly on the head can become an internal harness. Remove the bill with heavy scissors or shears. The adjustable band at the back of the cap should be left in place so that the costume head can be adjusted to suit different performers.

Baseball caps don't provide a rigid base for the head. Attach the framework to it using glue, which in turn stiffens the cap, or thread. If you build outwards with the cap as an anchor, you will need the performer or a lifecast to wear the cap while you work so that it retains its correct shape.

It's sometimes better to build the primary structure of the head first and then attach the baseball cap to it. If the costume head has enough space inside, the baseball cap can be suspended in the middle using taut wire or fishing line; when worn, the lines will carry force in the other direction, suspending the costume head from the cap.

The biggest advantage of using baseball caps is tha they are small and lightweight. If the underskull is built directly on the cap, it's possible to create a very close-fitting head.

The only disadvantage is that the back of the baseball cap needs to be reachable in the completed head. Although the adjusting band at the back of the cap is a nice feature, you will need to provide enough access to make the adjustments. It's also important when putting the costume on; being able to pull down on the adjustable band will help seat the cap firmly on the wearer's head.

Bicycle Helmets – Like our other harnesses, these helmets are designed to sit firmly on the head. However, they also come with chin straps. These can firmly anchor a costume with large or unevenly weighted heads.

Bike helmets do not usually have an adjustable fit, so they must be chosen based on the performer's head size. This can pose a problem if many different people share the same costume.

Bike helmets have the advantage of being lightweight and well-padded. They are inexpensive when purchased at local thrift stores or second-hand sports shops.

One disadvantage of bicycle helmets is their thickness. This adds bulk to the costume head. Depending on the design of the helmet, you might be able to carve some of this away. Some bike helmets feature an inconvenient front overhang which makes it hard to get the costume head to fit close to the wearer's eyes. This can sharply reduce the vision in the costume.

Wire Framework Heads

Creating a framework head is like building a sculpture. With this technique, lengths of heavy-gauge wire are shaped and assembled to form the framework for the head. This wire sculpture forms the underskull of the costume.

I recommend trying chain link fencing wire. Hardware stores sell lengths of this galvanized wire for tying fencing sections together and repairing breaks. It's most commonly found on large spools, but persistent scavenging can usually turn up straight segments of wire which are much easier to work with. If this appears to be unavailable locally, any equivalent gauge (10 AWG) straight wire could be substituted.

Straight wire is preferable to wire from a spool since we will be using this to sculpt the shape of the head. Wire from a spool has a strong curve bias forced into it, making it harder to control and match against other pieces.

Use heavy lineman pliers to bend the wire into shape. Don't try to use needle-nose or bolt pliers with such heavy wire. The small size makes them ineffective. Another essential tool is a pair of heavy-gauge wire cutters. There are several combination tools available, such as the Craftsman™ fencing tool, which combine wire cutters and heavy pliers.

The head is assembled by bending lengths of wire into contour shapes and then joining them together. Starting at the end of a length of wire, use the pliers to add bends until the wire matches the desired profile. Continue creating wires that follow the profiles of the other primary curves of the head. Joining them together creates a wire cage. Having the different wire shapes crossing at angles to each other reinforces the head and provides the necessary rigidity to the frame.

Once wire forms have been attached to define all of the major contours of the head's surface, exterior work can begin. The fur, eyes, nose, and other parts of the head cannot be easily mounted on the bare wires. We therefore need to create a mounting surface around the head to which we can glue these items. I like to use sheets of open-cell foam for this purpose, as shown in this chapter's example. Papier-mache or stiff fabric interfacing could also span the wire gaps to create a surface.

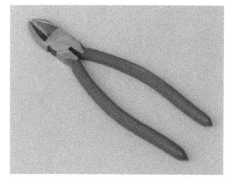

Diagonal wire cutters are good for clipping small gauge wire as well as plastic ties.

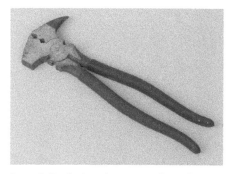

A specially-designed cutter, such as this fencing tool, is needed for heavy gauge wire.

Wire Joints

As you assemble the head, you will also need a way to create joints where the wires contact each other. An obvious choice is soldering, since it forms strong metal-to-metal joints. Soldering works well, and I would recommend it if you have soldering experience and the appropriate materials on hand. If you choose to solder your head, be sure to select a wire that will be receptive to the solder.

The only downside of solder is that the joints tend to be perfectly rigid. If insufficiently soldered, joints may crack if the head is impacted or stressed. Experience with soldering should be able to counteract this.

An alternative method is to use a glue to seal the joint between the wires. I recommend an adhesive that will form a semi-flexible bond, such as Goop™ or E6000™. Be sure to abrade the surface of the wires near the joint to allow the glue to acquire mechanical purchase. A quick pass with metal sandpaper or a metal file should be sufficient. While certainly not as strong as solder, the flexibility built into these joints can result in a better lifespan.

While still working the wire, it's helpful to create temporary joints with floral wire. This small-gauge wire (roughly 22 AWG) can be found in craft stores and florists' shops. Where wires cross, wrap the joint in both directions with the wire. A wrapped joint has a bit of flexibility and movement which will allow you to adjust it as you refine the shape of the wires.

When you're satisfied with the current wires, create a permanent joint. There's no need to remove the floral wire. Apply glue or solder directly over the wrapped junction to create a solid finished joint.

Alternatively, use nylon zip ties to create temporary joints. They are not as strong as glued wire, but can be use to hold other joints in place while you wrap each joint with wire.

Surfacing and Skinning

With a wire framework already in place as a basic structure, surface elements need to be added. In order to attach the fur, a sort of skin layer must be created. If the fur were attached directly to the wires, it would look like a tent. The substructure of the skin provides the final shaping for the fur based on the shape and strength of the wire frame.

Plastic canvas is an excellent surface or skinning material for wire-frame heads. It's lightweight, cheap, and easy to work with. I sew it to the structure using heavy upholstery thread. A modified blanket stitch works well to pull the canvast tight against the wire. The fur can then be applied on top of this skin using hot glue or some other adhesive. If you have time, and want a durable head structure, you can hand sew the fur to the plastic canvas skin.

Plastic Canvas Framework Heads

An alternative to wire is to assemble a framework-style head entirely from plastic canvas. This approach uses long strips of plastic canvas to create a foundation that is roughly helmet shaped. A lifecast or styrofoam mannequin head will greatly assist with the construction process. It's difficult to create the first key shapes of the understructure without being able to see it on a reference.

Additional layers of plastic canvas are added to build up the shape of the costume head. Hot glue will easily attach the plastic canvas together. Be careful not to let the glue get too hot, or it may melt the plastic. Cut and attach strips of canvas in bowed shapes to create bulges and ridges. Without some experience working with models and sculpting, this can be tricky.

Some advantages of this technique are that it is inexpensive and lightweight. Although individually the sheets are not very sturdy, the head gains structural strength when several layers of the canvas are glued together. The final head, with two to three layers of plastic on all surfaces, is quite resilient.

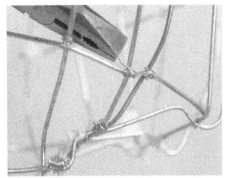

Detail of wire joint.

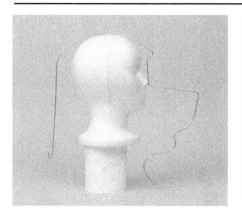

1. Create the Side View Profile

Bend a single long piece of wire into the shape of the profile, from the front to the back of the head. This wire goes up the center of the muzzle, between the eyes, over the crown of the head, and down the back. For characters with open mouths, this wire stops at the back of the roof of the mouth; for closed mouths, you can continue this profile line around the chin and down to the top of the neck.

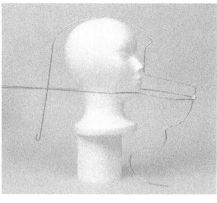

2. Mount the Profile on the Harness

For small-scale heads, you may be able to attach the first profile directly to the harness. For larger heads, it will be necessary to add a mounting strut to space the profile away from the harness.

On some closely fitted heads, I like to bring the front profile down to touch the wearer's nose. This fits very well in designs where the performer is looking out through the eyes of the character. By adding a small pad, some of the weight of the head can rest on the bridge of the nose.

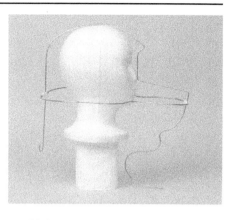

3. Add the Top View Profile

Now that the framework has some stability from the upper hoop, add a wire below it to define the extent of the cheeks. Carry this line forward to define the sides of the muzzle. If you extend this meridian to the back of the head, be sure that you leave enough access room to be able to don the head easily.

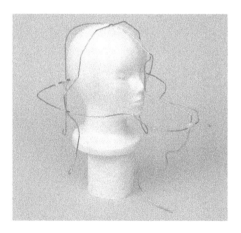

4. Add the Front View Profile

Use a wire to define the shape of the head as it is seen from the front. Place this wire so that it runs across the center of the harness and down the sides of the head to define the extent of the cheeks. This wire might not align with the peaks of the head or cheeks. It's preferable to run it across the center of the harness for better mounting and weight distribution.

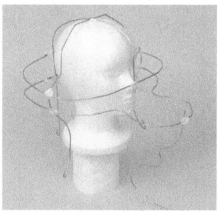

5. Add a Lateral Hoop Above the Nose

Create a loop that will circle the head parallel to the floor. This hoop should be mounted around the character's eye level. On most heads, it's convenient to place it across the bridge of the nose. This loop will add stability to the framework by tying together the other two profile pieces.

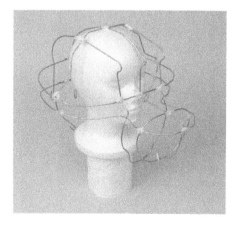

6. Define the Muzzle

Create and attach additional curves that define the shape of the muzzle. Most important are a front profile curve that wraps around from the top to the bottom of the muzzle and a lateral curve, if these weren't already accomplished as part of the previous step.

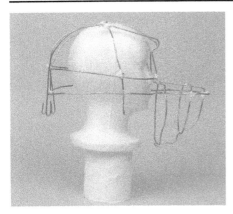

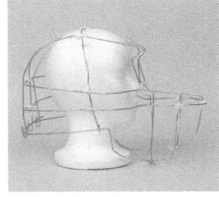

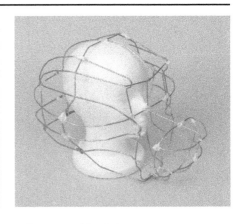

7. Add Radial Wire to Cheeks

Further define the shape of the cheeks by adding additional vertical wires. Depending on the shape of the character's head, it may make sense to extend these wires up to the top of the head. If not, try to extend them high enough to mount to the base of the internal harness.

8. Build the Lower Jaw

If your character design features an open mouth, attach long wires extending down from the cheek area to trace the jaw line. Continue these wires up and around the back of the head for extra security and redundant joints. Use at least two parallel wires to create the structure for the jaw.

9. Transitional Lines

Step back and take a look at the shape of the head as it's defined thus far. Wires should be in place to define the high and low points of the primary features. Add any wires needed to smooth the transitions between these shapes or to create extra details.

Larger ears will benefit from supporting wires. Smaller ears can be surface mounted on the head without any internal framework. If your ears require support, it should be attached to the framework at this point.

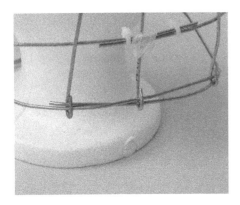

10. Neckline

Shape a loop of wire to define the lowest extents of the rigid portion of the head. Although I refer to it as a "neckline," this piece may be flush with the underside of the character's head. Building the character's neck from fabric provides better mobility for performance.

Once again, put careful consideration into how much of the back of the head is covered. Leaving the lower part of the back of the head exposed means that a zipper closure can be added later; this may make it much easier to don and adjust the costume head.

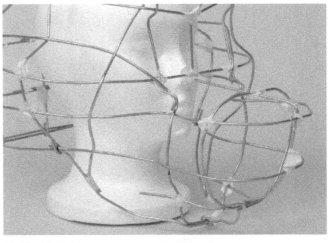

11. Final Reinforcements

Do a final check of the head's shape. The wire framework should define all of the essential curves and extremities of the head even though wires don't fill in all the details. Pick up the framework and attempt to flex it gently; it should be a rigid structure and resist any twisting or deformation. Proceed to skinning.

If you find any weak areas, add extra connecting struts. If a large portion of the structure isn't strong enough, add loops at opposing angles to existing wires. Additionally, if the head is large enough, you can add crossmembers through the interior space of the head.

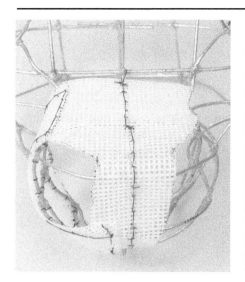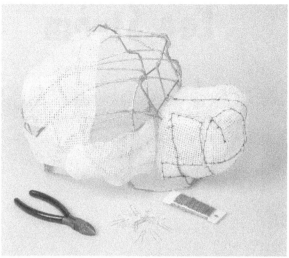

12. Supporting structure for fur

Apply supporting understructure to the wire framework. Using thread or wire, piece plastic canvas onto the head. Finish the head using the fur application techniques described on page 91.

13. Lion head in progress

This partially-finished head built on a wire framework just needs nose, teeth, and muzzle details to finish.

Lee Strom

Lee "Chairo" Strom creates and performs original costumed characters. He has also organized a number of fan events and been involved in running the convention Further Confusion. Pictured here is his raccoon character Chairo.

How did you get involved with costuming? What first attracted you to this hobby?

I don't really have a reason why I like it. Since I was a kid, though, I'd watch things like H.R. Pufnstuf and Zoobilee Zoo and shows with costumed characters. Once I tried performing, though, I found reasons in the excitement it drew and the happiness expressed by the children.

I never thought I'd be able to make good costumes myself because I'm not "artistically inclined." But a few of my friends said, "Just get a block of foam and try carving something." So I went out and did just that.

The biggest challenges for me, as far as constructing costumes, are proportions and symmetry. Symmetry can be really tricky. And you will hear a lot of people say "There is no symmetry in the real world. Nature isn't symmetrical." While that's true, you still have to get close.

But I would encourage people to give it a try. Don't spend too much time worrying or planning. Just buy some materials and start experimenting, seeing what you can create.

What sorts of performance work have you done?

Zoos, hospitals, parades, and other charity events, mostly. I've also done random street performance acts in cities I've visited, including San Fran-

cisco, New York, Toronto, St. Louis, Berlin, Paris, London... a lot of places, now that I think about it!

The only problem for me is that I almost always have to use my own costumes because of the height requirements. I'm on the tall side. Most paid bookings require character performers of smaller stature. So I don't get as many chances to perform as I'd like.

You've taken your suits to lots of different places. Any tips on travelling with a costume?

Well, these days, you can't ship locked boxes on the airlines. If you are travelling domestically and you're concerned, I recommend shipping it ahead separately. Use one of the courier services, insure it, and ship it before you fly out.

If you are flying, put it in a sturdy box. Make sure it's within airline size limits. Don't put anything else valuable in the box with the costume; just fill it with clothing. Having worked for the airlines myself, I know what can sometimes go on behind the scenes with unlocked boxes. If they think it contains valuables, they'll go through it. If they find a costume and clothes, which don't have much value to the average person, they'll probably ignore it.

What factor is most important to the quality of a costume, however you might define "quality"?

I'm pretty picky and, unfortunately, I don't always live up to my own standards. Too often I'm rushing projects. But I do enjoy costumes where people have taken the time with the details. I prefer details and visual appeal over general usability and convenience. If a costume is difficult to perform in but looks brilliant, it can allow for a better overall impression.

What's your favorite part about building costumes?

It's tough to explain, exactly. I like to build the heads more than the rest of it. For me, you can see the results sooner and you can see your art come to fruition as the character takes shape. It's also great motivation for me to get the head done; that's the part of the costume that people will primarily look at. Once that's done, it keeps the project flowing for me.

13 • Eyes & Vision

The purpose of a costume is to create the illusion of another creature. The critter costume trues to entirely disguise the human within the costume, obscuring it from the audience. Yet the performer must be able to to see out without being seen. This creates a design problem.

Various methods can be employed to make the performer's eyes invisible. Most of them rely on limiting the vision aperture, the area through which the performer is able to see, to the smallest possible area on the exterior of the costume. The theory here is that the smaller we make the vision surface, the easier it will be to hide it in the structure of the character's face. While this is sound design logic, it does mean that most costumes are built with severely restricted vision.

Performers are able to adapt to a great number of obstacles. Costume performers are used to having a very limited range of vision. In some cases, such as scripted stage performance, this isn't a big disadvantage. But I've always felt that costumes designed for interaction, particularly with small children, should have more attention given to the design of the vision surface.

Even with a small eye hole, it's necessary to hide this view port so that it doesn't draw attention. This is generally done by camouflaging it so that it appears to be part of the character's face. The effect can also be accomplished by simply hiding it among the details of the face without actually creating a surface. Fundamentally, all head designs rely on one of these basic techniques.

The visibility from a costume is determined by simple geometry. You have a fixed-size area through which the performer is able to look out of the head. If we consider the example of vision through the pupils of the character, then the performer is looking out through the small circular area of the character's black pupils. Taking this example, the vision area might be a circle about two inches in diameter. This seems a reasonable design. After all, I wear glasses and their lenses aren't even that large.

But the other major factor is the distance of the performer's eye from the actual vision surface. Most costume heads are designed to be oversized, whether to create a cartoony appearance, to be able to fit a variety of performers, or to provide for air circulation.

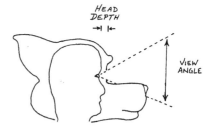

When your eyes are close to the vision apertures, you can see a wide angle.

As the location of the eye moves farther from the view surface, the actual vision in the costume is reduced. This can be understood by considering the view angles that define the performer's field of vision. The view angle is formed by the lines from the eye to the edge of the view surface. Each time we move the eye farther back, these lines get closer and the costume's field of vision shrinks.

Now consider that it is not uncommon for costume heads to have six inches of space between a wearer's face and the costume's eyes. Get a large piece of cardboard and cut two-inch holes to represent eyes. Holding this about six inches in front of your real eyes (about four inches, or a hand's breadth, from the tip of your nose), try to walk around a room; you'll probably catch yourself looking around the edges of the cardboard since your brain is simply not getting enough information through the eye holes. Keep this experience in mind when you're considering the vision requirements for your costume design.

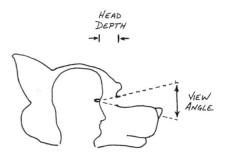

Move further back and you can't see quite as well.

Chapter 13

Possible Vision Locations

- Folds around the eyes
- Flared nostrils
- Mid-neck
- Jewelry
- Hair
- Hat
- Headband or Bandana
- Among Stripes or Colorations

If you use character eye on a large head, you may wind up looking a little cross-eyed.

A custom-built costume has the advantage of tailoring the head to exactly fit a person. This allows you to construct the vision surface as close to the eyes as possible. Minimizing the distance from the performer's eyes to the exterior of the costume widens the view angle. Even so, figure that enclosed costume heads will always need at least two inches of depth to hide the human nose, have some structural elements. Also account for the depth of the fur.

Seeing Through the Character's Eyes – One of the most common and intuitive ways to allow for vision is to have the performer see through the character's eyes. This is a good choice if the proportions of the character head roughly correspond to human proportions; the eyes of the character and performer should be in about the same spot. This isn't as simple in character designs emphasizing the realistic animal form, however, since animals usually have their eyes mounted much higher in the skull; the large human cranium doesn't match with the sleek head design of a fox, for example.

When using the character's eyes for vision, you can use the entire eye or just the pupil. It's easiest to use the pupil, since black is a color that makes it easy to disguise the vision surface. Being able to make the entire eye into a view port would greatly improve the vision of the performer, however; the tradeoff of a less realistic eye appearance might be worthwhile.

One benefit of designing the vision through the character's eyes is that it helps the performer create natural head movements. When they focus on someone, they automatically line up the character's eyes and head with that person. This makes the character seem to respond naturally and look around. When vision is built differently, such as through the character's mouth, it is easy for the performer to forget this and hold the character's head in an unnatural position.

Seeing Through the Character's Mouth – Costumes with particularly large heads can be built so that the wearer is looking out through the mouth of the character. This solves several problems by taking advantage of the large opening that people expect to see in a character's head. The width of the mouth can provide a good range of vision. Since the performer does not need to see through the character's eyes, they can be fabricated from opaque materials such as painted plastic. This provides the designer with the possibility of more complex and realistic eyes.

The largest downside of this strategy is that it requires the character head to be situated higher on the performer's head. This means that the character must have a very large head, as is seen in many sports mascots. This technique is less suited to costumes with more realistic proportions.

Other Vision Locations – It is, of course, possible to allow for vision in any number of different places on the character's head. The design decision will usually be determined by the proportions and geometry of the costume head. Try to make unusual shapes or folds work to your advantage for concealing vision surfaces. While sketching character designs, experiment with raising or lowering the character head relative to the performer's head to see how eye alignment changes.

Consider any special material choices which might allow you to integrate vision directly into visible parts of the costume. Some surface materials which will allow the wearer to see out may match a portion of the character's face. This allows you to build fairly large vision surfaces without any need to hide them. For example, on the foam costume head featured earlier, I took advantage of the black "mask" around the eyes of raccoons to create vision. The mask is constructed from reticulated foam. The performer looks through the foam between the character's eyes. Making the head larger horizontally allowed the character eyes to be situated farther apart. The viewer can't guess where the performer is peeking out at them. Be open to innovation. Experiment with materials and techniques.

Surface Materials

There are a variety of ways to build the vision surface; designers must figure out which techniques they prefer and which will match their characters. Anything can be used to allow for vision as long as it permits the wearer in a dark environment inside the costume to see out to some degree while preventing other people in a brighter environment outside the costume from seeing in.

This emphasis on light levels is deliberate and creates the illusion of a one-directional view. If you are considering a new material, examine it under different lighting conditions. Most importantly, take some test photographs using a flash. Some materials, such as metal mesh, can become more transparent under a flash than in ordinary viewing.

Solid Surfaces – Transparent plastic is a great choice for creating vision surfaces. Window tint film, available at automotive stores, will add enough reflectivity that it is difficult for people to see into the costume. The plastic can also be treated with dyes or paints to darken it and achieve the same effect.

A solid surface is very effective if the vision is through the character's eyes. Many characters, especially cartoon-style characters, tend to have large glossy eyes. Any break in the surface texture would be immediately apparent. It's possible to construct the eye from a single piece of clear plastic sheeting. Colored portions of the eye are painted onto the back side of the plastic, a technique similar to creating an animation cel. The unpainted pupil is covered with tinted film, thereby creating a vision surface which matches the rest of the eye.

The biggest disadvantage with solid surfaces is that they suffer from fogging due to condensation from the warm moist air inside the costume head. See Chapter 15, Ventilation and Cooling, for corrective tips.

Metal Screen – Many costumes, especially commercially available ones, utilize metal screens to disguise the vision surface. Screens do have some definite advantages, though the disadvantages outweigh them, in my opinion.

The screen material may be a fairly heavy perforated metal. That is, filled with an array of holes. Metal screen is very durable, making for a long-lasting, low-maintenance solution. Alternatively, screen door material can be used to create eyes. Since it is so thin, it is best to use two layers. Overlap them so that the mesh directions are diagonally offset to create the best effect.

Metal screen can be painted. The color will not be very saturated unless you use a heavy screen where the surface is predominantly solid. It can still be difficult to blend with other parts of the face, as the texture of the metal will stand out against fabrics and fur; this means it is harder to disguise screen surfaces believably.

One of the disadvantages of metal screen is that it doesn't stand up well to flash photography. In my experience, there's usually one of two outcomes: either the mesh becomes mostly transparent under the photographic flash, revealing the performer inside, or unpainted metal in the mesh reflects the light, creating an intense glare in the photograph.

Reticulated Foam – One of my favorite vision materials is reticulated foam. When cut into sheets ¼" to ⅜" thick (depending on pore density), this foam

Concealing Vision

Vision can be concealed in a variety of different ways. Try to take advantage of character geometry or facial features to incorporate vision. Using these more creative approaches can also make it harder for the audience to guess how the performer is seeing and therefore maintains the illusion of the character. If you're looking for inspiration on an unusual head, consider some of the options listed in the sidebar for vision locations.

The finished raccoon head provides vision for the performer through the mesh between the decorative character eyes.

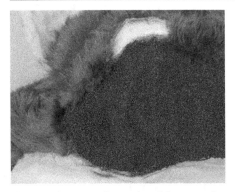

This is a close-up of reticulated foam used to cover the eye hole. The foam creates a vesion surface that allows the wearer to see out.

Smaller scale heads can be designed to line up with the performer's real eyes.

becomes excellent material for vision surfaces. It is black enough that people can't readily see into a dark costume head, yet the performer can see out.

I find that the rough irregular surface texture also makes the foam less noticeable than screens. Reticulated foam can be painted, though it will never have saturated color. Be careful not to clog the pores of the foam when painting, or it will hinder vision and create an uneven appearance.

One problem with reticulated foam is that it is not a very rugged material. It can be torn, especially when used as a thin sheet. For this reason, it should be used carefully in costumes that will be in direct contact with audiences and, especially, young children.

Using the Performer's Eyes

An alternative strategy is to use the real eyes of the performer as the eyes of the character. This style is limited because it requires that the proportions of the character head tightly match human scale. The costume needs to be designed with a close-fitting head, perhaps even custom-designed for a particular performer.

There are a couple advantages to this technique. Making the performer's actual eyes visible to the audience allows for a much greater degree of expression and emotion in the character; this can be very good for performances where the audience is close to the character. Using the wearer's eyes also adds to the realism, as long as human eyes match the character design. Finally, the performer will probably have excellent vision since his eyes are unobscured.

When wearing a head designed in this way, it's important to apply makeup around the eyes in order to blend with the mask. Usually black facepaint around the eye area and eyelids will be sufficient. Other head designs might require particular colors. While designing the head, realize that this choice adds a little extra time and material to the process of putting on the costume.

14 • Mouths, Noses & Other Details

Once the basic structure and furring of a head has been completed, there are many details that must be added. Your design of these features should be guided by the impression you want the costume to make. Cartoony characters or costumes geared towards children will need less detail work; instead, focus on creating a few large and caricatured features. Realistic critters should have greater facial detail to help complete the character's appearance.

In going through the following sections, consider which details are necessary for your character. Facial features convey more information than your species. Your mood and intellect are expressed through these details.

Teeth

If the character has an open mouth, it may be appropriate to give him teeth. These can make the character appear more menacing, beast-like, or cunning. Teeth identify a species. A costume can sport a full mouth of teeth or only a select few. Abstraction of tooth shapes lends more of a cartoon appearance. There are various techniques available for constructing different types of teeth.

Foam Teeth – Foam can be carved into tooth shapes quickly and easily. A solid coat of white or off-white paint will create a good surface finish. Though this won't make for particularly realistic teeth, it is a very effective way to create large, exaggerated teeth that are lightweight and harmless.

Sculpted Teeth – Individual teeth can also be formed from a variety of sculptural materials. Some popular products are Sculpey™ and Fima™ plasticine clays. They are worked by hand into the correct shapes and then "fired" in a household oven to harden them. Once dry, they accept paint well which creates a nice surface appearance.

Create multiple teeth by sculpting originals in clay and creating cast replicas. This requires a little bit of experience with casting materials, but it isn't too complex. If you're creating several costumes or a particularly large mouthful of teeth, then this approach has the advantage of easily creating a large number of copies from an original mold. Experiment with materials to find one that works for you.

Taxidermy Jaw Sets – Taxidermy supply houses offer a wide variety of animal jaw and tooth sets. These can be used, in whole or in part, to create realistic mouths. If you are trying to create a realistic character, they can be a terrific timesaver.

However, keep in mind how much you have scaled up the costume from the original animal. Costume heads are often twice the size of the actual animal's head. In order to account for this difference, you may need to buy a different species' taxidermy set in order to fit the costume proportions. For example, you may need to order a wolf jaw set for a fox costume. For the most accurate results, try to stick to species that are zoologically related.

Top: foam teeth. Midddle: sculpted teeth. Bottom: taxidermy jaw set.

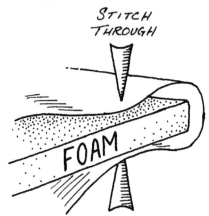

Chapter 14

A simple way to sew foam lips.

Tongues

A tongue can add a lot to a character's personality and appearance. A small tongue visible inside the mouth adds a degree of realism and color. A large, exaggerated tongue can be used to great effect to highlight a comic character.

Tongues within the mouth can be built from almost any material. They are usually only partially visible and need to provide more of the impression of a tongue rather than any details. I usually try to use a material which matches whatever was used in the construction of the rest of the mouth.

If the tongue needs to be more realistic, taxidermy suppliers are a good resource. They sell cast pre-painted tongue sculptures which can be used directly in a costume.

For larger tongues and those hanging out of the mouth, consider sewing the tongue out of fabric. A simple two-faced pattern can be created; a thin sheet of foam inserted between the fabric layers adds body. Choose a material that has an appearance that will help the tongue become part of the character. Depending on the desired effect, this might be fur or felt for a warm fuzzy texture, or spandex or taffeta fabric to create a shiny, wet impression.

Lips

Since animals often don't have pronounced lips, most character costumes don't feature them. Yet there are some species, such as lions and bears for which the lips can add to the recognition. Lips can introduce gender exaggeration, such as large colored lips for a female character.

My favorite technique for creating lips is to use an elastic material stretched over foam. For more realistic lips, fabric is wrapped over the edge of a small piece of foam and sewn down, creating a small roll of foam-filled fabric. Larger lips are created by carving a block of firm foam into the desired shape and then covering it with fabric, paint, or RTV rubber.

Whiskers

Whiskers are not commonly found on costumes that are used for close interaction with the public; they can poke someone in the eye, be grabbed by kids, and show wear easily. They are more commonly seen on stage costumes where they are an effective way to enhance the animal appearance of a character.

Most mascot costumes have whiskers pushed into the foam understructure of the muzzle and glued in place. Experiment on leftover foam to test your choices in whisker materials and glue.

Should you decide your critter needs whiskers, determine how thick and stiff you think they should be. These characteristics will help determine what material is a good choice for your whiskers.

Material	Thickness	Stiffness
Metal hobby rods (1/16")	Thick	Almost rigid
Broom straw (synthetic)	Moderate	Stiff
Fishing line	Thin	Some stiffness
Yarn	Moderate	No stiffness
String	Thin	No stiffness

Eyelashes

This feature is often added to female characters to exaggerate their gender. They can be particularly effective on more cartoony or stylized character designs. Eyelashes add subtle personality and look flirty.

Eyelashes can be constructed from a number of different materials, including actual false eyelashes. Other good candidate materials for eyelashes are thin sheets of closed-cell foam and felt (stiffened with glue). This is an area where it may be best to use materials similar to those used in the construction of other details, allowing the eyelashes to blend in and create a textural cohesion.

Flirty eyelashes

Noses

Of all the facial features, noses probably exhibit the widest variety among different species of animal costumes. There are many different approaches to designing and making an animal nose. Consider the size of your head, species peculiarities, and the amount of stylization you are striving for when selecting a method. The following techniques are just a few that I like for costume noses.

Underskull Noses – If the costume head is designed with a solid underskull, the nose can be incorporated as one unit. This is commonly seen in costumes with fiberglass or cast latex heads. The nose is sculpted during manufacture of the head and then painted to make it stand out. If fur is applied, the nose is left exposed.

Foam Noses – A large, soft nose made of foam painted or wrapped in vinyl, spandex, will balance a large head and create a cartoony effect. This is useful for making large and distinctive noses. The nose structure is first carved from foam. Next, a covering material like black spandex is stretched around the foam. The fabric is pulled around the nose and secured in the back where it will be attached to the head.

Sculpted Noses – It is also possible to sculpt a nose using a modeling compound. This is the same as the technique described for sculpted teeth. Noses can sometimes be a bit trickier to attach. Be sure to sculpt some good gripping surface onto the backside of your nose to accomodate glue.

Underskull nose

It is important that the material have a great deal of stretch in it to avoid excessive wrinkles and folds. It is possible to use folds to your advantage, though, if the nose is carefully shaped. Supple leather can be used very effectively as a nose surface.

Instead of fabric, you can put a surface on the foam sculpture using an RTV rubber product. Tool Dip™ is a common consumer product which works reasonably well for small applications such as noses. The rubber creates a solid and reflective surface on top of the foam.

Foam nose

Dennis Lancaster

Dennis Lancaster has been a professional costumer for many years, working under the name Mr. Dinosaur. He is now part of Intermission Productions, a company making custom mascots, props, children's shows, and character appearances. Find him online at www.ipmascots. com.

How would you describe your costuming work?

I set up Intermission Productions with my partners Sher Madison and Mark Rutchick. Part of the business is creating custom mascot costumes. We also write and produce educational kids' shows using our own characters. I'm involved in the design and construction of the different costumes.

A lot of costume construction is really hit and miss. You try things and you learn what works. I think of myself less as an artist and more as a "practical application technician." I rarely have the luxury of extra time to perfect something or make it really artistic. I need to get costumes together for clients, inevitably on a tight deadline, that will last through performances.

It's challenging, sometimes, to come up with something fast without compromising the character's design. I think my stuff looks pretty good and the construction is precise and durable, but it's not as artistic as some other costumers' products. It's a tradeoff you make in the business.

What factor is most important to the quality of a costume, however you might define "quality"?

The performer. That is the major factor in the final character's quality. I've made some beautiful costumes that had tons of potential and character.

But without a good performer, there's no life to it. On the other hand, I've seen some simple costumes look terrific because of the performer inside. It is up to the performer to make the costume into something real for the audience.

What do you think are some of the important aspects of your design and construction process?

Good construction can make performance easier. I like to build a costume from the inside out, starting with the structure and undersuit. Test it first. Wear it, roll around, jump, and whatever to see how it moves and reacts. Fix anything that doesn't look like it will be durable enough. Then add the outside onto this performance-tested base.

I don't use fur all the time in my work since not all of the characters I make are animals. When not using fur, I like to use polyester doubleknit fabric for the surface of the suits. It's a heavy fabric that wears well and is very colorfast. It does have the downside that it will show mistakes. Doubleknit will teach you to do clean stitching! You can't remove and restitch a seam without leaving marks on the material.

When designing a costume, I try to avoid putting too much around the performer's head. I like more open head designs that support the weight with the shoulders. I also don't like

to put fans in my costume heads, which is kind of unusual. Fans are white noise and they take away your focus. If you have a constant hum in your ear your brain just wants to shut down. I much prefer to use a cool vest and let my body cool down that way.

In your experience, how is designing a costume for a client different from creating your own character?

One thing I've found, when doing commissions for people that are not costumers, is that they tend to think in terms of animation, to the point of providing cartoons as reference art. Animation is two dimensional and the artist can stretch and fudge dimensions to make things look and move how they want. When it's a real physical costume, you can't do that.

Some designs also call for very elaborate costumes with lots of extra features and details. There's nothing inherently wrong with this as long as it doesn't make the suit harder to perform in. When you have a costume that has great visual impact, that's a great opening impression. But then people will expect your performance to keep the costume interesting.

If you are a performer, you'll become one with the costume. The bells and whistles won't matter. It's just important that you aren't struggling against the costume; the complexity of the costume shouldn't hinder the performer and make them focus on technicalities. There has to be a balance between performability and the "wow!" factor.

Any tips on designing costumes and performances towards a younger audience?

Respect their intelligence, first of all. If your characters don't challenge them, you'll lose their interest. Interaction is also very important with children. Kids like to be involved. Try to get them involved in the character, so that they share in your energy. Break down the wall between the kids and the characters.

Are there any words of wisdom you want to offer to someone new to costuming?

Ask yourself what you want to accomplish with your characters. That will guide you so that your costumes work for you. I think anyone who's trying to create some sort of fun illusion for people is doing something worthwhile. I don't mind if anyone disagrees with my own approach and opinions as long as they are inspired in their own way. Go out there and have a grand time! Find what works for you!

Just remember, the biggest performance sin is to be boring. Put an interesting creature out there and not just another person waving in a baggy suit.

The Dangerous Dinos, designed by Dennis Lancaster.

15 • Ventilation & Cooling

In costume head construction, ventilation is a very important consideration. If you don't immediately agree with the previous statement, I would guess that you've never had to wear an enclosed costume head for a long performance. It is amazing how quickly the heat and humidity can accumulate in a head during even minor physical exertion.

The most effective way to counter the twin problems of heat and humidity is to introduce forced air ventilation into the costume. The most logical place to do this is in the head. This chapter specifically addresses ways to improve the ventilation and cooling properties for a character head design.

Cooling Garments

There are many steps that performers can take to stay cool in their costumers. Some employ ice packs or cool vests worn under their costumes. I've never been fond of these since the cooling effect lasts only a limited time, after which they merely add weight. However, vests made with modern phase-changing materials integrated into their structure offer long-term cooling. These are effective but quite expensive.

A more passive cooling system is simply to wear undergarments. Something that is absorbent and will wick sweat away from your skin will help the body's natural cooling. Explore sports stores, motorcycle leather shops, and military surplus outlets for a variety of undergarment options.

Natural Ventilation

The easiest way to add ventilation to a head is simply to create holes and open passages to the outside that will allow for natural air circulation. Ventilation holes may be small and hidden, such as inside an ear. They might also be obvious but covered with a permeable material, such as a mouth opening.

You cannot have too much ventilation. Try to take advantage of the character head design wherever possible to introduce airflow. Holes near the top of the head can be particularly helpful for releasing the hottest air, which rises inside the enclosed head.

Openings on the front of the head are also very desirable. Every time you move forward fresh air is swept into the head. With sufficient natural ventilation of this sort and a little bit of heat tolerance, a costume head can be relatively comfortable.

Cooling Fans

Do you need a fan? Just because you can install a fan doesn't mean you need to. I usually recommend fans for newer costumers who may not be prepared for the heat of performance conditions. Building a costume head without a fan is easier and less expensive, but don't sacrifice comfort to save time and money. If the costume head has good natural ventilation a fan may be superfluous.

Deciding Whether to Ventilate

Pros

- Keeps the head and costume cooler during the whole performance.

- Usually easy to install and maintain.

- Allows you to wear glasses.

Cons

- Creates noise inside the head.

- May require some extra construction planning (vents and air circulation space).

Chapter 15

Unless a head has superb natural ventilation, you may consider installing a fan or two. It is fairly easy to install a basic cooling fan and it can make a huge difference to the comfort of the costume.

The effectiveness of fans depends on the amount of space inside the costume head. There needs to be some air cavity so that the fan can effectively move air around the wearer's head. Some tight-fitting heads, such as carved foam designs, may need to have open space added to allow for air circulation.

I prefer using computer cooling fans in my costumes. These are available at computer part stores for a few dollars. They are compact, move a decent volume of air, and are designed to run off 12 volts DC. You could easily use any small DC fan, though.

I usually hook my fans up to a 9-volt battery, so that the fan runs at less than full speed. This makes the fan quieter, yet it is still moving enough air to be effective in the small space of a costume head.

Mounting Locations

While it would be great to have an illustration showing possible mounting locations, every head is different and has its own ventilation requirements. You will need to experiment with your creation to find the best locations.

A number of different factors, including the shape of the character head, available air cavities, and personal preference, determine the ideal mounting locations for any costume. In general, I recommend mounting fans in the muzzle of the head blowing out through the mouth. In some cases, I like to install a secondary fan at the top of the head which pulls air in from the outside.

Remove Moist Air – As we breathe, water is transferred out of our bodies as moisture when we exhale. In an enclosed costume head, this moisture quickly builds up and makes the environment unpleasant faster than the heat! The optimal solution is to remove this moist air as quickly as it is created.

A fan placed in front of the performer's mouth can direct his or her breath out of the costume. Since the roof of the character's mouth is rarely a visible part of the costume, it's often easy to hide vent holes there. Critters generally have muzzles which allow for enough extra room to mount the fan, fuse, and wiring.

As air is blown from the costume, fresh air is pulled into the head through other openings. These are commonly around the costume's eyes and neck, creating good circulation past the upper face and neck of the performer.

Remove Hot Air – A secondary goal is to prevent the buildup of hot air within the costume head. Air gets heated both through exhalation and proximity to the skin. A fan in the muzzle can do a good job of removing hot and moist air. A secondary fan can improve the situation, too.

I like to mount the secondary fan near the top of the head. I prefer to mount it against a vent so that it pulls fresh air into the head and directs it downward, creating a strong flow of air from the top of the head to the muzzle. This conveniently passes the face of the performer, providing a constant low-humidity breeze.

Prevent Condensation – I wear glasses in my everyday life. In costume heads with enough room I like to wear my glasses, too. But even a little moisture can cause condensation to form on the lenses. The same problem is seen on solid eye designs, such as those using tinted film and plastic.

A muzzle fan helps remove moisture, but is not enough to prevent condensation. Some exhaled moisture, as well as evaporating sweat, will still remain in the costume head. Two-fan arrangements seem to create enough airflow to solve the problem. It is important that the airflow pass across the surface where we are trying to prevent condensation from forming.

Seals and Ducting

When mounting fans, ensure that they are moving air as your design intends. Since we are using small inaudible fans, we need to take advantage of their full air capacity. A few simple tricks will maximize the performance of the fans.

When installing a fan, ensure that there is a full seal to prevent air from going around the edge of the fan. Simply mounting it in front of a ventilation hole doesn't mean it will effectively pull or push air through it. A line of glue that seals the fan against the ventilation area will usually solve this problem. Be careful not to let glue drip into the fan and seize it up, ruining it.

For more complex heads, it is useful to create some simple ducting to direct the airflow. I've found this to be particularly useful for the top-mounted fan. A short duct can shift the airflow from straight down towards the top of the performer's head to the front of the head where it can move past the performer's glasses.

You can easily create a duct from craft sheets of closed-cell foam. Any thin, flexible plastic could also be used. Use glue or tape to assemble the pieces and secure them to the inside of the head.

Simple Fan Circuitry

A simple fan circuit can be created that includes a fuse, battery clip, and optionally a switch. All of these parts should be available at local electronics shops, such as Radio Shack, or by mail order. I like to order parts from Digi-Key (see sidebar).

I use a locking fuseholder that is fully enclosed. I prefer them over clip-style fuseholders because it prevents moisture from condensing on the outside of the fuse. I recommend a fuse because, although a short is unlikely, it's generally best to observe proper electrical safety with something that will be a couple inches from your face.

A switch is convenient but optional. Without a switch, you can turn the fan off by removing the battery from its clip. A switch allows you to leave the battery in the head between performances until it needs replacement.

The last step is to create some sort of battery holder to prevent it from dangling or rattling inside the head. I usually just use a rubber band to secure it to some piece of framework inside the head. In foam heads, I use a penknife to carve a battery-shaped hole.

Common Part Numbers

Radio Shack

Small 12V fan
Part #273-240

Inline Fuse Holder
Part #270-1238

Fast-Acting 0.50A Fuse
Part #270-1002

9V Battery Clip
Part #270-325

Slide Switch (optional)
Part #275-406

Digi-Key

Inline Fuse Holder
Part #F062-ND

Fast-Acting 0.25A Fuse
Part #F109-ND

9V Battery Clip
Part #2241K-ND

Slide Switch (optional)
Part #CKC5101-ND

Fan, battery clip, and 9-volt battery. Solder is only needed if a switch is used.

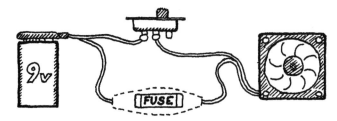

A simple wiring schematic for a cooling fan.

Part IV

Body Construction

There are millions of different animal species on the planet. Each one has a slightly different body shape! The challenge as a costumer is to capture the most important aspects of your chosen creature's physical form.

If that were all it involved, we would be talking about sculpture. In costuming, we have the added challenge of adapting animal forms to fit the human bod, or vice versa. The finished costume has to appear animalistic yet be mobile enough to allow for an effective performance.

To meet these challenges, the costumer's arsenal must include a variety of techniques for creating costume bodies. In this part of the book we examine everything from simple sewn jumpsuits to sculpted form-fitting bodysuits. We also look at the unique challenges associated with hands, feet, and tails for animal characters.

The style you select will impact the overall look of the costume. Here, the Dizzy costume has both a fully-furred suit and a spandex suit configuration.

16 • Sewn Suits

This chapter focuses on "sewn suits," costume bodies which are assembled and worn as a jumpsuit. This style of costume is nearly universal in commercial costume manufacturing. Mascot costumes are a canonical illustration of the style. Sewn jumpsuits also have many advantages which may make them attractive to the individual costumer.

Yet the simple description above doesn't allude to the many different variations and details possible with this technique. Beyond simple jumpsuits, it is possible to create padded and tailored bodysuits to good effect. While this may not be suitable for highly realistic applications, the simplicity and versatility of this construction technique make it worthy of serious consideration.

Making a Sewn Suit

If you sew, this process should be familiar to you. If not, don't fear! A simple bodysuit is an approachable project for the novice and can be a good learning experience.

The construction of a sewn suit is roughly similar to the construction of other articles of clothing. The first step is to acquire a sewing pattern. The easiest approach is to begin with a commercial jumpsuit pattern. The pattern serves as a guide for cutting and assembling the suit as well as aiding in the estimation of material requirements. Use the pattern as a basis for your own modifications.

Part of developing the pattern includes adjusting the fit of the jumpsuit. Depending on the amount and shape of the padding, the pattern needs to be adjusted to accommodate the changed animal form. It's important to note that all of this work is done during the development of the pattern, not the final costume. After many samples, you will arrive at a finalized pattern before passing expensive fur through your scissors.

Once the fur pieces have been cut and assembled the costume body is mostly complete. Further work is required to create the closure, coloration details, and padding. The level of additional work put into the costume at this stage will visually distinguish it and enhance the quality of its appearance.

Pattern Selection

Unless you harbor a secret desire to learn the intricacies of pattern-making, it's best to start with a commercially available sewing pattern and modify it for your costume's needs. (If you do harbor such a desire, more power to you! See the resources list at the back of the book for how-to books on pattern making.)

Most major consumer pattern companies produce jumpsuit patterns. Check the pattern catalogs at your local fabric stores. Jumpsuit patterns are usually available under a "Halloween," "costume," or "seasonal" section. Catalogs usually contain one or two generic animal costume patterns, with a simple jumpsuit body and an open hood face. Raglan sleeves, which are desirable for most costumes, differentiate these patterns from other jumpsuit patterns elsewhere in the catalog. A simple Halloween costume is the easiest pattern to modify.

Sewn Suits

Advantages
- Fast construction
- Repeatable/reusable pattern
- Can be made to fit different sizes
- Easy to put on and take off

Disadvantages
- Unrealistic appearance
- Subtle movements obscured by loose fabric

Durability
- Good, but varies with quality of fur

Primary Materials
- Fur fabric

Special Tools
- Sewing machine

If you are planning on using something other than fur or if your design calls for an especially tight-fitting bodysuit, then you should also consider unitard patterns. Some catalogs will feature an "exercise" or "dancewear" section with such patterns. However, if you're planning to use fur for the body, remember that plush fabrics have very little stretch. Be sure to check the stretch of your fur against the requirements of the pattern or to enlarge the joint allowances. Otherwise, the bodysuit will restrict movement and inhibit performance.

If the pattern that you are looking for is not available, see if the store is able to order it or if they have it at another branch location. Don't purchase an inferior or inadequate pattern simply because your first choice wasn't in stock at the time! A good base pattern is worth the effort.

Using Sewing Patterns

Consumer sewing patterns are printed on lightweight tissue paper. These patterns are designed to be disposable and will not stand up to wear and tear. Fur is a heavy and full-bodied material. If you're working with fur and pieces of thin tissue paper, one of them is likely to tear due to handling and it's not going to be the fur.

Commercial patterns for Halloween and mascot costumes can provide a good starting pattern.

I generally avoid working with the tissue paper pattern pieces longer than I have to. Using the size tables in the pattern, select the pattern size closest to the performer's measurements. Cut this set of pieces out of the tissue paper, discarding the excess. Trace these shapes onto thin cardboard and cut out the new pattern pieces.

When first working with a new pattern, I use cheap tagboard to create the copies of the unaltered commercial pattern. Once I've adapted and fitted the pattern, I create a sturdier copy of the pattern out of corrugated cardboard. You can salvage a lot of cardboard from packing boxes and stores; oversize pieces can be purchased from art stores and framing shops, where it's used as backing behind framed prints.

Cutting the fur is best accomplished on a large work surface. Lay the fur out flat, pile downwards. Align the pattern piece on the backing of the fur, checking that the nap of the fur matches the direction needed for that pattern piece. Then double check the direction the fur flows! When cutting out a lot of pieces for a costume, it is too easy to misalign the fur and cut an incorrect piece; do not use pieces cut with the nap out of alignment from the pattern. See the chapter on fur materials for more cutting tips.

After cutting each pattern, flip the pattern template over so that it's lying face-down, and cut another piece. This creates two mirror image pieces of fur. If placed next to each other with the nap running downwards, the pair of pieces will be left-right mirror images.

When finished using your pattern, make sure to store them so they will be undamaged and ready for the next costuming project. Be sure to label the pieces and put the date on them so you know when you made them. These large pattern pieces can be stacked behind doors or in portfolio envelopes for storage.

Bodysuit Patterns

In mascot-styled jumpsuit patterns, the legs and torso are combined into one long pattern peice. If you have never worked with commercial patterns before, read the directions on the pattern envelope. These instructions will give you the order of construction as well as hints on pattern layout and sewing techniqes. As you look at your pattern, you will see one front body piece and one back. Each pattern piece is cut twice, once face up and then, after flipping it over, face down.

Most patterns come with a two-piece raglan style sleeve. These sleeves have an upper seam that runs from the wrist to the neck and an under seam from the armpit to the wrist. They attach to the body with a diagonal seam that goes from the neckline to the armpit. This sleeve style eliminates the circular seam used in fitted garments such as shirts and coats, in favor of easier to sew straight-line seams.

A downside to the raglan construction is that the shoulders can be difficult to adjust. It also means that the neckline consists of eight fabric edges (two from each arm, two front body panels, two back body panels) rather than only four with single-sleeve patterns. If you're not familiar with pattern assembly, it can sometimes be tricky getting all eight pieces to align correctly.

Altering and Fitting Patterns

Fitting patterns can be a very complex process. It may seem like you need years of experience, but remember that costume bodysuits do not need to be precisely fitted. In fact, a sewn suit which was altered and fitted like clothing would be too restrictive for the majority of performance work. Costumes need more movement and flexibility because of their active use. Fur is a bulky and stiff fabric, and needs more allowance for movement. One up-side to fur is that it hides excess fabric and wrinkles so subtle folds and draping caused by a looser fit are obscured by the pile.

When working with a new pattern, make a test copy of the garment from cheap material. Use the original pattern without deviations for the first attempt. Use any medium-body low-stretch material that is inexpensive and stocked in bulk. I like to use cotton broadcloth, often available at clearance rates for colors that aren't selling well. Any color will work for a test suit as long as marking lines are clearly visible on it.

Sew the test garment and put it on the costume's intended performer. If designing for several different people, get the largest performer to model the suit. If your costume body requires foam padding, wear the finished pads or mock-ups during the fitting process. Keep the test garment inside-out so the seam edges are exposed on the outside. Use these exposed seams to make and test adjustments. As the wearer tries different extremes of movement, mark where there is extra fabric to eliminate and open the seams if the area is too tight. Pay particular attention around the shoulder and knee joints. Your goal is to strike a balance between good fit and free mobility.

To reduce a seam, pinch it together farther in from the seam and add a line of pins or basting stitches. Have the actor test the range of movement. If it's satisfactory, draw the new line on the fabric, tracing the position of the pins. Leave the pins in until the fitting is completed, however, since one altered seam can affect others. The marked lines will serve as new contours for the pattern pieces. Be sure to mark the fabric faces on both pieces. Should an area be too tight, use a marker to note this on the fabric near the seam. Use any convenient system of marks or symbols you like as long as you will be able to understand it unambiguously once the test suit has been removed and disassembled. Consult a sewing book for more detailed directions.

Once the fitting session is complete, remove all of the pins marking alterations. Check as you go that each row of pins is marked on the fabric. Removing

Necks

Depending on the size of the costume's head, you may need to add a neck to the bodysuit to prevent the performer's neck from being visible. Jumpsuits don't include neck pieces, so this is a pattern alteration. Incorporating a neck into a raglan sleeve pattern is tricky, because four pattern pieces would need to be modified and numerous seams would be on the inside of the collar. Instead, the neck can be added as separate pattern pieces which are assembled and then attached to the top of the existing jumpsuit.

the pins first makes it much less prickly for the performer to remove the suit. When the fitting sample is off the body, make sure to transfer any additional markings from pins to an inked line. Use scissors or a seam ripper to take the test garment apart into its original eight pieces. Each piece of fabric should have its own marks to indicate how the pattern should be reduced or expanded. Since two pieces were cut from each part of the pattern, there will be some redundancy if you fitted both halves of the test suit.

In an ideal world, both pieces of fabric would indicate the same changes to the pattern. Since we don't live in that ideal world, I'll tell you what to do when they inevitably don't align: make the smaller alteration. It's better to err on the loose side. Synthetic fur won't grow, so if your pattern is too small, you will have to do some tricky piecing to make it fit.

Once all alteration marks have been transferred back to the pattern pieces, trim them down to their new shapes. If the test suit was too small in some areas, you will need to make new, larger, pattern pieces. If you're unsure of your alterations or they were particularly numerous, then it's probably worthwhile to create another test suit. It's preferable to find out that something wasn't altered properly using inexpensive fabrics!

Once if everything looks good, clearly label all of the pattern pieces, e.g., "Bodysuit XYZ, front/back, sleeve/body."

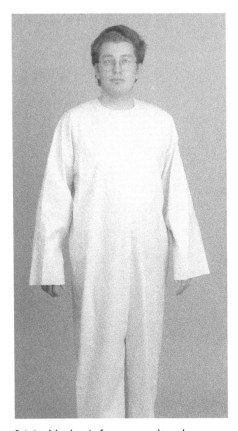

Original bodysuit from an unaltered commercial pattern.

The same pattern after alteration. Markings were drawn on the bodysuit to position the color boundary.

Fur bodysuit assembled based on the tested pattern.

Coloration and Markings

Coloration describes the broad blocks of color pattern on a costume. This is in contrast to markings, which are localized color effects (e.g., black tips on ears). The reason for the distinction is that it's usually easiest to approach them in different ways based on how large the color effect will be on the finished suit.

The coloration pattern of the animal is generally represented by translating the colors into large regions on the anthropomorphic form of the costume. The costume has a number of color boundaries that divide regions of different coloration. More realistic costumes will blend these lines while cartoony or mascot costumes often leave them as distinct (or even contrasting) color changes.

Adding Coloration

It is easiest to incorporate broad expanses of color into a costume by including it in the pattern. The costume is assembled from fur materials of different colors (and possibly textures). The different colors of fur can be purchased or, if a precise color is required, created by dyeing.

To determine the sewing pattern for your body markings, use the test bodysuit. Use a marker to draw the desired color boundaries directly onto the suit. When the test suit has been removed, it can be laid on top of the original sewing pattern pieces to determine how these coloration boundaries line up. Transfer the color lines to the pattern.

Each boundary line becomes a seam in the original pattern piece. Cut the pattern apart on these new seam lines. Add seam allowance to the pattern pieces to ensure a good finished fit.

When sewing the bodysuit, assemble these multi-color pattern pieces first. Test the composite piece flat on your original pattern piece to check your alignment. The piece you have just assembled from several different colors of fur should match the size and proportions of the original piece it replaced. Then continue assembling the sewing pattern as usual.

Adding Markings

Markings, or smaller areas of coloration, are more easily added after a suit has been assembled. Tipping or small details can be easily added by dry brushing inks into the fur. (See the "Acrylic Paint and Inks" section of Chapter 7.)

Small areas of solid color, such as tiger stripes, can also be added after the sewn suit has been assembled. Cut the appropriately-shaped piece from the contrasting fur color which will form the marking. Hold it against the suit (ideally while it's being worn) to check that the shape and placement of the marking is correct. Mark the shape onto the suit.

Carefully shave away the pile of the fur on the suit in the same position as the marking piece. The goal here is to inset the new piece of fur into the original fur. In order to maintain the integrity of the suit, don't cut through the backing of the original fur piece. Use a beard trimmer or thread scissors to cut the fur pile down to the knit backing. When nestled into this hole, the marking should blend in with the other fur.

Glue or sew the marking piece into place. Sewing is a good approach, and ensures that the edges of the inset piece will never become visible due to wear

Finished racoon costume with light grey fur to enhance the animal's markings.

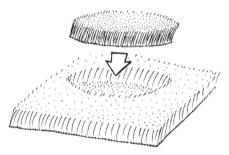

Pieces of a contrasting fur can be sewn into the main color to create small inset markings.

Chapter 16

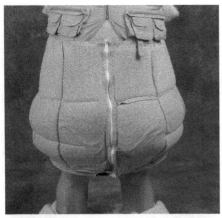

More complex padding can be assembled to dramatically alter the apparent shape of the body.

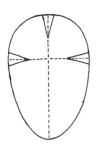

A simple pattern to create a shaped hip insert from a piece of sheet foam.

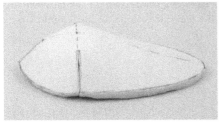

and fraying. Use a simple hand stitch from the backside of the fur around the edge of the marking.

If you're in a hurry, use a thin coating of hot glue. Make sure that the bead of glue gets close to the edges of the insert piece. Before you set it in place, brush the base fur outwards from the hole to avoid trapping any loose fibers in the glue. Handle the glued piece carefully to ensure it doesn't fold up on itself. Hot glue has a tremendous ability to curl synthetic fur backing, which will distort or shrink the marking.

Padding and Inserts

Plain bodysuit patterns, though common on commercial and mascot costumes, don't disguise the shape of the human body. Simple bodysuits are sufficient for most applications and are an easier project goal for beginning costumers.

For projects where the animal's body shape needs to be more realistically defined, foam pads can be inserted into the bodysuit. Padding is used just under the fur to add extra shaping and volume to the body. This is practical if the shape of the body needs to be modified in only a few key areas to create the suggestion of the animal form. More complex transformations may require a padded undersuit, a technique covered in Chapter 18.

The most convenient material for creating body pads is sheets of foam. Urethane foam is commonly available in one-inch-thick sheets at fabric stores. Stiffer, washable inserts can be fabricated from reticulated foam.

Sheet foam is made into more complex three-dimensional shapes using simple darts. Cut a wedge from the foam and then glue the interior edges together. A foam-specific glue such as Fastbond™ (see Chapter 10) is ideal, but hot glue also works well. The simple pattern at shown here creates a rounded shape which, worn just off the hip, adds definition to the haunches.

Foam insert pads can be covered with fabric to allow them to slide against the fur. Otherwise there is too much friction between the foam surface and the backing of the fur to allow for movement. (The friction is usually not enough to actually do something useful and hold the pads in place, however.)

Covered pads therefore need some form of support to anchor it in the proper location. Loose pads will tend to drift slowly downwards during performances. To retain the proper shape of the character, it is necessary to rig some support for the various pads or attach them to the inside of the fur body.

If you're planning a suit which requires more complex padding or support strategies, it might be worth considering a complete padded bodysuit. This entails adding a separate undersuit to which all of the padding will be anchored. Sewn suits tend to become cumbersome with more than a handful of inserts.

Closures

Since fur is not a very stretchy material, it is almost always necessary to construct the costume with a hidden opening so that it can be taken on and off. This is usually a long opening on the spine or stomach area. Some sort of closure will be necessary to hold the costume closed when it's worn. The key to realism is to conceal the costume's opening so that it does not attract attention.

Zippers – These are the best choices for suit closures. They have the advantage of being easy to install and use, and they fit readily into a sewn suit design without adding any additional pieces. However, zippers can be tricky to blend or camouflage.

The first thing to consider is the placement of the zipper. The ideal location is up the seam along the back. The zipper should close upwards from the waist to the neck. This is the best location for a zipper, since the spine has the least amount of movement and stretch. Zippers are slightly less flexible than fur, so this location can hide that stiffness.

The zipper can be somewhat hidden in the fur. Leave some extra fur on each side. These pieces will need to be shaved prior to sewing, as shown in the diagram, so that the inward-pointing fibers won't snag the zipper. When closed, the two rolls of fabric should abut, concealing the teeth.

Zipper selection is also important. Look for the largest teeth you can find. I like to use nylon zippers to avoid any possible rusting or metal discoloration, since costumes do get damp when they've been worn for a while. Avoid zippers that completely separate. These are meant for outer garments where the two pieces must completely detach. For costumes, we don't need the bottom of the opening to separate entirely. Getting the zipper back together again can be very difficult.

Velcro™ – Another option is Velcro, generically known as hook and loop fabric. A strip of Velcro two inches wide has sufficient staying power to keep a costume closed. This requires that a two-inch overlap be factored into the pattern where the closure is located. Design the opening so that the pieces overlap, and connect one underside to one outer face. Don't fold the outer surfaces inwards to meet, as you would with a zipper.

The big advantage of using Velcro is that it won't get snagged and snarled by stray fur fibers. Zippers require a bit of careful handling around the pile of the fur. Velcro isn't affected by fur, but it requires occasional cleaning.

The main disadvantage of Velcro is that it's not as strong as a zipper. The lateral stress in the fabric creates a peeling action that can undo Velcro. This is not a major problem unless too little Velcro is used in construction or the costume is put through unusual paces.

Snaps – Large sew-on snaps can be useful as a closure on smaller openings. Snaps are easy to attach and can be nestled in the pile of the fur so that they are disguised. I don't recommend using snaps for larger openings since the spaces between the snaps can buckle and reveal themselves. I tend to use snaps for smaller details such as cuff and collar closures.

Find the largest snaps you can when working with fur. Larger snaps are generally stronger, more tolerant to errant fur fibers, and (perhaps most importantly) are easier to open and close while wearing paws.

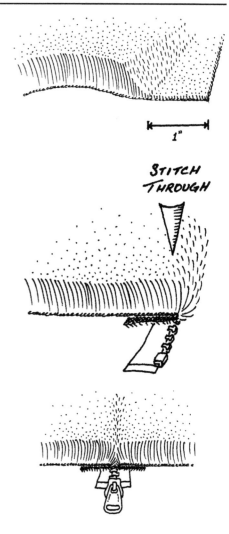

STITCH THROUGH

A simple zipper closure. A more complex version is shown on p. 136.

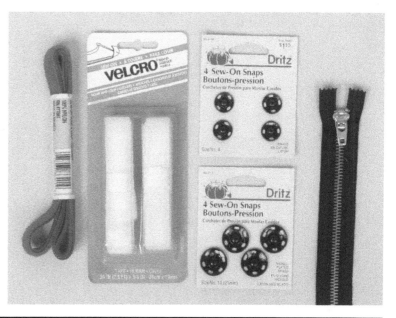

Lance Ikegawa

Lance Ikegawa creates original and commissioned costume characters. His work has appeared in television and video programs. Shown here is one of his characters, Reales.

How did you get started as a costumer?

At one point in the mid-Nineties, I needed a costume for a no-budget project and had no filthy lucre to hire a professional costumer, so I did it myself. I've always been good with 3-D stuff and I had a great time sculpting the foam for this endeavor. I owe a great deal of credit to Kathy Sanders (a master costumer) and Lynette Ecklund (a great special effects costumer) for their help.

I don't consider myself to be a professional costumer. While I do commissions, I still have a day job. I was approached to make costumes when I started entering costume masquerades. I worked out material costs, added any sub-contracting costs and gave myself a rate that worked out to just above minimum wage.

I have friends who work in the special effects business and a few who are professional costumers. I have done some corporate mascot costumes and television work but I don't generally forage for that kind of work. I learned a long time ago that doing costuming professionally takes a lot of the fun out of it.

What do you enjoy most about costuming?

It's "showbiz" without having to show one's face? Acting for shy people? Art that moves? I suppose I enjoy the creation of the character the most. While I enjoy masquerades as a place to share my work, going on stage and performing is a lot of stress.

I like taking a concept or drawing and bringing that creature to life. I am happy if I can create a suspension of belief in a creation. I pride myself on being able to take a two-dimensional character and translate that into a costume, while still retaining the look of the original character.

What factor is most important to the quality of a costume, however you might define "quality"?

I like to disguise the human form, to make the costumes I make look like a creature and not a man wearing a mask. Creating the illusion of life in a non-living covering. Expression is important: the actor can add the spark of life with good movement, but the personality of the character has its foundation in its expression.

For me quality is creating something that succeeds at doing what it was intended to do. If a costume needs to last five minutes on-camera and it lasts for six, that's a success. Generally most commissions should last several years with proper care; for those, I put extra work into the structure and assembly of the suit. I avoid mattress foam and shag fur and hot-glue "stitches." I utilize high-end foams, quality furs, and a combination of hand and machine sewing.

When creating a sculpted bodysuit for a new costume, what is your general design process?

Once I have preliminary design drawings, I grab my two workhorse reference books: "Anatomy for the Artist" (Jeno Barcsay) and "An Atlas of Animal Anatomy For Artists" (Ellenberger-Dittrich-Baum). I use these to understand how the bones and muscles of the animal correlate to those of the human body. Since my specialty is form-fitting costumes, the muscles and structure of the creature need to lay on their human anatomy counterparts so that they move smoothly and correctly.

Some creatures I can do by heart (canines) because I've done so many, but others need a lot more R&D. For new designs, I will use paper to start making patterns of muscles and pin them on the unitard which I've put on a mannequin. I use cheap sheet foam to rough out the muscles themselves. Then comes the final foam carving. The foam is pinned to the unitard and then covered with spandex, which is then sewn to the bodysuit. The muscle suit is then tested to see how well the muscles move. This is the big test… and the point at which I've had to start over on more than one occasion.

Another part of the design process involves trying to make the costume as comfortable as possible. Using reticulated foams and NFT (National

Fiber Technology) fur is my ideal solution since they both breathe exceptionally well. On a tighter budget, I will vent the unitard with an open nylon mesh every place that I can without losing too much stretch. I also cut vent holes or slits any place that they won't be seen and won't compromise the muscle movement.

You then need to cover this muscle suit with fur. This is basic draping to develop a pattern by laying cheap fabric on the costume. Be sure to note the direction the fur needs to lay on each pattern piece. Also be liberal with your labeling and registration marks so that you know how the pieces fit together.

Once the draping is complete, it's finally time to get down to cutting the fur and pinning it together. Lay it on the muscle suit to make sure it fits, make adjustments, then sew it all together. And then probably un-sew it, make adjustments, repeat until the fur "skin" fits snugly.

What advice would you give to a beginning costumer that is undertaking a challenging new project?

For what it's worth, on tricky costumes or new designs, I might end up building the costume three times. I end up with a pile of parts that you could literally use to build two other costumes. I have created foam muscles and sewn then onto the unitard only to not like the result, take out the seam ripper and start over, muscle by muscle. It's just a matter of not being satisfied until the final product is what you originally visualized.

Shenandoah, designed by Lance Ikegawa.

17 • Spandex Bodysuits

Fine-tuning the appearance of the costume is often achieved by sacrificing movement and flexibility. Stage productions, particularly those featuring dancing or gymnastics, require a different approach. In these cases, the goal is to create an animal appearance with minimal encumbrance. Spandex bodysuits are the solution.

The bodysuits required for costuming need to cover as much of the performer as possible. Ideally they will extend to the wrists and ankles and feature a high neckline. If the bodysuit is going to be used with a costume head or mask, the high neckline is particularly important to accomplish this transition.

The basic bodysuit can then be embellished with color effects or fur accents to create the desired animal character.

Purchasing or Building?

Unless you plan to produce a plethora of bodysuits, it's more convenient to purchase a unitard than to create one from scratch. Spandex unitards are available from dancewear and theatrical suppliers in a variety of colors and styles. Below you will find tips to use when shopping for a commercially produced bodysuit.

You may still choose to create your own unitards if you are creating a lot of costumes, have very specific material or patterning requirements, or if you just want the experience. Working with spandex is different from working with static fabrics. A standard sewing machine will sew spandex fabrics, but a serger will provide a professional look. Being able to sew a bodysuit correctly will require practice in order to avoid sags and pulls along the seams. One downside of fitted spandex is that any mistakes will be evident to the audience. Someone with sewing experience should be able to adapt to the challenges with just a bit of practice, though.

Shopping for Bodysuits

When shopping for a unitard, choose one with the highest collar possible. Many dancewear shops stock unitards with scoop necks and no zippers. This is not suited to costuming, since it leaves a large open area of human skin at the neck. Undersuits used as foundations for costumes will also require zippers, for it is impossible to don a spandex bodysuit through a collared neck.

Look for bodysuits made from a relatively heavy material. Fabrics that contain spandex come in many different weights and blends. Heavier materials with higher spandex content will be more durable and serve as a better base for paint coloration or fabric surface effects. Some companies will create made-to-order bodysuits based on the performer's measurements. This option offers the best fit possible and you can specify additional details such as cuff styles and zipper placement.

Spandex Bodysuits

Advantages
- Inexpensive
- Can be purchased off the shelf
- Does not hide performer's movements

Disadvantages
- Unrealistic human appearance

Durability
- Very good

Primary Materials
- Spandex

Special Tools
- Serger, if making the bodysuit

Chapter 17

Creating Custom Bodysuits

Creating your own bodysuits is always an option. This may be practical if you need to produce a large number of costumes or if you have unusual material or pattern requirements. As mentioned above, creating a bodysuit requires a serger. Stretch inherent in the material creates the snug fit of a spandex unitard. In order to maintain this, the seams must be able to stretch equally well. Only a serger can create a stretchable seam that won't cause the suit to bind.

The first step in creating a bodysuit will be developing a pattern. Many commercial pattern companies offer bodysuit patterns in their catalog. These make good starting points. Given the difficulty of patterning for high-stretch fabrics, I would caution against developing an original design unless you have pattern-making experience.

The orientation of the material is important when planning the pattern. Spandex fabrics usually have much more stretch along one axis. The stretch of the fabric should be oriented so that it wraps around the body, while the less stretchy grain of the fabric should flow up and down along the body's vertical axis. This alignment of the spandex's stretch affects the fit of the garment. The extra elasticity in the horizontal direction allows the suit to conform to the underlying body curves and stretch during movement.

Adjust the fit of the pattern so that the garment fits snugly on all parts of the body. It should conform to the wearer's skin without either sagging or constricting. Areas which are too loose can be fixed by serging the nearby seam farther in the fabric. Areas which are too tight cannot be so easily fixed and will necessitate creating a new suit. Better too loose than too tight on the first fitting!

Coloration and Markings

As mentioned in the previous chapter, coloration is the term I prefer to describe the broad color pattern of a costume. This is in contrast to markings, which are localized applications of color. The reason for the distinction is that they represent different costuming challenges which may require different techniques.

Coloration is best achieved by assembling the bodysuit from multiple colors of fabric. The process is the same as described for adapting bodysuit patterns in the previous chapter. The only additional complication is determining the curve and placement of the color boundaries on the pattern pieces for an elastic fabric.

Dyes

If you need a special color, dye. Dyes are the best route to coloration if fabric is not available in your color of choice or if you require transitional colors. Use a synthetic dye with good washfastness and you can make a costume that has both strong coloration and easy cleaning.

Most spandex materials are actually blends of spandex and other fibers. A blend with cotton improves the garment's absorbency and opacity. A common reactive dye will provide good color effects. This is an easy dye process and will produce reasonably pure colors. Reactive dye has little effect on the spandex fibers so you won't get absolutely intense color results.

Notice how this custom bodysuit was pieced to add a distinctive white chest patch.

More dramatic colorations are achieved by using disperse dyes. Although these are more complex to work with, the resultant colors can be brilliant and washfast without affecting the texture of the fabric.

Dyes are used to create colored material from which the costume is assembled. This will create composite pattern pieces with defined coloration boundaries. It's also possible to create transitional effects by controlling the dye immersion of the different pieces. This is more complex and will usually take a bit of experimentation to get good results.

The completed bodysuit can also be dyed to achieve other color effects. By deliberately dyeing unevenly, by bunching up the fabric, a mottled effect will be created. If the dye is a darker color being applied on top of the base fabric color, this could create interesting chromatic texture.

Painting Effects

Markings can be added to a bodysuit by painting directly on it. If the actor is wearing it at the time, be sure to use only nontoxic materials. Otherwise a fitted tailor's dummy is required.

A variety of colorants can be used. Low temperature dyes can be thickened and brushed onto the fabric. Once the dye has had time to affix to the fibers, briskly rinse away the excess.

Art and craft stores sell a variety of fabric paints. These are easy to use and unlikely to run or migrate within the material. The disadvantage is that they can change the texture of the fabric. If applied too thickly, they can also inhibit the stretch of the spandex. Results obviously vary by brand.

Acrylic inks can also be brushed onto suits. These will have much the same effect as fabric paints. They will preserve the original texture of the fabric better but will probably not wear quite as well as fabric paints. Neither inks nor paints will stand up to heavy washing.

Do not usepermanent markers on bodysuits. Spandex is very resistant to ink and it will rub off over time. Since the bodysuit is in direct contact with the performer's skin, this usually means the ink will stain the skin and possibly rub onto different areas of the bodysuit.

Airbrushing

Airbrushing works very well as a technique for applying markings to bodysuits. It can be used to create blended edges and color transitions not otherwise possible.

Airbrushing is probably the best way to apply fabric paints to a bodysuit. The thin even spray helps the paint cover the spandex with minimal interference with the material's hand.

Airbrushes can also be used to apply dyes to the fabric. This is not necessarily a good way to do it, though. The diffuse application of the dye makes it difficult to predict exactly how much is being absorbed by the fabric. The final coloration of the piece may not match your expectations!

Alternative Materials

Despite the chapter title, it's possible to use materials other than spandex for costume bodysuits. Spandex is simply the most common and easily available choice.

Any fabric with a large amount of stretch can be used. One interesting alternative is stretch velvet. It has almost as much stretch as spandex but it features a wonderful surface texture. The texture is similar to its namesake except that this material features a flexible construction.

Airbrush detail work. Costume by Lance Ikegawa.

Fur Accents

When combined with paint effects, fur accents on a bodysuit will complete the appropriate animalistic appearance.

During the design process, select several locations on the suit for fur accents. Consider locations that might help create the impression of a fully furred creature. Examine your reference materials for pictures. Take note of places in the coat where fur is especially prominent, differently colored, or unusually long.

A chest ruff is a diamond-shaped piece of fur starting at the neck, partway spanning the breast, and descending to mid-chest. This is effective for canines and large cats, which have a prominent line to the chest.

Wrists and ankles are excellent locations for fur accents. Fur will enhance the costume's appearance and hide the transition to the paws. Ankle fur accents are particularly effective on equines, where they create the impression of shaggy fetloch hair, as on draft horses.

Attach fur accents to a spandex bodysuit using sparse tacks rather than with a continous seam, as doing so will reduce tho stretch around the area. While this won't make the suit unwearable or cause binding, it may cause the spandex to stretch and pull unevenly around the seam.

Use localized tack-stitching to anchor the fur at key points. Start by attaching the outer corners of whatever fur shape has been chosen. Then add more anchor points as necessary to prevent the edges of the fur from rolling or folding. Anchor the fur every two inches along the edges for best results. More complex curves will require more tightly-spaced tacks.

Position the fur accent on the bodysuit when the suit is on the body and fully stretched. This ensures that the fur accent won't restrict the motion of the performer. When that portion of the spandex is under less tension, the fur will naturally relax but not sag.

Closures

Zippers are the best option for bodysuits. They can handle the stresses in the stretchy material without opening. Zippers are also compact, occupying only a narrow line up the back. They do make "invisible" zippers which are subtle when closed and will suffice for most projects.

Given the thin nature of the material, it's not really possible to hide the closure in the way that we would with heavier fur costumes. Fur accents can be applied around the zipper, but if you end up using fur to cover the full length of the closure, you're getting dangerously close to building a sewn suit.

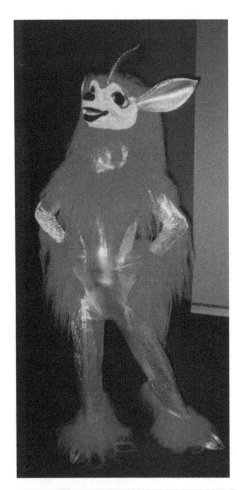

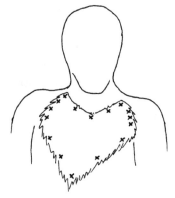

Sewn anchor points on a sample chest ruff.

18 • Sculpted Bodysuits

A sculpted bodysuit is a more sophisticated costuming technique that incorporates sculpted or tailored foam padding into the bodysuit. This is a good technique for designers who want to create a more realistic character than can be achieved through a traditional jumpsuit-style costume. Extensive padding and sculpting will create a more "animal" appearance. Perhaps you want the fur to move and fold more realistically. In such cases, constructing a costume around what I refer to as a sculpted bodysuit is the way to go.

The sculpted suit is much more complex than the simple mascot-styled jumpsuit. It is comprised of three layers. The foundation layer is made from a spandex base with an applied foam body sculpture. An intermediate padding or structural layer adds bulk and form to the costume. Lastly, the surface layer of fur or other skinning material covers the substructures. The beauty of this multi-part structure is its washability and multiple uses.

Creating a Foundation

The foundation layer creates the semblance of musculature. The inner suit has two requirements: it must fit the actor comfortably and serve as a firm base for the application of foam padding. This layer is the foundation for the rest of the costume. A spandex unitard is the best and most versatile choice for the undersuit.

Select a heavier fabric, one with a higher spandex content. The suit will distribute the weight of the padding or other costume elements over greater surface area. Lightweight spandex is more likely to sag or distort if heavy padding is attached to it. However, a spandex bodysuit or unitard of any spandex percentage can be adapted to the purpose.

Spandex unitards fit like a second skin, fitting and moving in coordination with the actor's body. This can be a key element in costume design since we now can associate points on the unitard fabric with fixed points on the performer's body, something which would not be possible with a conventional jumpsuit. Anchoring sculpted foam pieces to different parts of the spandex undersuit creates shaping that moves with the actor's body.

Padding and Structure Options

Depending on the size and shape of the overall costume, different structural options can be employed. For creatures that roughly correspond to human stature, it's easiest to attach the foam padding directly to the undersuit. The placement and shaping of the padding can build out the body to create the desired proportions.

Larger creatures may require more sophisticated structural designs. Semi-rigid foams can be used to extend cantilevered components from the body. This can work well to create relatively lightweight shapes as long as it is sufficiently anchored to the bodysuit in order to prevent swaying or drooping.

Sculpted Bodysuit

Advantages

- Realistic appearance is possible
- Shows movements well
- Extensize reshaping of the body is possible

Disadvantages

- More expensive
- Takes longer to build
- Fits only one person (or people of similar build)
- Slower to put on and take off

Durability

- Good, but must be stored carefully

Primary Materials

- Spandex
- Foam
- Fur fabric

Special Tools

- Serger, if making the bodysuit
- Sized mannequin, if actor isn't present during construction

Even larger designs can be realized by building a rigid framework into the costume. I recommend PVC pipes for structural elements. They are relatively strong for their weight, easy to cut and assemble, and they come with pre-made joints. While a single pipe length may flex significantly, attaching pipes to create cages (ala trusses) will allow for mutual reinforcement and create a relatively rigid structure.

Any rigid structure must be attached to the actor in such a way that the weight of the structure is distributed in a manageable fashion. The structure must also connect over a large enough area to prevent it from swaying or wobbling. Keep in mind that the farther a structure extends away from the actor's body, the more its weight acts as a lever against the mounting. Always mount extensions as firmly as possible and over as large an area as possible.

Internal structures are usually not necessary; they invariably limit the performance capabilities of a costume. Foam buildup is much more versatile and will suffice for most creature costumes. The following sections offer different techniques for creating foam padding for a bodysuit.

Sculpted and Patterning Pieces

The padding for a bodysuit is composed of a large number of individual foam pieces. These are applied to create the final composite shape. You can think of each foam pad as a particular muscle or anatomical structure. When put together, they create the full body shape.

Carved Foam – Carving is the most straightforward technique for creating these foam shapes. They can be carved with an electric knife, similar to the carved foam head in Chapter 11. Smaller pieces can easily be created with a pair of scissors.

Don't worry too much about the surface detail of the pieces if they are going to be covered by fur. Small scissors marks and surface ridges will be hidden by the pile. If you are planning on using something other than fur as the outer surface of the costume (e.g., spandex or rubber), then you may choose to enclose the foam padding in spandex to create a smooth appearance.

Sheet Foam – An alternative to carving solid blocks is to assemble pads of sheet foam. Cutting the foam and assembling it with a few darts can quickly create a shaped foam piece. These pads are hollow, and won't translate all of the details of movement as well as solid foam.

Patterned foam pieces have the advantage of making the suit lighter and cooler. The cooling comes from the air pockets introduced under the foam pads. As the costume moves, they have a slight bellow effect, moving air into and out of the suit. Although minute, anything that improves cooling in heavy costumes is welcome.

It's best to create the foam pieces while the undersuit is worn by the performer. This is a time-consuming process and will likely require several fitting and placement sessions. If this isn't practical, find a full-body dummy of the same proportions as the performer.

Fitting directly onto the body is a requirement because the foam padding builds upon the person's body shape to create the final costume shape. If the suit is worn by someone with different proportions, it will distort the proportions of the costume character. If the body shapes of the people are similar enough, the changes may not be noticeable in the final costume.

Undersuit with foam muscle shaping.

Selecting Appropriate Foam

Most padding is constructed from versatile and inexpensive open-cell poly-urethane foam. This foam is easy to work with and well suited to complex layered structures because it is readily available in different densities. Suits constructed with polyurethane foam can only be surface cleaned and are prone to waterlogging and mildewing.

Layering and abutting foam pads of different densities allows you to control the way the suit flexes. Heavier foams are resistant to movement; nearby pieces of soft foam will compress instead. By using softer foam around joints, you can concentrate the compression in that area of padding while leaving nearby stiffer structures undistorted by the movement.

Reticulated foam is also well-suited for use in sculpted bodysuits. It improves cooling because air can circulate through the foam. It is waterproof and easy to clean.

Reticulated foam is generally stiffer than open-cell foam and the structure and arrangement of the padding should take this into account. It is possible to find different densities of reticulated foam, though it can be difficult.

Building for Movement

Ensure that some foam is placed around all of the major joints of the body. This is especially important for suits that will be covered in fur or other low-stretch material. If fur were attached over the surface of the bodysuit directly, the resultant costume would bind at the joints as they tried to flex. As the joints of the body move, the skin surfaces near the joint stretch and fold. We can accommodate this movement with foam padding.

Consider the knee joint as an example. It improves the movement of the suit to add at least a thin foam pad over the kneecap area. When the leg is straight, the fur lies smoothly over the foam, preventing visible wrinkles from appearing in the fabric around the joint. As the knee flexes, the foam padding compresses as the fur fabric gets taut; the "extra" length which has appeared over the top of the knee is created by flattening the foam against the knee. Soft foam is best, since it will offer the least resistance to compression and, thus, the least resistance to joint movement.

Put at least minimal (½") padding around the outside of all of the major joints to ensure sufficient mobility in the finished suit. The shoulder area is particularly important. From standing with your arms and shoulders back to reaching directly forward with both hands, the length between the shoulders around the back almost doubles! Foam padding in the area of the shoulder blades is a good way to provide the extra material to allow for this flexing. Since many animal have more pronounced scapula than humans, this often works well with the design of anthropomorphic characters.

Attaching Foam Padding

The foam pads can be attached directly to the undersuit using an appropriate surface glue. Super 74™ works well in this application since it's thick enough to prevent it from immediately soaking into the spandex. It bonds reasonably well between the foam and the spandex. What holds the padding securely in place is the addition of another layer, either the surface material or an intermediate spandex layer.

Gluing will be less successful with patterned foam pieces, because they present less surface area for the glue. Carved pieces can be shaped so that their underside matches the contours of the spandex suit. Apply glue to both the spandex and the foam piece and then press them together to attach the padding to the body. I recommend using a few straight pins to tack the edges of the foam in place while the glue sets in order to prevent accidental shifting.

An alternative to gluing is to sew the pads to the bodysuit. It's impossible to sew foam directly since it will tear. Instead, make spandex pouches that enclose the foam pads and prevent them from shifting. These pouches are easily created by draping a cut piece of spandex across the foam pad. Trim it close to the edge of the foam piece. Use several pins, pushed straight into the foam, to anchor the center of the spandex. Hand-stitch around the perimeter of the foam piece, tucking the cut edge of the spandex under as you do so. This is an excellent way to use up spandex fabric scraps.

As you work, stretch the spandex cover piece so that it is under gentle tension. This creates some pressure against the foam and will discourage it from moving. It is important that the tension in the covering spandex be less than the tension in that part of the spandex unitard. If the outer piece of spandex is under greater tension than the inner (bodysuit) piece, then the elastic pieces will try to reach equilibrium and the foam will warp away from the body surface.

A simple hand stitch tacking around the edge of each foam pocket should be sufficient for the undersuit. What is important is that the sewing be done while the spandex is under tension. Pinning and removing the spandex makes it difficult to sew a seam that will lie flat when the suit is worn. Small changes in the tension of both pieces can lead to buckling and gathers.

Attaching Fur to Spandex Fabrics

Once the padding on the undersuit is complete, apply the final surface of the costume. For this discussion, I'm going to focus on fur since it is the most popular choice for animal costumes. Any number of surfaces could be created, from rubberized skins to feathers. Some designers use the spandex as a surface and airbrush it with animal patterns.

The fastest way to attach fur to the suit is to use a surface glue. Fur will adhere well to both spandex and foam with Super 74™. However it will not stick firmly enough to resist wear and tear; it will be necessary to sew all of the edges together in order to make the fur layer properly secure.

Gluing Fur

During this process, the undersuit needs to be on the body of the performer. Begin by marking all color changes and animal pattern boundaries. Use chalk or soap to mark all of these lines directly on the suit. Placing these lines ahead of time will help to maintain symmetry through the furring process.

Start attaching fur to the bodysuit. I like to start with the largest, flattest areas first, such as the stomach, legs, and lower back. Begin by cutting a piece of fur to a workable size that roughly matches the area you'll try to cover. Always cover as much as possible with one piece, since it means fewer edges to sew later.

Spray a palm-sized area of the fur fabric and undersuit with glue. Press them together, being careful to align the direction of the nap correctly. Hold it

---

Duct Tape Dummy

Making costumes is easiest when you have a life-size dressform to tailor the fabric and/or fur on. But dressforms are expensive. An easy, inexpensive dressform that fits your body perfectly can be made from duct tape. There are many websites on the Internet with directions. See www.crittercostuming.com for links.

for about thirty seconds so that the glue forms a good bond. Put a few pins around the edge of this area to hold it while it cures.

This area anchors the fur piece you're working on. Spread the fur outwards from that point, pinning it occasionally. You may need several pins at a time, as the weight of the fur can pull heavily on the spandex undersuit. As the flat fabric spreads over the curved body shape, it will reach places where it naturally wrinkles (crossing convex areas) or doesn't cover (crossing concave areas). If the fur doesn't have enough area to cover inside all of the concavities of the sculpted suit, then you'll need to end this piece of fur and create a seam in that area.

Where there is excess fur over convex curves, dart the fabric to eliminate wrinkles. Spread the fur as flat as possible, gathering the excess material into a single fold. Make a cut along one side of the fold, from the edge of the fabric up to the place where it flattens. This side should now lie flat. The other edge creates a flap of overlapping fabric. Carefully trim this piece of fur so that its edge conforms to the first cut you made. Now the cut edges should lie together and also follow the shape of the padding underneath.

Fur pieces should end at the color boundaries you've marked on the suit. Keep an eye on the nap of the fur. As you make darts and wrap the fur around the body surface, the alignment of the nap can shift. Once it drifts too far from the direction you want, you should end that piece of fur there.

When you place a new piece of fur, don't start at the edge of the previous piece. Rather, anchor the new piece to a salient convex surface near the previous piece. Starting pieces at the prominent curve of a surface makes it more likely you'll be able to dart the fabric and successfully contour it to the undersuit.

Continue placing fur and gluing until the entire surface of the bodysuit has been covered. It's useful to leave extra fur around the neck, arm, and leg openings to create finished cuffs. Don't make the cuffs on the arms and legs too tight. The hands and feet have to squeeze through these openings, and fur won't stretch. The use of some extra foam padding for compression can help.

Sewing After Gluing

The edges of the fur pieces should be stitched down after gluing. Glue will not hold or stick to the spandex for long periods of time, and adding a perimeter of stitching will make the costume more durable and prevent the pieces from moving or sliding.

Sew all of the edges of the fur pieces together using hand-stitching. A blanket stitch is effective with long fur, which will hide exposed stitching. Shorter pile furs will require a hidden stitch such as a ladder stitch. This stitch pulls the edges of the fur pieces together and finishes the suit.

Use the strongest possible thread for this sewing. As the suit flexes, these seams take a lot of force. The stitch holding the fur together limits the motion of the pieces and transfers stresses between them. It's not unusual to have to repair these seams regularly. Without the sewing step, the fur pieces would have visible gaps, showing the undersuit.

If the fur edges are in a concave area of the padding, it's a good idea to sew the edges down to the bodysuit. Otherwise the seam might rise up out of the fold, creating a loose pouch of fur and obscuring the sculpted shape of the suit.

Movement of the suit will put stress on the fur. Make sure it is firmly attached.

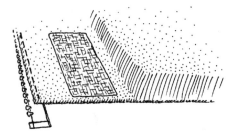

Whether the seam includes the undersuit or just passes between the fur pieces is a matter of preference. Including the spandex in the seam anchors the boundary to a specific line on the performer's body. Seaming only fur to fur creates an outer skin with a little latitude in its movement. Select the technique that suits your preference.

Sewn Outer Suits

Instead of gluing the fur directly to the foam padding, many costumers elect to create a top or outer layer to wear over the sculpted undersuit. This process is similar to the way in which a regular sewn suit is created except that it's tailored to fit the sculpted body shape.

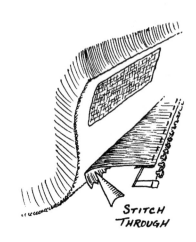

STITCH THROUGH

A free-floating outer suit allows greater movement of the fur over the undersuit's padding, especially if the padding is covered in spandex. This results in a more natural skin movement, although you may lose muscle definition. One of the down-sides is that you now have to create separate outer and inner suits, lining up not one, but two closures.

A separate outer suit simplifies washing by allowing all the pieces to be washed separately. Since excessive washing can degrade the texture and markings on fur, it can be beneficial to wash only the inner suit. Be sure to use waterproof reticulated foam for the padding.

Closures

Since the undersuit has a zipper, a closure is already present. If you have glued the fur, you can leave loose edges of fur overlapping the zipper. If the fur has a reasonable pile, the zipper will be sufficiently obscured. The fur will have a tendency to snag in the zipper, so operate it carefully.

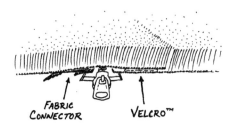

FABRIC CONNECTOR   VELCRO™

One of the strongest yet invisible closures is a combination of zipper and Velcro.

Top – Design your suit to have a 2" overlap at the closure. Shave a valley in the fur the length of the closure. Install the hook-and-loop side against the body and follow up with one side of the zipper.

Middle– Stitch the other half of the zipper 2" in from the edge. Apple the Velcro between the zipper and edge as illustrated.

Bottom – When closed, the zipper will hold tight and the Velcro will line up, holding the flap that conceals the zipper closed.

A better way to hide the zipper on the undersuit involves creating a second closure in the outer fur layer. The zippered closure is secure and serves as the primary force keeping the costume closed; the outer closure is more cosmetic.

One way to create such an arrangement is to have an outer flap of fur that covers the zipper. The edge of this piece of fur seals with Velcro to the opposite edge of the outer suit. The advantage in using a flap that covers the zipper is that there is now no fur near the zipper to snag in it.

If your design allows for it, the Velcro closure can be hidden at a color boundary. The change in fur color already requires that the fur pieces have edges there.

19 • Clothes & Partial Suits

Some characters are always featured wearing certain distinctive clothes that help define who the character is. In critter costuming we can follow this model literally by designing costumes that are composed of modified clothing.

In the case of a clothed character, we only need to construct the "exposed" portions of the character's features. The rest of the costume is simply clothes worn by the character. This can save construction time while simultaneously developing the character's personality.

The concept is simple: a character is built from only a head and paws. The rest of the costume are "clothes" the character appears to be wearing. This sort of costume is popular at Halloween, where purchased masks and gloves are combined with themed clothing.

More sophisticated costumes combine clothes with other constructed components. For example, most people have come to expect animal characters to wear gloves. Taking the extra step of incorporating furred sleeves poking out of a character's shirt greatly enhances the costume.

Using Clothes in a Character Body

Certain characters seem to work better with clothes. Clothing as costume presents the designer with a myriad of clothing options that can reflect the character's status or occupation, or a special event, holiday or occasion. A professional outfit, a combat uniform or tattered clothes all convey specific messages about the nature of the character wearing them. Your budget will determine the quality and variety of clothing options available.

The clothes become the body of the costume. Only portions of the creature not hidden by the outfit need to be built, which can translate into a great savings of time and money. This technique also makes the costume lighter and cooler than a full fursuit. Unless the clothes are particularly heavy, they will probably be much more comfortable and less restrictive for the performer.

Using clothing sidesteps the issue of building costume closures. Clothing already requires obvious closures. By using clothing, you completely sidestep the issue of installing and hiding an unsightly zipper or Velcro™ closure. If you plan on adapting clothing for wear over a full fursuit, you can find garments that disguise or cover any unsightly openings.

Integrating Clothes and Costume

The effect of the costume can usually be improved by planning "exposed" areas of fur around the clothing. For example, a button-front shirt worn open will expose the furry chest underneath, which creates a much more convincing animal effect for a small investment in materials and time.

The key to maintaining the illusion of a furry body is to keep the fur elements taut against the skin. Fur body elements can be mounted onto tightly fitted

Clothes and Partial Suits

Advantages
- Materials less expensive
- Cooler to wear
- No need to hide closures
- Excellent movement and flexibility

Disadvantages
- If attached, clothes cannot be changed for different performance situations

garments so they don't add bulk to lightweight or draping clothes. For instance, a tightly fitted shirt makes an excellent base for upper body fur details. Chest panels can be tacked onto the front of the shirt and allowed to spill out of shirts. Sleeves of fur mounted onto the base undergarment will prevent the outer garment from pulling or sagging under the weight.

If you absolutely must add fur body details to existing clothes, be sure to install them so the weight is either evenly distributed throughout the garment or is transferred to sturdy seams that can handle the weight. For instance, a sleeve of fur mounted onto a short-sleeved garment will cause an awkward pulling of the fabric. Rather, extend the furry sleeve all the way up to the top and attach at the strong shoulder seam. Test your costumes by putting them on a body and looking at them from all angles. If you see the clothing pulling or buckling around the fur, you may want to rework how the fur is attached.

Sewing all of your clothing components together will shorten your dressing time and shorten your list of items to carry with you to events. One example is the executive furry. If your character wears a shirt, vest, jacket and tie as part of his costume, sew some of these pieces together. Stitch the shirt and vest together along the shoulder seam to keep them firmly attached. Even though you have constructed one garment, the modification doesn't interfere with the button front closures.

Finding and Creating Clothes

This is not a good method for costumes with large changes in body shape. In these cases, you will need to heavily modify clothes or create them from scratch.

Experienced sewers shouldn't have trouble modifying clothes to fit. Commercial patterns are readily available for almost every type of clothing you could want. Select a pattern several sizes larger than the performer and adjust the seams and darts to accommodate unusual body shaping.

Many costumers buy large, oversized clothes at thrift stores and size them down, tailoring them to fit over the unique contours of a padded furry understructure. Poke around in thrift stores to see what's available. If you have a bigger budget, check out department stores and specialty big/tall stores in your area for clearance deals.

Once you have your base layer of foam and fur finished, put it on the performer and then put on the oversized clothing inside out. Carefully pinch out excess cloth and place a row of pins where you new stitching line will be. Since most bodies are symmetrical, work both sides evenly, making the same changes to both the left and right sides.

When the costume fits, carefully remove the pinned garment and proceed to sew where you have marked. Stop periodically to test the fit on the understructure until you achieve your desired results. When you are finished, you will have custom tailored clothing for your critter costume.

Understructures

A potential barrier to using clothing as part of the costume is that it does not hide the shape of the human body. For small alterations or suggestions of a different shape, consider individual foam pads as described in Chapter 16, "Sewn Suits." More complex musculature can be suggested by creating a sculpted bodysuit, as described in Chapter 18.

Transitions and Sagging

Something to be mindful of when attaching fur to clothes is how the weight of the fur will affect the fit of the clothes. Fur is much heavier than clothing fabrics. When fur pieces are connected to regular clothes, the weight of the fur can pull the clothes, causing unsightly sagging. To prevent this, it's necessary to anchor the fur to portions of the clothing which can support the added weight.

For example, consider a furry sleeve being attached to a short-sleeved shirt. If we attach the fur to the hem of the shirt sleeve, the weight of the fur will pull down and make the shirt sleeve obviously taut. This looks unnatural, since shirt material is normally lightweight and would not hang this way; it draws the viewer's attention to our trickery!

Instead, anchor the fur to a major seam in the garment which can better support the additional weight. In this case, we should use a longer fur sleeve and connect it to the shoulder seam on the shirt. The fur sleeve goes inside the shirt sleeve and is sewn into the underside of the original shirt seam. If the fur connects at the shoulder, the weight of the fur is more easily borne by the performer's body.

Additionally, the shirt sleeve now hangs as it should… almost. The bulk of the fur near the seam may cause the sleeve to have a puffed effect. This is because the pile of the fur, beginning at the shoulder seam, is pressed against the shirt fabric. We can easily eliminate this by shaving away the top two inches of the fur pile near the seam; over these two inches, gradually increase the pile to its normal height. This will let the shirt sleeve hang and move naturally over the fur.

Gary Allen

Gary Allen is a Halloween enthusiast and costumer. He often goes by the moniker Marrok, the name of his werewolf character. He has built a number of werewolf costumes for his seasonal performances.

How did you first get involved in costuming?

I got involved through my interests in wolves, werewolf legends, and Halloween. I always wanted to have a really kickin' Halloween costume yet I could never bring myself to get a store-bought one. I thought most of them were pretty generic and cheap. I considered professional costume companies but I couldn't justify paying what they would charge. So, I got the materials and tried to do it myself.

Did you face any unusual challenges when you began making costumes?

Definitely. When I started, I couldn't sew two pieces of material together to save my life! But I've always been a pretty crafty person. I enjoy home improvement projects, working with wood, tile, drywall, and such. But I had never done any sewing before I started making costumes.

I learned through trial and error. Through my mistakes I learned what techniques produced the effects I wanted in the fabric. I kept at it through four revisions of my costume. I wasn't quite happy with it each time, but I was also learning.

Have you used any unexpected materials in your costumes?

Most of what I used, except the fur, can be found at home and craft cen-

ters. Probably the most unique item is GE's Silicone II, a rubber silicone compound. I find it very useful in making paws and paw pads. It's resilient, tractable, and comes in a variety of colors in large caulking tube sizes for relatively cheap.

What factor most defines the "quality" of a costume?

Personally, I prefer realistic style costumes, since I enjoy the fright aspect of Halloween events. Quality comes if the creator pays attention to the details. Take all the little things that really complete the look and focus on each as if it is it's own project. Integrating all of these elements seamlessly to produce the illusion that the creation really is alive is what makes it for me.

But I wouldn't overlook the toony or mascot style costumes either. Again, focusing on little things is a mark of quality. The overall look must be consistent and well executed. Every costume has a theme and the creator must carry out the theme in all aspects of the work.

What is the most important piece of performance advice you can give?

Know your limits. It's easy for someone who's never been out in their costume to overdo it. Heat exhaustion is a killer. Likewise, know the limita-

tions of the costume. I designed my suit for active wear in mind, allowing for full range of motions. This allows me to be fairly active without harming myself or the costume.

As a realistic wolf, your character might intimidate children. Is this something you deal with a lot?

Yes, very much so. During parade outings, for example, it's expected to see strange characters. That's the nature of parades. But I always find a good number of the kids shy away from me.

I approach children like this much in the same manner you would try to win the friendship of a nervous dog. I crouch down, so that I'm not taller than the kid, and extend a paw. I keep the palm/pad side up as a non-threatening gesture.

Since I'm a canine, I find it works better to tilt my head. Then I look like I'm confused and wonder why they are afraid of me. Some of the time they'd warm up to me, other times, they wouldn't.

Where do you like to perform? What makes for a good venue?

I enjoy performing just about in any venue where characters are expected. I've participated in parades, out at a Mardi Gras celebration, and at conventions. I'm also out and about during Halloween, of course!

20 • Paws: Hands & Feet

Five-fingered paws.

Unless your character is going to wear gloves and boots, you will need to construct suitable paws.

Do not underestimate the power of paws to define a character's attitude. Claws can represent a dangerous creature or, with exaggeration, a true monster. On the other hand (so to speak), large rounded, clawless paws can be used to indicate youthful characters and playfulness. During the design process, consider the impression you want your character to project when he or she waves to people.

Paws are also very useful from the standpoint of costume practicality. It is easier to get into, remove, and clean a costume that has removable paws. It is also very convenient to be able to remove paws at key moments – such as trying to find your key to get into a changing room.

Four-fingered paw.

Four or Five Fingers?

Many fur costumes feature stylized four-fingered hands. This is partly a reflection of a long animation tradition that simplified the drawing of hands. But it also stems from the practical costuming consideration that fur is a very bulky material. A thick pile fur takes up a lot of room between your fingers. Joining two fingers can eliminate some of this bulk and keep the paws smaller. Ultimately, the decision is one of personal preference. Five fingers is certainly more realistic, while four fingers is often more practical.

The two middle fingers are usually grouped together. This makes the center finger on a four-fingered paw the largest. This can be somewhat hidden by adding a little padding to the outside edges of the other three fingers if it is a concern.

Simple Paws

The easiest way to create a set of paws is to use a single-piece pattern. This involves cutting two pieces of fur (a forwards and reversed copy of the pattern piece) and sewing them together. The result is a simple fabric sandwich. This is a quick, easy, and surprisingly effective way to create basic gloves.

Creating the pattern is very easy. Lay your hand flat on a piece of cardboard. Spread your fingers as far apart as possible. If you're planning a four-fingered paw, keep your middle two fingers tightly together. Trace the contour of your hand. I suggest that you make the pattern based on your subordinate hand so that you can trace with your dominant hand. Keep the line directly below your hand as if it were casting a shadow onto the cardboard. This will be the shape of the glove.

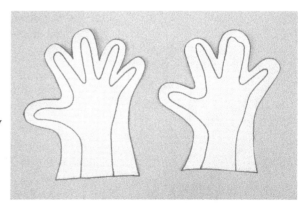

Simple five- and four-finger patterns.

Finish the pattern by adding seam allowances. Draw a line around your hand contour that adds a half-inch or so. This can be tricky in the troughs between the fingers; just do the best you can.

Cut the pattern along this outer line. You can now assemble a glove by cutting a forward and reverse copy of this pattern out of fur. Sew the fur pieces together along their matching edges except at the wrist.

Glove Pattern

Understructure of a lion's paw, ready for fur.

True glove patterns are much more complex than the simple two-faced paw we created above. The problem with the simple paw is that the human hand is not symmetrical front to back. You can see this by relaxing the muscles in your hand for a moment. Notice the position of your thumb: it projects forwards, almost perpendicular to the palm. The simple paw doesn't address this anatomical detail and therefore doesn't conform to the human hand very accurately.

Glove patterns were developed long ago that can fit the hand accurately… they fit like a glove. But these patterns involve many more pieces than our simple paw. If you want a really comfortable fit or if you're using a material without a pile then this might be the way to go.

Paws with Shaping

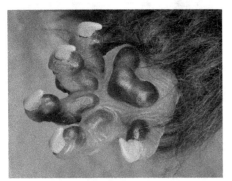

Forepaw with pads for added realism.

You might also want to create paws that have a distinctive shape or structural element. This technique allows the designer to create paws with an exotic, inhuman look. Such paws require building out from the foundation of a glove to create the correct structure for the character's paws. Shaping elements are added to create new paw proportions. As you design, consider how these paws will translate the actor's hand movements.

Build a foam structure on top of a set of well-fitted gloves. I have had very good results with fleece mountain climbing gloves. Other designers recommend thin leather gloves.

Glue foam pieces directly to the gloves. The foam can easily be carved with scissors to get the correct shapes. Fur is applied on top of the foam and glove combination. Depending on the structure of the gloves, you can leave portions on the underside exposed to create the effect of paw pads.

Should your critter require claws, incorporate them into the paw construction. Sew claws down to the fingertips of fur paws. This isn't the best solution, though, since the fur gloves may be loose enough that the claws will wobble. If you've constructed paws on top of fitted gloves, the claws can be glued or sewn to the gloves for a firmer mount.

Claws on the toes are easier since feet usually have internal structure. They can be mounted to the structure of the foot. Be sure to mount them high enough that they won't scrape the ground or be dislodged by walking.

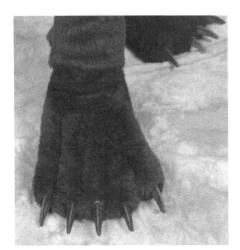

Exaggerated foot with claws.

The line of the claw should extend from the axial line of the finger or toe. Test your new clawed paw before furring to get a feel for the claws. Make sure that you can curl your hand and manipulate any required objects for your character. Also make sure that your claws are not too sharp when interacting with other people.

Designing Feet

Most characters have feet. Even if they aren't immediately visible, the performer needs some place to put his feet. These are not the most important part of the character, in terms of appearance. Yet they are essential to the performer because they can determine the mobility and comfort of the costume!

Feet need to be the most rugged part of the costume. They support the weight of the costume and performer over a variety of abrasive and dirty surfaces. The easiest solution is to rely on the work of footwear professionals and build your costume feet around existing shoes. Since constructing feet from scratch is a rather advanced topic, I've chosen to focus on recycling existing shoes. You can use any footwear you like as long as it meets the following criteria:

Comfortable – The shoes should be comfortable to wear when walking for long periods. They need to fit well and not slide around. If the costume is going to be worn by multiple people, you will need to find something that fits everyone. I think that one of the best things for this scenario is to use inexpensiv bedroom slippers that are not quilted or padded. They usually have a little stretch to accommodate different feet comfortably.

Durable Soles – The soles should be able to handle exposure to asphalt, gravel, and other outdoor conditions unless this costume is exclusively for indoor or stage use. Don't use shoes on which the soles have been worn dangerously thin or are peeling around the edges.

Easy to Put On – Make sure that it's easy to get in and out of the shoes. If you're planning on adding shaping and structure on top of the feet, laces might be hard to reach in the finished paws. Slip-on shoes, sandals with a single securing strap, and slippers work well.

Making Paws from Shoes

Once you have a pair of shoes selected, construct the paw around them. Most animal costumes tend to have fairly large feet so it is not a problem to scale up the paw design to fully enclose the shoes. It is important not to make the feet too long, front to back, or it can become very easy to trip over your own toes.

Carve foam pieces to create the proportions and shape of the paws. I usually create solid foam pieces as the structural elements of the feet. This can be done by stacking layers of sheet foam or carving shapes from a foam block. Fur is then glued on top of the foam. Be aware that any foam shaping added above the ankle level can impede movement.

If you are more inclined towards sewing and patterning, you can also create the shape of the foot in fabric. Use cotton cloth internally to divide the shape and create pockets. Pack these with fiberfill so that the paw holds its correct shape. Then glue or sew the completed fabric shape around the shoe.

One consideration is how low the shaping hangs. To properly hide the shape of the shoe, it seems natural that the padding should be flush with the sole of the shoe. But once the fur is attached, this adds the length of the nap. You can compensate for this by shaving the fur on the underside of the foot or raising the padding above the ground by just less than the height of the nap.

Soles

By using existing shoes we have circumvented the need to attach soles to our feet. But it is sometimes still desirable to attach new soles in order to further disguise the original shoe. When the character lifts its feet or, even worse, sits with its feet up, the outline of the original shoe soles are clearly visible on the bottom of the feet. They can be hidden by attaching new soles, cut to the out-

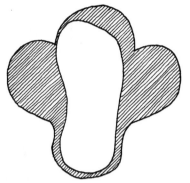

Pattern to add padding to a foot to create a paw shape.

A slip-on shoe forms the base for a lion's rear paw.

Glue foam padding onto the shoe to create the sculpted form of the foot.

Glue fur onto the foam understructure. Add claws for a realistic effect.

Chapter 20

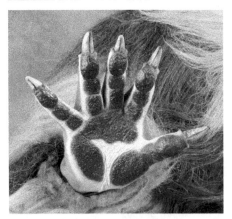

Above and below: paw pads add a sense of realism and detail to a costume.

line of the character's feet, over both the original shoe soles and the new foot structures.

Vulcanized rubber sheeting is a good material for soles. You can often find this at hardware and home supply stores as flooring material. Look for something with a flat surface, a little pliability, and not much thicker than an eighth of an inch. Overly thick soles make it more cumbersome to walk because they are heavier and less flexible. If it's textured on one side (i.e. it's intended to be flooring or a mat), make sure it's a pattern that would be suitable for the soles of your character's feet.

Attach the sheet to the underside of the foot. Although it is possible to sew it down, gluing is probably a better option. You will need to use a very strong adhesive such as Barge™, since vulcanized rubber tends to be fairly resistant to glues.

The Issue of Paw Pads

If you are aiming for realism with your animal interpretation, you may be considering paw pads on your feet. While they work well in nature, paw pads can be a difficult, but not impossible, item to recreate.

The trick is to find a material that will be durable, shapeable, and provide traction. It must be durable because all of the performer's weight will now be concentrated on a much smaller surface area. The material must be shapeable—whether cast, carved, or sculpted—so that we can create the paw pads to fit our feet. Finally, the material must provide adequate traction so that the performer can maneuver while supported on a small number of contact points.

A variety of rubbers and synthetic polymers seem to be the products which meet all of these criteria. Research, experiment, and determine what material you think will be best suited to your character's precise needs. I have seen effective paw pads constructed from slush-cast latex, pour-cast silicone, and pour-cast RTV compounds. I have also had some luck with carving dense closed-cell polyurethane foam into paw pads for indoor use. If you have access to industrial RTV mixtures, you could probably coat firm open-cell carved foam to create effective paw pads.

Spats

If you don't want to build a complex foot, spats are a convenient option. A spat is simply a fur covering that is slipped over a regular shoe. While they are less realistic and don't provide any interesting shaping, they have a number of advantages.

A simple spat allows the wearer to slip the costume on over his everyday shoes. The pattern has only one piece and is easy to construct.

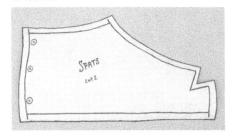

Spats are not limited to a specific shoe size; this makes them a good choice for costumes that must be worn by many different performers. Spats are easy to make, to put on, and to launder. They can be sewn from a simple two-piece pattern (see diagram). Snaps, laces, hooks, or a zipper can be used at the back of the foot to secure the spats. In order to keep them from flopping off the shoes, use a couple of flat elastic cords run underneath the sole. They hold the edges of the spat down against the edge of the sole. The elastic is small enough that it won't affect the traction of the shoes.

Part V

Masks, Makeup & Accessories

Creativity is the most essential skill in the costumer's art. It takes time to develop a designer's eye and the skill of mixing and matching techniques, materials and styles to achieve your vision. There are many other approaches to critter costuming beyond the full-body costumes described in previous chapters. In this part of the book, we'll explore some other costuming techniques.

One of the most versatile, easy and inexpensive methods for replacing a full-head mask is face and body paint. Makeup has the power to transform the human face into an animal without sacrificing expression. There are a tremendous variety of products available, from professional makeup and custom prosthetics, to store-bought cosmetics and inexpensive Halloween kits. Products are available at every price range, and there are many resources that offer advice on application techniques.

Makeup can be further enhanced with the addition of other animal details like ears and tails. While these can be purchased from costume outlets, making your own gives your character that personal touch. Ears, tails, paws and other costume pieces can be used as just a single eye-catching focal point, or incorporated into a larger design.

For those who don't want the trouble of makeup, but don't want to build a full head, masks are an excellent alternative. While mask-making techniques could easily full an entire book, in this section we will present the basic methods and techniques used by designers to create critter costumes.

21 • Facepaint, Makeup & Prosthetics

The quickest way to transform your face into an animal is by using makeup. Using face paint allows you the freedom to use your facial features to define your character. Makeup is great for kids who, for safety's sake, need to have their faces exposed for maximum visibility. Makeup can also become a base layer, used in conjunction with prosthetics that reshape the face and partial masks that expand beyond the limits of human anatomy.

Face paint reached its height with the Broadway musical *Cats*, and since then, painted faces have been popular for theatrical costumes. Face paint is also good for those folks who may be battling issues such as claustrophobia. Animal makeup is also a great alternative for costumers who need to travel light to events, and cannot take along a large furry costume.

Types of Makeup

Makeup is available in a wide range of styles, formulations and prices. Animal faces can be created using all sorts of makeup products; from a simple black eye-liner used to draw on sexy cat eyes, to completely colored and lined tigers. Check the availability in your area of professional makeup, costume or Halloween grade face paint, and commercial cosmetics.

Before investing in a full range of products, take the time to experiment and find items that work for you. Buy a pencil from one line, a pot of colors from another, and experiment on your face. Some people are extremely sensitive to cosmetics and may develop irritations, breakouts or even rashes. If you are new to makeup, experiment with different products to find out what both you and your skin are comfortable with. Also be aware that professional quality makeup caries a professional price, so make sure you stick to your budget.

Theatrical makeup is available from many different companies and comes in different formulations.

Theatrical Makeup

Expensive specialty makeup is designed to really "stick" to the face during performance. It holds up well to heat and perspiration, but is tricky to apply. When using professional products, make sure to consult their product literature, website, or ask at the store about application and removal instructions. Manufacturers often recommend their own specific setting powder, makeup removers or special brushes. Remember, you can often mix and match product lines, using inexpensive drug-store varieties for the basics while using expensive professional quality color and foundation.

Halloween Kits

These pre-made kits are inexpensive and easy to use. Although widely available at Halloween, they can be found at specialty costume shops year-round. Most kits are composed of inexpensive grease-paint products that are easy to apply and can be readily removed with soap and water. Use plenty of powder to set grease-paint formulations to prevent them from rubbing off on your costume. Many costumers find grease-paint irritating to the skin, so test these products before a long performance. Wash it off immediately if you feel burning, stinging, or itching.

Commercial Cosmetics

Makeup is widely available and ranges from dirt cheap to fabulously expensive. In generally, this style of makeup falls into two categories. Drug-store varieties are self-service and can be found in grocery stores, discount department stores and pharmacies. Counter cosmetics are those found in upscale department stores and have an upscale price to go with it. Let your budget guide your choice, and remember there are lower price alternatives to every expensive product.

Commercial cosmetics have some advantages over theatrical makeup and Halloween kits. Cosmetics are excellent for costumers with sensitive skins. Upscale brands offer consultants who can demonstrate applications and introduce you to tools and techniques. And of course, commercial cosmetics are widely available. The down-side to commercial cosmetics is that colors are dictated by fashion. You may need a bright orange eye-shadow and find it's simply not available in spring. Also, colors come and go, so buying seasonally and stocking up will ensure you have the colors you need when you need them.

Tools for Applying Makeup

Regardless of what type of makeup you choose to use, you only need a few basic application tools. Tools fall into three major groups: disposable items, permanent brush sets, and mirrors.

Disposable Makeup Sponges and Cotton Swabs – Cosmetic sponges come in round and wedge shapes and are handy to have around. They are inexpensive and disposable, but can be washed and reused to conserve cash. Sponges are ideal for applying liquid products and for blending colors in most types of makeup. Sponges are great to take to events because you can share them with other costumers if you need to and they are inexpensive to replace. For more detailed or finer lines, eye-shadow sponges and cosmetic swabs are useful tools. Most drug-store brand eye-shadows come with a handy sponge applicator. You can buy these separately and use them with any type of makeup.

Brushes – Makeup brushes come in a variety of different shapes and sizes. If you are just starting out, you can invest in an inexpensive kit that has a basic assortment of shapes and styles. Brushes vary from inexpensive, produced by the drug-store cosmetic bands to outrageously expensive versions available in upscale department stores. You don't need expensive brushes to do a good job. Even inexpensive brushes will produce excellent results if you practice your skills and techniques.

If you will be doing a lot of makeup application, invest in the best quality brushes you can afford. However, if you are going to be doing an inexpensive or one-shot costume, you can find inexpensive makeup brushes at discount drugstores. If you have a special painting technique, you may find what you need on a trip to the brush display at your local fine-art store.

Fingers – One of the most versatile and useful makeup application tools is your fingertip. Make sure to wash your hands thoroughly before you apply makeup products to prevent contamination of your makeup jars and bottles, and help keep your skin bacteria free.

Fingers are especially good at applying broad patches of color, liquid products like foundation or makeup base, and for blending colors. And the best part, you don't have to invest any additional money, or worry about misplacing them!

Mirrors – A magnifying mirror will help you get it *just* right, allowing you to easily see the details that you are painting on. While hand-held mirrors are portable and good for taking to events, tabletop models leave both hands free. Having both hands available to work on designs will give you better control. When you go to events, make sure to pack a portable hand mirror so you can make minor touch-ups.

Assemble a makeup kit that contains all of your essential items and can be easily transported.

The Makeup Process

Transforming your face from human to animal can be intimidating, depending on the style and feeling you want to evoke. It's important to develop a plan before beginning. A photo of an actual animal or reference artwork of the character can help you plan your project. A simple line drawing of a face with lines to indicate the color placement is a handy reference tool to have beside your mirror. If you have created this character before, a photograph of your actual painted face can be used as a guide to recreate the look.

Practice makes perfect, and if you are new to face-painting, you may want to work on developing your application skills and refining your design. If these are new skills you are building, use simplified lines and a minimum number of colors. Once you have become familiar with the makeup application process, you will be able to apply your makeup quickly, but no matter what your skill level, always allow enough time to do a good job applying your character face. If you are planning multiple appearances, remember to moderate the level of complexity so your face can be easily put on before each performance.

Designing Your Animal Face

Start with a reference photo of the animal or character you portray. Look in a mirror and compare your face that of the animal. Decide what features, markings or colorations really identify this specific animal and its species. Now look at yourself in the mirror. Remember, the features of your face can be painted over, but your eyes cannot. So plan your design based on the position of your eyes.

Take a photograph of yourself and make a photocopy, or scan it and make a printout. Color your face with pencils or makers to 'practice' your design. Once you have perfected your design, use it as a guide when applying the makeup. Before you buy new makeup, look at your makeup box first and see if you have the colors you will need for this project.

Practice, Practice, Practice

Practice makes perfect, so take the time to practice before your debut. Allow yourself plenty of time to really experiment with application and blending techniques when you aren't pressured. Gather all your tools and supplies together and experiment.

If you're not experienced in makeup design, experiment with different design variations and product application. If possible, take photos of your attempts for a later side-by-side comparison. Practicing different designs and techniques will allow you to learn which products and tools are best for specific visual effects.

Striped Kitty, Step by Step

Although brands and formulations of makeup are different, and some specific products will require special application techniques, the process of putting on makeup is almost always the same. Here is a demo that uses a variety of tools, makeup formulations and techniques for application. You may want to try and follow this step-by-step and see how your cat face turns out.

A reference photo. This is the effect we are trying to achieve.

1. Begin with a clean face and hair pulled back. Apply a smooth, even coating of your foundation or base layer. Allow to dry fully.

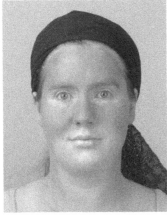

2. Begin your design in the center of the face. Trace the main lines that demarcate broad areas of color. Fill in the areas of color, working on both sides of the face to maintain symmetry.

3. Continue applying the blocks of colors and lines until you get your design on your face. Make sure to blend and to sharpen up lines where you need to.

4. Powder the face to fix the color and help prevent it from sliding. If you are using very dark black lines, you may want to go over the darkest places one more time.

Recording Makeup Designs

When you are finished and like your look, take a photo of your finished face. If you have made a costume or are working with a mask that you will wear again and again, you will want to repeat this makeup. Try to get photos of head on, three-quarter and profile views of both sides. These reference shots will help you apply your makeup consistently, so store these photographs with the costume or makeup kit. Include a written list of the products you used and the order in which you applied them to create the desired effect. The more information you have, the more consistent your results will be.

Prosthetics

If you are dissatisfied with your human face, and want to change their contours, why not try prosthetics? In a nutshell, makeup prosthetics are molded pieces of foam or latex that are applied directly to the face with glue. Makeup is applied to blend the prosthetic appliance into the actor's face to create a seamless transition.

Complex and detailed prosthetics are used in movie and television effects work. Advanced professional prosthetics are sculpted over life casts of the actors' faces for an exact fit. The creation of these makeup effects requires a great deal of experience and I would not recommend this for most costumers. Instead, there are commercially available prosthetics for many popular animal forms. Although not custom-fitted, these ready-made facial appliances are designed so that they will mold well to most faces.

A lifecast, such as this one, serves as a base for sculpting prosthetic pieces.

When you get down to it, prosthetics are just pieces of rubber that are glued to the performer's face. But this superficial (and superfacial) summary doesn't acknowledge the variety of styles and materials commercially available. Each type has different strengths and weaknesses and are suitable for different roles.

Foam Prosthetics – Most movie and effects prosthetics are solid pieces of injection-molded foam latex. A clay sculpture is built up on top of a life-cast of the actor to create new physiology for the character. A mold is created from this sculpture and then the clay is removed. When this negative mold is paired with the original life-cast, a void exists between the two. Foamed liquid latex is injected into this cavity and baked to create the prosthetic. Since the foam is in contact with the entire surface of the face and is quite flexible, movements are translated well, allowing the prosthetic to show every nuance of expression. The downside of foam prosthetics is that they are expensive, complex to make and are quite fragile.

Shell Prosthetics – Prosthetics can be made that create a hollow space between the wearer and the shape of the latex. For this type of appliance, called a shell prosthetic, latex is cast inside a mold to create a pliable shell. The edges of the shell are thin and feathered so that they can be easily glued to the face. The advantage of this technique is that the appliance can fit a variety of performers since it isn't molded to lie directly on top of the skin. Shell prosthetics need to be thick enough for the appliance to hold its shape. The disadvantage is that these appliances don't show subtle movements. They do benefit from increased durability and can be reused dozens of times if handled carefully.

Check in the Resources appendix under Lyonshel for one supplier of animal prosthetics.

Chapter 21

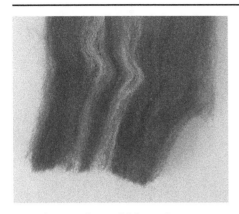

Crepe hair can be useful for makeup transitions to fur.

Fur, Makeup, and Transitions

Creating believable transitions from fur to skin is one of the most difficult effects to achieve. This style of costuming will have a region, usually around the edge of the face, where the fur ends and the face paint begins. You may need to address this issue, and so here are a few approaches to consider if this is one of your costuming challenges.

Covering the Transition

The simple and obvious solution is to hide the problem. Flowing hair and large wigs are good for covering the hairline and sides of the face. Scarves, elaborate hats, or other costume elements can also be used to surround the face and mask the transition from fur to skin. The transition at the neck could be wrapped with something bold, such as a bright bow tie or necklace. A large and contrasting item will draw the eye to it and overshadow the fur transition behind it.

For some characters, it's possible to integrate the fur during the makeup process. If the character design is constructed like a fur hood, the edges can be glued directly to the face. Prepare the edge of the hood, shaving the hair down towards the edge to make the transition smoother, by making the fur shorter and sparser.

Crepe hair is a a lightweight imitation hair product that's used for makeup special effects and full wigs. If your fur is a natural hair color, use crepe hair to create blended transitions between the costume and makeup or between your costume and your hair. If your fur is an unusual color, use fur trimmings to create patches to glue to your face and smooth over the transitions.

Punched Prosthetics

A more advanced technique for transitioning between costume and makeup is to use a punched hair prosthetic. This style of latex appliance is flat, and isn't designed to change the shape of the face. It serves instead as a method for holding the thinning fur together in a reusable format. Hair is ventilated into the latex, and can be as thick or sparse as you require. In the theater, punched prosthetics are used as stage moustaches. This same technique makes excellent fur-blending patches. While this is an excellent technique, it requires advanced skills. For details, check the bibliography for books on theatrical makeup.

22 • Ear Sets

Creating a set of ears is a relatively quick and easy project that is a good introduction for novice costumers. Ear sets are a versatile costume accessory which combine easily with other outfits, wigs, and makeup. The most simple critter costume is simply a set of ears and painted on whiskers.

Headband Ear Sets

Creating ears is really only half of the challenge. In order to create a set of ears that is useful, they need to be easy to wear. One of the best ways to assemble a set of ears is to build them onto a purchased plastic headband. Pick plastic headbands without fabric coverings unless you plan on sewing it, in which case, you'll need a wider band in order to get a secure mount without too much wobble. I prefer plastic because I use hot glue to hold the ears in place. In addition, you may find that a headband with teeth will help keep it stable on the head. Remember, ears that stick up add a lot of extra weight, and the better the anchor, the higher the ears can go.

Hats and Caps

Headbands are just one of the many ways to mount a pair of ears. Any head-gear can be adapted to the task as long as it fits securely on the head and has enough surface to attach the ears. Some characters have distinctive head-gear that becomes part of the overall costume.

For heavier ears, select a more secure mounting system, such as a baseball cap. Hats provide a sturdier base, since they have more contact with the head. When attaching ears to a hat, you may need to cut through it to invisibly connect a supportive substructure. For characters with wigs, many costumers use a snug baseball cap, bill removed, as a harness for the ears. The cap is then disguised by adding a wig to create the character's hair. This allows you to pre-style the hair around the ears. And best of all, it's easy to put on!

Ear Design and Structure

My technique for building ears is based on simple triangles. Vary the shape according to your intended species. Reference photos are helpful for determining the shape and proportion of the ears. In order to add dimension and shape, I use darts in the pattern. The darts create folds in the ears, bringing the edges inwards and creating a natural curvature. When planning your design, remember that most animals have lighter colored fur (or skin) on the inside of their ears.

The goal is for the ears to stand upright, so they need an internal structure under the fur. Unless they are exceptionally long, such as rabbit ears, you don't need a very strong or rigid structure. Any thin and relatively stiff item can provide the structure. For the sample ears in this chapter I chose plastic canvas mesh. It's lightweight, resilient, easy to work with, and inexpensive.

Chapter 22

Create the structure for longer and more complex ear shapes using wire. Select wire of thick enough gauge that it's sturdy yet flexible enough to bend into your desired shape. I recommend using wire around 12–14 AWG. A simple long loop will define the outer edge of rabbit-style ears and using wire means you can go pretty high. However, beware of making long ears too heavy. As the length increases, the ears act more like levers. The mass of the ears will create a lot of motion in response to head movements and may dislodge the headband completely. The longer the ears, the more support you will need at the head as well, so make sure to mount tall ears on a wide supportive headband.

Mounting and Positioning

The position of the ears conveys both emotions and aspects of the character's personality. Mount your ears so that the base of the ears closely corresponds to the placement on the animal. Take into consideration that when animals gesture with their ears, the base doesn't shift position. If you construct your ears with wire supports, you will be able to manipulate the quality of emotions.

For most species, pointing the ears in a more upright position creates an alert or perky appearance while rotating the ears outwards, projecting more to the sides, will create a sad or despondent look. How closely the ears lie against the head adds another dimension of emotion. If the ears lie relatively flat, perhaps even folded, it can represent fear or aggression. Ears that point away from the back of the head can indicate interest, friendliness or playfulness.

Ear Construction

Glue is my favorite mechanical approach to attaching the ears. A generous amount of glue will secure the ears to the headband. Remember, since the uncovered headband has a smooth, hard finish, you must abrade the surface with sandpaper so the glue gets a better grip. Hot glue is probably the best adhesive for this application.

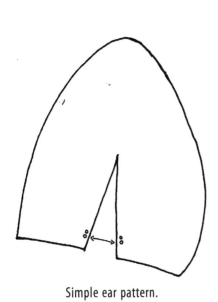

Simple ear pattern.

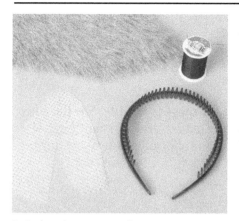

1. Gather the necessary items

Choose a headband that will form a secure base for the ears.

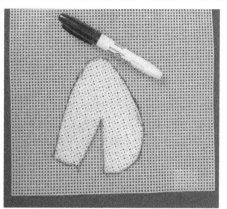

2. Cut the ear supports

In this example, I'm using simple plastic canvas to provide the ears with their perk. The plastic is easily cut to shape with scissors. This shape then slips into the fur ears.

3. Sew the fur pieces

Cut out the inside and outside pieces for each ear using your pattern. Use the provided pattern drawing as a starting point. Make sure the nap of the fur runs towards the point at the top of the ear.

Assemble the fur pieces by sewing them inside out.

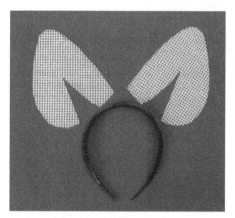

4. Create the internal structure

Lay out the pieces so the angle of the ears looks correct. Bring the darts in the supports together to create a cupped shape. Glue or tie them together.

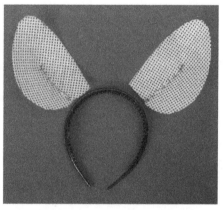

5. Attach ear supports to the headband

Mount the ears on the headband (or other base). I began by gluing the plastic canvas to the plastic of the headband. To secure the fur edges, I stitched the fur together around the headband.

6. Cover supports with fur

Once the framework is attached to the headband, slip the fur ears over them. Hand stitch or glue the fur to the headband. You may want to add a hand-stitched tack to the center of the ear to control the cupped shape.

Since these ears are somewhat large, I put a little foam padding in them for extra shaping. I simply cut down a piece of foam into a wedge; this pushes the backs of the ears out a little to give them a better shape.

Michelle Sams

Michelle Sams has worked in theaters for most of her life. She has been a theater tech, lighting designer, stage manager, and assistant director. Over the years, she has dealt with a number of practical costuming challenges.

How did you get started in theater work?

I started out in grade school with acting and have been involved with it ever since. I got into tech work and backstage operations in high school and fell in love with it. I've been doing effects and stage managing ever since. These days, I am primarily a stage manager and light board operator.

You've worked on shows featuring creature costumes. What sorts of costumes have you dealt with?

A number of odd costumes, over the years. In one recent play, "On the Verge," there was a baby yeti character. That was quite a large costume to deal with. Also in that same production was a character, Madame Nu, which was a fairly extensive face mask with attached hair. I'm currently working on *Midsummer Night's Dream*, so we have, of course, an ass.

Are you involved in backstage setup and costume prep?

It really depends on the show and the company. For one theater I worked at recently, I was in charge of setting up all of the props for the show. I had an assistant who worked primarily with the costumes since that was a very costume-intensive show. In other productions, costume handling gets added to my other duties.

What's involved in the storage and handling of such stage costumes?

Febreze™ became our best friend! A normal actor's costume, like everyday clothes, you can throw it in a washer at the end of a performance. Most theater costumes are designed to be washable in that way. But you can't really do that with a full fur suit. Washing it is a much more laborious process and not something we can do between every show. But you have to clean it somehow. Since the suit is so hot, the actor sweated a lot. So we had to Febreze it a lot after each performance.

In terms of handling masks, I had to make sure that I was the only one handling it other than the actor. Stage masks are sometimes very delicate so you want to minimize any chance of damaging them. We had to repair masks almost every night for minor damage.

What materials do you use to fix damage to the masks?

I usually use either hot glue or gaffers' tape. As a stage manager, my first option for fixing anything that breaks is usually gaffers' tape. It's fast and it's handy, though it might not be what the costumer would have wanted. Actually, I'm sure it's not what the costumer would've wanted. When you're working on a tight schedule, though, you don't have time to wait for glue

to dry and so forth. You have to fix things as quickly as possible so that you can get on with the show.

Do you tend to hear any particular comments from actors who perform in such creature costumes?

Yeah... Normally four-letter words are involved! It's really just because of the heat. The costumes are very heavy and insulating; adding the hot stage lights on top of that doesn't help. So the actors know it's going to be hot and it's tough to deal with it night after night.

For some plays, such as in "On the Verge," there's also the matter of a quick change. The actor plays multiple characters and needs to switch costumes between scenes. In this case, he had to get into the full fur costume really quickly, do the scene with the yeti, then get out of that and into something else for the next scene. It's tough!

It's important to have the costumes backstage and ready to go so the actors don't waste any time. It's also good to make sure there's plenty of water backstage since they tend to dehydrate faster from the heat in the costume.

23 • Tails

A critter costume just isn't complete without a tail! Perhaps some animals don't have them, but in other cases tails can be one of the most engaging parts of the character, lending them personality and style. Most mascot-style costumes have a tail that extends from the body. To make it really sturdy, they are supported from the inside with belts or harnesses attached to the wearer.

Separate tails can also be worn with regular clothing and a set of ears to create a cute yet inexpensive critter appearance. So, to make up for the tail-less animal population, I'll also cover how to build tails to be worn separately from costumes. It all balances out in the end—so to speak.

Practical Considerations

When designing the costume, spend some extra time thinking about the shape and proportions of the tail. While many animals may have long, flowing tails, costume designers find these difficult and impractical. Animals have specialized skeletal and muscular support in order to hold their tails aloft. Humans, lacking these support systems, have to rely on belts, bands and harnesses to support their costume tails. In most costuming projects, this is too complex and mechanically intensive to be practical. So, during the design phase, consider adjusting the proportions of your tail.

Cleanliness is also a big issue. Most costume tails hang from the back of the costume. If the character tail is longer than the wearers' legs, some portion will come in contact with the ground, causing the fur to discolor and creating unnecessary wear and tear. It's a good idea to keep tails at least a couple inches above floor level.

Tails are an irresistible lure for children. Fishermen only *wish* they had fishing lures this effective! If you work public venues with crowds of children, you will find that large hanging tails inevitably get pulled. This is something you should expect and plan for when designing and constructing your tail. Consider making it a little smaller, so it's less of an obvious target, and always be sure to sew it very securely to the suit.

Stuffed Tail Designs

Perhaps the easiest tail to make is a stuffed tail. Movement is generated from the overall movement of the character. To give the tail thickness and dimension, the tail is stuffed plush, making it much like a stuffed toy animal. The tail is a tailored pouch, patterned to create the correct animal shape. The tail is filled with lightweight stuffing and attached to the suit, If it's heavy, it may be given additional support with an internal waistband. The tail usually connects at about waist height in the dorsal seam. If the tail is small, stitch it directly into the seam. Alternately, tails can be surface mounted to the bodysuit. I prefer to attach the tail with a surface mounting method since layering many pieces of fur into one seam makes it bulky and difficult to sew.

The easiest stuffed tail is made with a two-sided pattern based on the silhouette of the desired shape. Cut the pattern from the fur, making sure to reverse the pattern (flip it over) for one of the pieces, creating left and right sides.

(CUT 2)

A simple two-face tail pattern.

Pattern for creating a double belt loop for your tail.

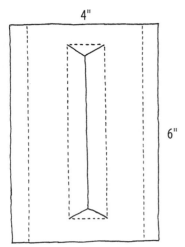

1. Cut along solid lines, fold along dotted lines.

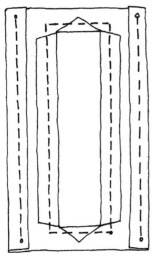

2. Stitch on dashed lines.

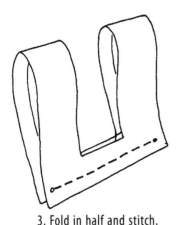

3. Fold in half and stitch.

Sew these two pieces together, leaving an open space at the top or side of the pocket for stuffing. While this simple two-piece construction is quick and easy, the resulting tail can sag along the bottom seam.

A three-piece pattern will improve the shape of the tail without having to overstuff it. A third panel is added to create width along the bottom of the tail. Many animals have a contrasting fur color on the underside of their tail, and this technique makes color blocking easy.

There are many different options for tail-stuffing materials. Loose polyester fiber stuffing, or Fiberfill™, is effective, inexpensive, and easy to locate at fabric stores. It is light and will fill out a tail nicely, but may compress over time, requiring additional stuffing. Quilted batting, fiberfill in sheet form, is a good alternative, especially for tubular tails. It can be tightly rolled up, giving the tail a more defined shape. Another alternative is shredded foam. You may have foam pieces left over from building your body padding. These pieces can be chopped up and used to stuff your tail. However, this tends to be heavier and less durable.

Foam Tube Tail Designs

Long, narrow animal tails, such as those of some felines, are built using a tubular design. Narrow tails can be difficult to stuff evenly using fiberfill or loose foam. Instead, foam pipe insulation is an excellent choice for giving the tail body. This ethafoam insulation is available at hardware stores in several different diameters.

The fur for the tail is made into a simple cylinder by sewing together the long edges of a rectangle. A curve of stitching at the end will create a rounded tip. The width of the rectangular piece should be slighter longer than the circumference of the foam, plus seam allowances.

The foam pipe insulation is stiff, so the tail won't have much movement along its length. To make a tail you can bend and shape into position, run a length of stiff-gauge wire down the hollow center of the foam tube. The thick-walled foam insulation will safely enclose the wire. This type of construction allows you to bend the tail into specific shapes to represent the posture of the animal's tail. When combined with swing generated by your motion, the tail will have a good appearance of movement.

Tails Worn With Clothes

There are several approaches to combining a tail with a character's clothing. The tail can come out through the clothing, if only through something as simple as a hole. Alternatively, it can be integrated into the structure of the clothing, stitched directly into an outside seam. A third possibility is to wear the tail monted to an external belt.

Both stuffed and tube tail designs work well for this application. The top of the tail is simply modified so that it can be worn with the chosen clothes. Stuffed tails must also be stitched closed. A character sporting an untucked shirt can easily use it to hide the top of the tail. The tail can attach to the wearer's belt; the back of the shirt hangs down past the belt line so that the top of the tail is obscured.

The tail can be worn by simply affixing loops to the top of the tail and slipping them onto a belt. A single belt loop is simply a rectangle of fabric sewn to the topmost part of the tail. However, most pants have a belt loop centered at the back of the waistline. If the tail has a single belt loop then either the tail must be worn off-center or the belt can't be threaded through the pants' loop. One way to solve this conflict is to create a split belt loop on the tail. A split tail loop allows the tail to be positioned at the center of the pants. An added bonus to this configuration is that by straddling the loop on the pants, the tail will remain centered and not slide around the belt.

Some costumes may require more complex adaptation. Skirts and dresses do not need modification if the tail is going to protrude from beneath them. Pants are more of a challenge. It's possible to adapt the leg pattern of a pair of pants to create a tail sleeve on the back of them. Taking a regular pair of pants, cut a vertical oval opening centered on the rear seam just below the waistband. A "tail sleeve" can be inset to match this opening by adapting a leg and cuff design. Be sure to keep the tail sleeve loose enough that it has movement around the tail in the same way that the pants have movement around the wearer's legs. With such a design, however, the tail can't attach to the belt, so something else must be devised. One possibility is a second belt worn under the clothes to which the tail attaches as described above.

Internal Structure, Cantilevers, and Mounts

An internal structure refers to tail designs that use something other than the basic fabric and stuffing in order to create a particular shape, posture, or movement. The guide wire used in the foam tube tail is an example of an internal structure. Wire is often used in tails that need to have an upward curve or hang away from the body.

If the structure is only used in the body of the tail, then the entire assembly can still pivot where the tail connects to the body. This allows the entire tail to act and move as a pendulum. This is the case in the simple foam tube tail described above and also in a regular stuffed tail. In many cases, such as a wolf or fox tail, this is acceptable because the movement mimics the actual animal.

Tails with a larger curve or which are designed to hang away from the legs, such as a curled husky tail, will need extra support. To solve this problem, we can mount the tail more firmly to the wearer's body to restrict its motion and brace it against gravity.

If wire is being used to construct the structure of the tail, it can be extended to create the mount as well. Without making assumptions about the understructure of the costume, we can design a tail supported from a belt. In order to stabilize the tail side-to-side, wire is used to create a horizontal span; this loop of wire rests against the wearer's back at waist height, tracking the movement of the hips. To prevent this segment from twisting or rotating downwards, a vertical spur is required. This should hit near the base of the spine and the tailbone. As long as the belt is kept snug, this wire mount will track the performer's movements and prevent the tail from drooping.

For best results, keep the tail construction light. Remember that the length of the tail allows the mass to act as a very effective lever. The tail is a cantilever based on the mount at the hips; even if the mount is strong enough to support the tail, heavy tails will be very uncomfortable to wear for extended periods.

Tails that are unusually large or heavy will need a secure mount or attachment in order to distribute the force over a larger area. It is possible to even create a fully rigid framework for more extreme tails. Something such as a mountaineering backpack frame could connect to a tail's rigid internal structure and convey the weight to the wearer's back and shoulder area. A setup of such

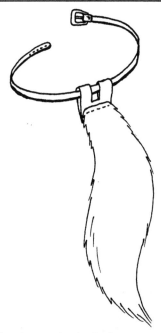

Use the opening in the loop to center the tail around the center-back belt loop of your pants. The slot goes on either side of the belt loop.

A stronger, more substantial waistband is needed for larger tails.

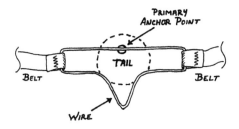

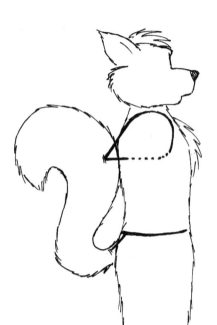

complexity should only be needed on unusually massive or suspended structures, such as a cantilevered dinosaur tail.

Upright Tails

Some character styles require raised tails such as cartoon skunks and squirrels. The size and the weight of the tail and the stresses caused by the upright posture make construction of this difficult.

It is possible to create such a tail using the techniques already described but I don't recommend it. Hip mounts and cantilever structures can work but, for a tail that is supposed to be held largely upright, it is difficult to engineer and the necessary bracing may inhibit the wearer's mobility. The main problem is that we are trying to support a vertical weight from a single point at the bottom, which is a dynamically unstable arrangement.

We can stabilize the tail by adding a second mount near the top. This can help support the weight of the tail and also keep the top of the tail from swaying too far to either side. In order to make this mount invisible, or at least unnoticed, the tail needs to be upright against or very near the back of the critter.

If the tail curls against the back of the costume, you can actually connect the tail directly to the body. Consider, for example, a cartoon squirrel with a tail that arcs away from the body at the base of the spine then curves upwards and curls against the shoulders. Where the tail contacts the shoulders, sew the tail directly to the bodysuit for support. The tail still requires internal structure in order to create the right shape. I would assemble this upright tail style with sheet foam to create an internal form that defines the arch and curl of the tail.

Tails that do not contact the body at the top arc of the tail can still be supported with fishing line. When used over short distances between the back of the body and the top of the tail, clear fishing line will be largely invisible. Use the heaviest transparent fishing line possible. Connect the fishing line to the tail's internal structure at a point near shoulder height. If the tail is quite wide, such as a skunk tail, you may need two parallel lines that will provide greater lateral stability.

The most difficult part is mounting the fishing line on the wearer's body in a manner that will be comfortable and secure. Mount the fishing line to a harness worn under the suit. Simply connecting the line to the bodysuit is insufficient because the pull of the fishing line will create an obvious tenting effect and make the front uncomfortably tight. Again, a backpack style harness structure will bear the added weight of the tail. The fishing line passes through the outer layer of fur to connect to this shoulder harness. If the tail has two connection points then shoulder movements will transfer to the tail.

Sewing a Stuffed Tail

The simple patterned fur tail is, by far, the most common design. It is generally easy to assemble, although colored markings can complicate the issue. In the case of the raccoon, each of the three basic pattern pieces had to be divided into alternating color panels. These were assembled, as shown, to recreate the original pattern's shapes.

When stuffing a tail such as this, I use loose fiberfill batting. But I have found that, over time, fiberfill can work its way through the weave of the fur's backing. To prevent this, I create an inner bag to hold the stuffing. This can be made according to the same pattern out of any tightly woven fabric. This pouch is then put inside the fur tail, stuffed, and sewn closed at the top.

The tail then needs to be attached to the costume. It can be sewn directly to the bodysuit or connected to a belt for support. The approach will usually depend upon the size and weight of the tail. If the tail is connected to a belt, the stuffed tail can protrude through the bodysuit by adding a hole in the dorsal seam. If the tail is narrower at the top, as in our raccoon example, a small closure will need to be introduced underneath the tail so that the tail hole can be sealed and disguised.

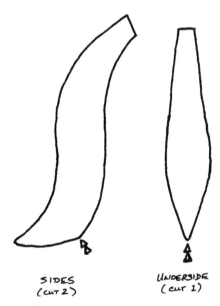

SIDES
(CUT 2)

UNDERSIDE
(CUT 1)

A fuller three-face tail pattern.

The pieces, cut out and ready for stitching.

Finished tail attached to costume.

Wolf Corlett (Ysengrin)

Ysengrin has been building and performing wolf characters for over two decades, including his work as a professional haunted house manager. He currently runs a horror costume and prop company called Running Wolf Studios (www.runningwolfpack.com).

How did you get involved in costume construction and performance?

It started in first grade with an eagle costume made out of plastic grocery bags for a school play. Then, senior year in high school, our school staged "Reynard the Fox," a one act play. And that decided it for me. I thought the animal costumes were really fun.

Freshman year in college, in my dorm room, there were little fur clumps everywhere from making my own suit. That was the first werewolf costume I built. Halloween was really an excuse to make and perform them. Of course, later, it got to the point where it's just all the time for me.

You've worked and managed a haunted house. Other than your interest in werewolves and all things Halloween, how did you get involved with that professionally?

I worked at Verdun Manor for fourteen years, actually. As it happened, I met Lance Pope, owner and operator of Verdun, at one of the science fiction conventions in Dallas. He was running around in his wolf suit and I was running around in mine. I saw him for probably three years at conventions before I knew he had a haunted house! I thought he was just doing costuming for fun like I was. As soon as I found that out, though, I went out to Verdun with my costume, and I started working that first night.

What factor is most important to the quality of a costume, however you might define "quality"?

Suspension of disbelief is the key. Do you believe this creature is really here? On the other hand, from a performance standpoint, costumes need to have good durability. You want a costume that will hold together for hours of wear at a time.

For the faces of your wolves you use cast latex. What do you use to paint them?

What are you supposed to use or what do we actually use? For safety reasons, try PAX paints first and see if they work for you. These paints are a colorant plus a special adhesive that can be thinned enough to work in an airbrush. It does the job pretty well but, to be honest, we find that it rubs off latex too easily. The depth in the color also isn't as good as we'd like.

Something that we like using – and here's my disclaimer: don't try this at home unless you're using a respirator and lots of ventilation because it is very toxic – is rubber cement paint. That's rubber cement that's been thinned down with acetone to the point where it will go through an airbrush. A little paint or colorant is added to it to create the color you want. It sticks wonderfully to the latex mask. It's also somewhat translucent so you can paint in layers; we air-brush on veins and then come back over it with a skin tone, for example. It's fairly durable, too.

But this rubber cement mixture is very toxic while you're working with it. It's not really dangerous after it sets. While using it, though, the vapors and liquid can be easily absorbed into the body and cause lasting damage. I can't stress safety precautions and proper handling enough!

From a performance standpoint, what is it like performing in a haunted house professionally?

We were different from most haunted houses in that people were going through without a "tour guide" we provided. So what they bring to the house determines what they're going to get from it. We have to read the guests as they're going through the house and determine what they want. Do they want a big scare? Do they want to just look at everything? There are some people that want to go through and not be scared!

Some guys want to go through with their girlfriend and be the big macho type. They're the ones that, yes, you can scare the heck out of them but they're also the ones that are most likely to take a swing at you. So you have to tailor it for everyone going through the house. The ability to read people is really something you develop as a job skill.

Ysengrin and Darkfang

Other than that, it's learning how to hide in shadows. Learn how to move around really quietly in a big suit. That's needed to really give a surprise. Working in a haunted house is also very unusual since you're deliberately trying to frighten people. This is just the opposite of what you want to do in other costume characters!

Character performers almost never talk in a full costume... We're sort of an exception because of how our wolves' faces are built. Even then we don't do much. We mostly just growl and chuckle. The body language is what you really use to communicate. You have to remember to make your gestures big and visible.

How would you describe the feeling of giving someone a really good scare?

Oh, it's wonderful! You're just bouncing along afterwards thinking to yourself, "Yeah, yeah! I got him! That was a good one!"

24 • Alternative Mask Techniques

There as many ways to create costumes as there are costumers. The quickest way to create an animal appearance is to simply put on a mask. While it is impossible for this book to detail every possible method for constructing masks, I do want to provide an overview of several popular techniques. This will help to provide a sense of the larger scope of the costumers' repertoire as well as to potentially inspire you with future possibilities.

Commercial Masks

A wide variety of commercially-produced Halloween and party masks are available at seasonal stores and costume shops. While by themselves they might be too simple for your designs, they may provide the raw materials for creating a costume head. Most commercial Halloween masks are made from slush-cast latex. The surface of the mask is composed of several layers of hardened latex rubber. This can be cut with heavy scissors or shears to disassemble or modify the mask. Portions of the mask, or even different masks, can be glued together with a strong adhesive capable of bonding hardened rubber, such as Goop™.

It is also possible to use commercial masks in their original shape as an understructure for a head. Fur, wigs, painting, or detailing can be added to the mask to alter its appearance. When starting with a commercially available mask, the goal is to significantly alter the final appearance so that your costume strikes the viewer as an original creation rather than a commercial product.

Some examples of commercial Halloween masks which might be used with costumes.

Sculpting and Casting

It is possible to create elaborate and inventive masks using latex casting. This results in finished masks similar in construction to the widely available Halloween costume masks. However, this is a complex process and involves a variety of skills, so it is not suitable for beginning costumers. If you are interested in learning this technique, the bibliography lists several books that are quite instructive.

Life-casting

The process begins with a life-cast of the person who will be wearing the mask. A life-cast is a plaster bust and is commonly used in the creation of special effects makeup. The advantage of using a life-cast is that it gives you an exact model of the performer's head and facial proportions so that your final mask can fit precisely. If a looser mask is desired, such as would be the case if it needed to fit a wide variety of people, a life-cast is still helpful for providing basic head proportions and eye placement.

Creating a life-cast is, by itself, a complex process best approached by a veteran costumer or someone familiar with molding and casting processes. The first ingredient in the process is alginate, a derivative of seaweed that is more

commonly used to make dental impressions. Available in powdered form, it is mixed with water to form a thick mixture with about the consistency of pancake batter. At this stage, it is applied to the performer's entire head, coating it evenly. Over the course of a few minutes, the alginate will progressively thicken until it stops flowing and becomes a soft, pliable solid.

Since it was applied as a liquid, the shape of the inner surface of the alginate captures the contours and details of the person's face. But alginate is a fairly flimsy material; it is not strong enough to remove and use as a mold by itself. To lend it strength, plaster is applied on top of the alginate to create a mother mold. Plaster-infused bandages, a common medical supply item, are generally used for this step. The mold is typically created as two halves, with the seam line running across the ears.

This combination of molds is then removed together from the person's head. The two halves are reassembled and strapped together. The alginate halves should be glued together to recreate the inner surface; cyanoacrylate is one of the few adhesives which can get a grip on the slippery alginate. Breathing holes in the molds can be plugged with small pieces of clay or extra alginate.

A casting is then poured in the upturned mold. A dense casting stone, such as ultracal, is best for the job. However, any casting material can be used. If the lifecast does not need to capture tiny facial details, ordinary plaster can be used. Once the casting has dried, the molds are opened to reveal the new lifecast.

Mask Sculpting

Working directly on the lifecast, begin sculpting the shape of the animal's head using plasticene or oil-based clay. The lifecast provides a working foundation and will ensure that your final mask is large enough to encompass the actor's full head. When designing particular facial masks, you can precisely gauge its boundaries.

The clay sculpture builds outwards from the human head shape to create the surface of your character's head. Over the full surface of the lifecast, the clay should cover to at least a quarter of an inch depth; this accounts for the thickness of the cast latex plus the slight shrinkage usually seen in alginate molds. Also keep in mind that the widest cross section of the human head is at about nose height. Unless the head features an opening in the back, the bottom or neck opening must be large enough to admit the actor's head.

Once the clay sculpture is complete, a mold is made on top of it. This will be a negative mold, meaning that the inside surface is the one carrying the detail. Plaster or casting stone can be applied to the clay original to create this mold. The mold needs to be carefully segmented to avoid excessive undercuts; books on casting technique will provide details on how best to divide the mold for different shapes.

Casting Latex

Liquid latex is the most common material for creating slush-cast masks. The slush-casting technique, or slip casting, involves pouring the liquid into the mold and swirling it around. The mold is then tipped to pour out most of the latex. A thin coating remains on the inner surface of the mold where it dries. The process is repeated between three and ten times, depending on the thickness of the latex formulation and the desired rigidity of the finished mask.

After a final drying period, the mold is opened and the latex casting is pulled free.

The resulting mask will need to be powdered or painted to remove any lingering stickiness and provide a finished surface. Latex masks can be used as a base for attaching fur to create a fuzzy face.

If the shape of the sculpted head is much larger than the actor's, the cast mask may need internal padding to hold it in place. A simple yet effective solution to this is to use pieces of foam applied inside the mask. This will make soft and comfortable bracing and will prevent the head from shifting.

Papier Mâché

This classic technique uses layers of glue-impregnated paper to create a surface. It is still a popular costume material because of its low cost, light weight, and easy preparation. Papier mâché can be a good choice for both theatrical masks and fully-enclosed costume heads.

Papier mâché strips can be applied to a clay sculpture, negative mold, or shaped chicken wire mesh. Applying the strips in layers and at different angles will strengthen the final piece. Papier mâché created from mulched paper also works but will not have the same strength.

Since it is constructed from paper pulp, it can be prone to moisture problems. It is important to fully coat the finished papier mâché item in order to seal it from moisture. This can be done by something as simple as applying several coats of paint. Lacquer is an even better sealant, although it does require a bit more work.

Fur and other surface materials can be glued directly to the papier mâché understructure. Hot glue and epoxy will form a good bond with papier mâché. Parts of the sculpture can even be left exposed and painted in order to create facial features such as the nose or eyes.

Vacuum-Formable Plastic

You've probably seen plenty of vacuum-formed plastic in commercial packaging. A heavier version of this plastic can be useful in costuming projects. It is often referred to as "vacuform plastic" or simply "vac plastic."

These products can be used to form a base for papier mâché.

The key principle behind the vacuum-forming process is that the sheet of plastic can be heated until it is very soft and pliable. It is then stretched over a positive sculpture, the shape that we want to produce, and a vacuum is used to pull the plastic tight against the form. The vacuum is used to remove the air space between the plastic and the sculpture so that the plastic conforms to it. You have to be careful to avoid pockets and undercuts in the sculpture or the vacuum won't be able to remove air from these areas; one solution to pockets is to drill holes in the form to allow air to be removed.

The quality and thickness of vacuform plastic varies. Heavier sheets should be used for costuming so that the final product has enough stiffness. The temperature at which the plastic softens also varies by manufacturer. It is best to observe the sheet as it heats and, through practice, learn to judge when the plastic is ready. As the plastic begins to heat up, it will warp and sag unevenly. It will later tighten up and rise slightly, taking on a more taut appearance, as the sheets gains elasticity. Watch for it to reach this point, where the wrinkles are disappearing, and then try to form it.

POSITIVE AIR PRESSURE

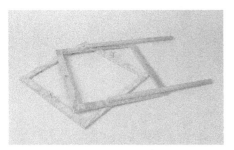

THERMOPLASTIC
FRAME
VACUUM
PERFORATED SURFACE

Above: vacuum forming frame.

Below: vacuum box.

Scratch-Built Vacuum Forming Equipment

Since most vacuform equipment is designed for industrial use, individual costumers and small shops are left with the alternative of building their own. Four pieces of equipment are needed for the operation: a heating system, the vacuum box, a frame to hold the plastic sheet during the process, and (naturally) a vacuum.

Heating System - The heating system is a mechanism for softening the plastic prior to forming. If you have access to an oven, then you can probably use this and avoid having to build a special heater. The disadvantage of an oven is that the size of your sheet is limited by the dimensions of the oven.

It is possible to assemble a custom heating system for working with larger sheets of vacuform plastic. The easiest approach is to construct a box containing ni-chrome (nickel-chromium alloy) heating elements. It is akin to building an oversized toaster oven. You should only attempt to build your own heater if you are comfortable with electrical and carpentry projects.

Frame – The frame to hold the plastic is relatively simple and may be built in a number of different ways. Its primary purpose is to clamp the plastic so that it can be manipulated while hot. The sample frame shown was constructed from plywood and wooden dowels.

Vacuum Box – The vacuum box, sometimes called a vacuum table, is one of the more complex pieces involved. The upper surface of the box, on which the forming takes place, is covered by a dense grid of tiny holes. Hand drilling this piece of wood requires patience but is an essential step.

The holes in the forming surface should be between a half-inch and one inch apart. More holes will produce a slightly better fit around the base of the positive sculpture; unless great detail is required, a one-inch spacing will work for most applications. The holes should be drilled with an 1/8" drill bit.

This surface is attached to a box that serves as a vacuum chamber. There should be at least an inch of internal height to allow for plenty of air movement in the chamber and thus a more even vacuum pull on the forming surface. The vacuum hose should connect to the interior space of the box through a mounted fitting or precisely drilled hole.

Foam weatherstripping is applied around the perimeter of the forming surface to encourage a good seal with the frame. The clamping frame for the plastic needs to be the same size as the forming surface. During the casting process, the frame is pushed down and aligned with the edges of the vacuum box, creating a vacuum-tight seal with the weatherstripping.

Vacuum – The vacuum may be anything from a household vacuum to an industrial pump; the strength of the vacuum required depends on the size of the forming box.

It's important that the vacuum be controlled by a switch that is easily accessible during the casting process. The vacuum needs to be applied after the plastic sheet has been pushed down over the sculpture and the frame is firmly resting on the vacuum box. The vacuum only needs to run for ten to twenty seconds to pull the plastic into position.

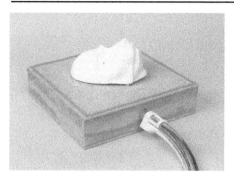

1. Put the parts together

Center the original positive form on the vacuum box. Note that the indentations around the eyes have had holes drilled through the sculpture to allow the vacuum to pull the plastic taut in these areas and prevent tenting.

2. Soften the plastic

Heat the sheet of plastic, clamped inside the wood frame, until the plastic softens. Here, we're using a household electric oven.

3. Place plastic on the form

Remove the plastic from the oven. Quickly and firmly clamp it down over the positive form so that the frame seals against the weatherstripping.

4. Turn on the vacuum.

This pulls the plastic tightly around the sculpture. After 20 seconds the plastic will cool and hold its shape. The vacuum can then be turned off.

5. Remove the plastic

The plastic can be removed from the frame and the edges trimmed. The sculpture can be reused in future castings.

This is the finished mask created from the sculpture. Fur and fabric have been glued directly onto the formed plastic to create the facial features.

Feather Masks

Although used extensively on carnival and theatrical masks, feathers are less common on critter costumes. Durability is a factor here as feathers are fragile and much more susceptible to wear and tear. Avian mascots almost always have their feathers represented by shag fur. The fur is sometimes cut with triangular edges and layered to enhance the effect.

But fur approximations cannot match the beauty in a feather mask. These masks are created by adhering individual feathers onto a shaped surface. The underlying surface can be created through any one of the many mask techniques, including papier mâché and vacuforming. Since the feathers are rarely layered so deep as to be fully opaque, this base layer is painted an appropriate background color to match the feathers.

Feathers are applied from the outside in, working against the flow of feather vanes and gluing them down along the quill. The goal is to overlap the feathers as they would lay across a bird, concealing the base of the quills. As you progress, lay the feathers in corresponding sizes based on the character design and mask contours.

Inexpensive plastic masks can be quickly decorated using hot glue, acrylic glue, or Barge™ cement. Purchasing feathers can be tricky. Feathers can be very expensive, so unless you are working on a small project, order your feathers in bulk from a theatrical supply house.

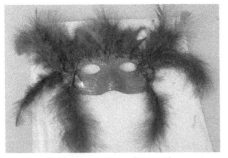

1. Key the mask base by painting with a color that coordinates or matches your feathers.

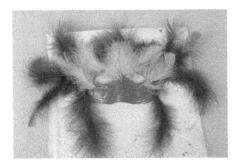

2. Glue the feathers onto the mask, moving from the outside edge towards the center of the mask. Make sure to lay in a row at a time, allowing each layer to dry completely before adding another.

3. Continue working in, row by row. Watch the shape of the feather tips.

Finished Feather Mask

25 • Costumes & Props

When is a character actually complete? It's not simply when the last piece is glued into place or stitched onto the costume. The character may not be complete even at the moment of its first public appearance. Why? Because a character is more than the sum total of the costume's parts. The character is only complete when you decide the details, accessories and performance nuances have fully captured your original design.

Two of the ways that you can give your character added, well, character is through your choices of clothing and props. While you may not need finishing touches on your project, these are things to consider while completing the character.

Clothing

Does your character wear clothes? Clothing is a very powerful tool for giving your character more depth of personality. Like a language, clothes send messages and give clues about the identity of the wearer and add depth to a character's persona. With a simple glance, clothing can tell you which team your mascot plays on or what your character's profession is.

Accessories

Sometimes just adding one important garment or accessory can change the context of your character. Consider using a costume element as a visual shorthand for a complete ensemble. Hats are an excellent way to quickly change the look of a character while providing a wealth of visual information about them. Look for hats that fit a particular period, social standing or occupation. For example, a chef's hat is so distinctive, most viewers will instantly recognize important facts about the character.

Complete Outfits

Some costumers like to develop complete outfits for their character, creating pants, shirts, and even outerwear such as coats. These full ensembles give the character a lot more visual interest and change the character's context, mood, or job. The difficult part of putting together a clothing ensemble for your character is finding clothes that will actually fit over a mascot-styled costume.

Carmichael in Tuxedo – Notice how the costume gives this bear a dignified air.

Shopping for Costume Pieces

Many costumers find that with a lot of hunting, patience and luck, they can find garments that they can modify at resale shops and thrift stores. This is an excellent source for inexpensive garments suitable for deconstruction and repurposing. Before you go shopping, take the measurements of your character or the performer. Be sure to take the circumference of the thighs, upper arms and neck, as well as the chest, stomach, and hips. Take a tape measure with you when you go shopping and measure potential finds. If you have a big enough budget, check out retail clothing stores too. You never know when you will find something at a great price on a clearance rack.

Making Your Own

If you have an exact idea of what kind of costume you want for your character, or if your character has an overly large body, unusual proportions, or more appendages than standard human anatomy, you may have to make your own costumes. Simple patterns from commercial pattern companies can be modified to fit. If you feel intimidated by the task of sewing costume pieces, remember to keep the pattern simple and make test samples from inexpensive fabrics. For hints, tips, and ideas on how to achieve your goals there are many excellent books on the subject of pattern manipulation and fit. Consult the bibliography for recommended titles.

Using Clothing to Unify a Group

Clothes are also a clever way to unify an assembled group of characters. Clothing and accessories made from the same fabrics, featuring unifying logos, or that otherwise match in some way, will usually tie the group together. If the costumes were not all built in the same style or by the same person or company, then it might not be immediately apparent that they are interrelated. Providing similar clothes or accessories to all of the characters immediately makes them identifiable as a group.

Seasonal Clothing

Holiday scarves and hats are a great way to give the character a nice seasonal appearance without any modifications to the actual costume. Keep an eye out for post-holiday sales to pick up accessories at great prices. Remember, accessories should be pinned in place to prevent them from coming loose. After all, you probably won't feel a scarf slipping off when under a layer of thick fur! Large safety pins, applied from the inside of the costume, will do the job.

No matter if you buy it new, used, or make it from scratch, costumes and clothing accessories will greatly enhance your character. Eye-catching clothes will make your character more distinctive and memorable!

Props

Some performers enjoy working with props. Like clothing, props can help define the role and personality of a character. Think about what associations you would make for a cane, an umbrella, a book, a paintbrush, pom-poms, or even a bone? Unusual items draw attention to characters and simultaneously convey information about them. Props are useful for directing attention during performances. The prop becomes a focus for the characters' actions, giving them an object on which to focus their attention, play with, and use to entertain onlookers.

Props fall into two major categories. The first are ready-made items that are simply appropriated and used during performances in much they way they would be really used. The second type of prop are those created for specific purposes. No matter which type you choose, props can really add sparkle and life to your character and performance.

"Have I got a bone to pick with you!"

Readymade Props

This is the easiest and quickest type of prop. Readymade props are simply objects that you appropriate for performances. There are many kinds of readymade props that work realistically without adaptation. Sports equipment, cooking utensils, and children's toys are just a few of the props that I've seen effectively used by critter costumers during performances. Simply choose the themes that support your character and performance and you're on your way!

Homemade Props

There are as many ways to build props as there are props themselves. Prop items can be built by adapting many of the different construction techniques presented in this book. There are also costuming reference books on the creation of stage and theater props that are very helpful for construction techniques. But why would you want to create a copy if the real item exists? Props are most often recreations for these reasons:

Safety – The original item would be unwieldy, have sharp edges, or otherwise be inappropriate for use in a crowd. Consider the issue of swords. A metal sword, even without an edge, can be dangerous. A mock-up made from fabric-covered foam is much safer.

Expense – The genuine article might be too expensive. Stagecraft abounds with techniques for recreating items on strict budgets for this very reason. This is the same principle as costume jewelry. Who could afford a diamond ring for an overlarge furry finger?

Scale – Character costumes are often significantly scaled up from human proportions. If the prop is something that relates to the head, such as a phone, an actual version of the item might look out of place. Also keep in mind that small objects will be mostly obscured from view when held in a large furry paw.

Durability – the original item may be too fragile for repeated performance use. A flower is a great example of this. Your character might need to hold a flower, yet a real flower would quickly become bedraggled. An artificial flower should be built or purchased.

Holding Props

One of the downsides of using props is that you must hang onto them through your entire performance. Character costumes usually don't have pockets and, even when they do, pockets are surprisingly challenging when you're wearing large furry paws! With this in mind, you should plan to continue holding the prop for the entire length of your performance.

Consider adding wrist straps to your props. A wrist strap will prevent you from accidentally dropping the item. It also means you can quickly and easily free your hand, leaving the prop hanging by its strap. When adding wrist straps, make sure they fit around the character's arm without binding.

Props help establish a character's mood. Here, a snazzy fox-about-town is off to do two different things. The props help indicate he's on a shopping adventure (left) or going to the beach (right). What props can you use to contextualize your character?

Part VI

Performing Animal Characters

Do stuff. Be funny. There ya go.

Okay, perhaps it's a *little* more complex than that. The chapters in this section cover the various aspects of performance. The hints and tips throughout this section are geared towards mascot and public performance of children's characters. However, many of these principles are broadly applicable to many other public appearances and performance situations.

This section introduces you to performance tips specific to critter costume work. It gives advice on what sorts of moves to rehearse, different ways of interacting with the audience, and proper planning for events. In short, the following chapters present you with background on how to do stuff and be funny.

26 • Character Commandments

These are some basic rules which should always be followed when you're performing in public venues. These apply particularly to walk-around and mascot characters; to some degree, they will apply to other costume situations as well. If you've never had a chance to perform a character before, study these well to avoid rookie mistakes.

1. Never Take Your Head Off in Public

For obvious reasons, removing the head will destroy the illusion of the costume. Always make sure that you are fully out of public view before removing your head. Be sure you know which areas are "onstage" and which are "offstage". Remember that the public is your audience and they should not see any part of the transformation between your human self and your animal character. This will preserve the reality of the character.

2. Never Talk in Costume

Again, this is about preserving the illusion of the costume. Sometimes it can be hard to resist saying *something* to people; this is where good pantomime skills will help out. Do not give in to the temptation to speak!

There are several good reasons not to talk while performing. First, if you're playing an established character, then it probably has a particular voice; a different voice would spoil the effect. Additionally, your voice will be muffled when speaking from inside a costume head. Finally, it will look odd to see the character speak without moving its mouth!

An exception may be made for costumes with an articulated mouth. Some costumes are specially designed to speak and be able to do so convincingly. Unless your costume is in this rare category, avoid speaking!

3. Know Your Venue

Be sure you know the layout of the area where you'll be performing. Walk around at least once out of costume.

Know which areas will be "onstage" and publicly visible. Know which areas will be "offstage" and hidden from view. Find out if there will be anyone in the offstage areas should you need assistance getting into or out of your costume. Note any stairs in the area that you might later have to navigate with reduced vision and large feet.

Chapter 26

4. Maintain Your Costume

It is your responsibility to make sure that your costume is cleaned, repaired, and ready before every outing. When packing, double check that you've included all of the pieces. Check pieces periodically for any seams coming loose or other wear and tear problems. Use a hair brush or pet slicker brush to comb out and detangle the fur before you perform.

After your performance, spread out the pieces of the costume to air dry. If possible, use an antibacterial spray or deodorizer before repacking the costume. Wash the suit at regular intervals. See the section on Cleaning Supplies for additional details.

5. Mind Your Hands

You occasionally hear allegations about costumed characters feeling people up or committing some other inappropriate act. I suspect that most of these are due to the limited vision and sense of touch of the performer rather than lecherous intent. Nonetheless, you should take care to steer clear of any gestures or contact which might be misconstrued. This also includes reaching near purses, wallets, or handbags.

Never make rude gestures, even as a joke. It can be tempting sometimes to make gestures when you know they won't be taken seriously. Photos out of context are very unforgiving! A poorly chosen jest could have serious repercussions.

6. Do Not Retaliate

As unfair as it is, you should not retaliate if you're hit, shoved, kicked, or otherwise attacked. Characters have to take a lot of abuse, it's true. But as soon as you make an offensive move, that's what the onlookers will remember and that's what will get you fired!

Try to anticipate assaults by spotting and avoiding possible troublemakers. Working with an escort can help greatly. If you are attacked, leave the area. Alert your escort; they should step in and take care of the situation for you. Otherwise, steer towards more friendly (i.e. mature) audience members. If nothing else is available, make a beeline for an "offstage" area.

Never hit, push, or yell at anyone.

8. Never Hold a Child

Parents will sometimes want you to hold small children for photos. They don't realize that you have limited vision, your coordination is impaired by a heavy costume, and you can have difficulty gripping squirming kids while wearing thick fur gloves. Be smart and don't set yourself up for an unfortunate accident.

Instead, encourage the parent to hold onto the child. Stand next to them in the photo or lean over the child to pose. If the child is in a stroller, crouch down next to it to pose.

With all of the limitations presented by a mascot styled costume, never be tempted to hold a child. Never assume you can see and feel well enough to control the situation. Mistakes like this one can be costly.

9. Keep Moving

It is essential to character performance that you remain mobile and active. As soon as you stop moving, the character seems to droop. Move, wave, and walk!

Be sure to circulate around the full area of your performance venue. Spend time with people and children who want to see you but then continue moving. If you are in a crowd, try to avoid following the movement of the crowd so that you are visible to new people.

10. Be Prepared for Emergencies

Always try to be prepared for unexpected problems. Keep track of the nearest offstage area at all times. If you're working with an escort, be sure that you have worked out an emergency hand signal. Pay attention to your own health and don't risk injury to yourself.

7. Never Approach Someone Who Wants To Be Left Alone

Some people do not want to interact with costumed characters. Really! It's true! These aren't necessarily the people loudly and theatrically declaring they don't want to meet you. It's more likely the people who back away, exhibit closed body language, or bluntly say, "Don't bother me."

If they don't want to interact with the character, any attempt you make to force the situation will likely make things worse. Some performers try it, thinking they'll "win them over," but this rarely happens if they sincerely don't want to get involved. It's much easier to avoid such people and move on. Then everyone will be happier.

Bottom line: be respectful. No always means no. Learn to read people and have a spotter sensitive to these issues.

27 • Travel & Storage

The key to travel: always be prepared! Always carry a small kit of supplies when travelling to performances. Being prepared when you arrive at a performance is a mark of professionalism. If you plan on showing your costume frequently, having a dedicated bag ready to go at a moment's notice will help reduce the stress of getting yourself ready. Additionally, having a repair kit can solve unexpected last-minute problems. You can even win new friends if someone else has costume troubles!

The Travel Kit

You never know when you'll need to make an emergency repair. Despite the laws of statistics, repairs seem to be needed most often when you're at a remote location about to begin a performance. Keep your tools and supplies in a small bag or plastic box to keep them neat, together and easy to find.

In your kit, pack basic sewing materials including scissors, safety pins, needles, and thread. Black and white thread is sufficient for most emergency repairs. If space isn't an issue and you want extra security, pack a small hot glue gun. Other items you may wish to take with you include zip ties and duct tape.

Towel, Bottled Water, and Clean Clothes

Costume performance is hot work! It's nice to have a clean towel and a handy drink of water ready for when you get out of a suit. Wearing a critter costume can leave you hot and sweaty. If you wear your regular clothes under the costume, have a clean change of clothes available.

Costume Packing Cases

Get a set of travelling cases sized to fit your costume. I like to use hard-sided cases even though most critter costumes are usually durable. When deciding what size boxes to purchase, consider storing and transporting not only your costume, but your repair kit and cleaning supplies.

Check your local hardware store for large plastic storage bins. Utility bins made for outdoor use or truck beds are a good choice. Look for something made from durable plastic that will stand up to abuse. Select a case with a locking lid, to allow you to secure it during freight shipping. (Check airline regulations before checking locking container lids.) If you already own cases you use to transport costumes, keep in mind these dimensions when designing future suits. It's easy to build a costume in shapes that are awkward to pack. Designing a costume that will easily fit into containers will make travelling to your next venue a snap.

Event Packing List

Directions & Site Contact

Repair Kit

Bottled Drink of Choice

Towel

Extra Clothes

Deodorizer

Batteries, if applicable

Snack

The Actual Costume!

Above: a small toolbox can store a good traveling repair kit.

Below: The Action Packer™ by Rubbermaid is a large, sturdy bin that can be used for storing and transporting costume pieces.

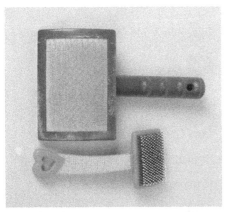

Chapter 27

Slicker brushes

Cleaning Supplies

Antibacterial sprays are great to quickly disinfect and deodorize your costume. There are several good products available though they can be difficult to find. My personal favorite is EndBac II™, a hospital sterilization product available in an aerosol can. A more widely available product is Nature's Miracle™. Although it's designed to remove pet odors, it is effective on human sweat as well. This is an excellent antibacterial product and widely available. Other common commercial deodorizing products, such as Febreze™, can be used though they are not antibacterial. Avoid any heavily perfumed product.

If you're concerned about the possibility of staining, you may also want to pack a bottle of spray-on carpet cleaner. This is good for removing surface stains in the fur before they set. Always test these cleansers on a scrap of fur before use on the actual costume. One last item that is handy to have is pre-moistened towels that can be used to clean you or your suit.

One old theater trick: make your own antibacterial solution by mixing one part vodka with one part water. This mixture evaporates quickly, is non-staining, and costs much less than commercial products.

Stain Removal

Since washing a full suit can be quite time-consuming, it's often easier to maintain the suit by cleaning only soiled areas. Some suits, such as those with built-in padding, may not even be washable. For those cases, surface cleaning is the answer.

Tougher stains can be attacked with a dilute mixture of bleach. Apply the mixture with a sponge, stroking along the fur in the direction of the nap. Use a damp cloth to clean the fur and remove the bleach. Follow with a dry cloth to remove the moisture.

Note that these surface cleaning techniques should not be used on a costume with painted markings! Some of the colorant may be removed from the fur along with the stain.

These are many other cleaning products are used to keep mascot costumes clean. Test a sample of fur with these cleaners before washing an entire costume.

28 • Escorts, Spotters & Handlers

Spotters protect both you and the crowd from problem situations.

These are some of the names used to identify the people who accompany costume performers when they're out and about. But no matter what you call him, your handler is essential for your safety and supports you as a performer. A good handler will work with you as a team. If it's not someone who's worked as a handler before, be sure to brief him on what you expect him to do and to arrange signals. I always recommend pre-arranging to have an escort during character appearances.

Duties of the Handler

The handler is responsible for making sure that your character appearances go as smoothly as possible. The escort serves as an extra set of eyes and ears that can watch for trouble. They are also a useful source of information for people, since the character cannot speak. Handlers can distribute information and pass out business cards, perhaps even getting you future bookings!

Ideally, the handler shouldn't appear to be leading or guarding the character. The escort generally follows behind you and hangs at the edge of the crowd. The ideal distance is just far enough away not to be in the crowd's focus, but just close enough to step in at a moment's notice.

Taking Photographs

Groups often want to take photos with a character. Unless they are busy dealing with another issue, it's good form for handlers to step forward and volunteer to take photos so the entire party is included. Having your photo taken is one of the best parts of being a mascot. If you think there will be a lot of people taking photos, you may want to take an extra escort to help exclusively with photography.

Spotting Opportunities

Handlers can also keep an eye out for kids looking at the character but unnoticed by the performer. The escort has a less obstructed view, and will be scanning the crowd, paying attention to things that you cannot see. He will be able to point out things you may miss, like people or events that are happening behind you. Let your handler know what types of things to look for in the crowd. This way you won't miss out on opportunities.

Chapter 28

Providing Information

People often ask questions about the character and why it's visiting an event or location. The handler is in a great position to field these questions. He can provide information on the character and background information about the event. If you're a performer for hire, make sure that your handler carries your business card Make it easy for people who are impressed by your performance to contact you. Your escort can help you generate future bookings.

Withholding Information

Handlers should also be discrete. It's important for them to know when not to volunteer information. One question people often ask is whether it's a man or woman performing the character; this seems to be the number one question for some reason. Whether you want your handler to answer questions about the performer rather than the character is your choice. Talk to your handler before your performance to go over your needs.

"Let's keep moving."

Establishing Signals

Before performing, meet with your handler and set up hand signals to use while in costume. You shouldn't need to use these often but it is a real comfort to have this level of communication with the handler.

At the very least, establish signals for emergency situations. Use them only if you need to get out of the costume immediately. For example, you might be feeling heat stroke symptoms. Your handler should separate you from the crowd and quickly lead you to the nearest offstage area.

Watching for Trouble

At any public appearance, there are bound to be a few kids looking for trouble. Since costume characters are designed to stand out in a crowd, you will be an obvious target. The handler should watch for kids and teenagers that have that look in their eye, that telltale "mischievous look" that says they may mistreat the character. Never assume that parents will be around to keep kids in line!

"Keep your eyes open."

"Time check."

"Emergency!"

Mischievous Children

With a little practice, handlers can quickly learn to predict the behavior of kids in the audience. They should encourage kids who want to interact with the character while simultaneously discouraging any troublemakers. The clearest indication of trouble is groups of kids trying to maneuver into the character's blind spot. Anyone pointing or hesitating behind the character might be considering something inappropriate. I try to avoid stereotypes, but this one seems to be supported by my experience: watch for groups of two to four boys, ages eight to twelve. Be especially aware of children without parental supervision.

Tail pulling is the most common offense. If a costume features a tail, kids will feel compelled to pull it. Since it's behind the performer, it's also the most difficult place for the performer to guard. With limited hearing it's not even possible to listen for kids sneaking up. The handler needs to be alert to these situations and be ready to step in if necessary.

The quickest way to resolve problem situations is for the handler to step forward and make it obvious that he is there to protect the character. If they know someone is watching, the kids will usually back off without causing any trouble. Encourage your handler to be an authority figure.

Maintain Distance

A good handler will accompany the character without looking like a bodyguard. If the escort has a strong presence and stands next to the character, it may discourage crowd interaction; people will be more reluctant to approach. The handler needs to always keep in mind that the character is supposed to be the focus of attention.

Handlers can maintain a more subtle presence by standing behind and to the side of the character. This will allow the escort to keep the vulnerable backside of the character under watch. Ask your escort to follow along behind you and not keep a tight pace. The handler should avoid standing directly behind the character so they don't end up in people's photos.

Escorts need to vary their distance from the character based on the density of the crowd. If there are a lot of people pressing around the character, they should stand closer. The handler will help establish a small circle of space around the character. If the crowd is thin, the escort should hang farther back; standing a little farther away will help them survey the public and reactions.

The handler should remain behind the character to protect the back side and keep an eye out for opportunities.

Brian Hagen

Brian Hagen has been a professional character performer for theme parks, corporate mascots, and stage shows. He has played the mascots of several sports teams, including the Oakland A's and the Bay Area Cyber Rays. He has recently returned from his role in the U.S. *Bob the Builder Live* tour. Shown here is his creation, Violet.

What different types of character work have you done?

I began performing costumed characters at Paramount's Great America in 1994. Following that, I played the mascots of several sports teams, including the Oakland A's and the Bay Area Cyber Rays. I've also done some corporate work, portraying well-known characters such as Bugs Bunny and Sonic the Hedgehog. I've just recently returned from my role in the U.S. *Bob the Builder Live* tour.

What do you enjoy most about performing costume characters?

The chance to be uninhibited and in disguise. In addition to doing stuff you're normally too shy to do, you can do stuff that you're not really supposed to do such as slide down escalators. Mascots get away with more. You don't want to push it too far, though; if the security guard starts yelling at you, then it's not funny any more.

What type of performance work is your favorite?

Scripted stuff on stage is good because it's more controlled. Less can go disastrously wrong... sort of. You know you're not going to get tackled or anything like that. There's also less idle time since you always have something scripted to engage in.

On the other hand, interacting with kids is more fun and rewarding. You can make the kids feel personally recognized by the character, which is cool. Kids at a young enough age won't think "Scooby Doo waved at me and all the other kids," they'll just remember "Wow, Scooby Doo waved at me!" When you're up on a stage, it's hard to get that much connection with the kids.

What factor is most important to the quality of a costume, however you might define "quality"?

I personally like the costumes to look good from a technical perspective. I feel kind of cheap in a poorly made suit with the ankles gaping. Apart from the quality of the costume, the person in the suit is very important. It's not as bad to have a suit that's not too great if the person inside is a really great performer.

What are some of the performance challenges you've faced?

Changing space. It's sometimes tough to get it through people's heads that a public bathroom is not a good place to change, for both logistical and character reasons. I've had to change in public bathrooms several times. I even had to change in a handicapped Port-a-Potty once. It kind of wrecks the effect when a guy carrying a bulky bag staggers into a Port-a-Potty

and then the character comes out... Kids tend to pick up on that kind of thing.

Not having escorts is a huge risk. A lot of people who just want to hire a character to walk around at their car sale or whatever don't understand that it can be hazardous for the person in the suit. The character is very visible and can attract troublemakers. If you don't have someone to shoo them off, other kids see that they're getting away with it and then they join in... It can snowball very quickly.

What performance advice do you think is most important?

Keep moving at all times. Don't necessarily be running around but keep looking around. If you see a kid, wave to them. Things like that. The trouble is that the suit has big wide-open eyes. Sometimes you're feeling tired and want to take a break, but you forget the suit is still out there looking happy and alert. People will still be waving at you and if you ignore them, well, the kids will remember that.

The most important part of preparation is building up this endurance. You want to be able to run around without falling over and collapsing. Pace yourself! But be aware that you're going to be wearing a heavy suit and it's going to be hot, so you might need extra endurance over and above what you might expect.

How much would you guess the average costume you wear weighs?

Professional suits can be pretty heavy. I've worn some heads that were seventeen pounds by themselves. Generally, I'd guess costumes weigh around thirty pounds, total. Keep in mind that most of that is hanging off of your body; a heavy head is much worse than a heavy suit.

How would you describe the feeling at the end of a show?

I'm often too tired to notice but it sure feels good in retrospect! I watched the *Bob the Builder Live* DVD the other day and saw all the kids clapping at the end and it felt good knowing that they were doing that for me when I was doing the show. The trouble is, a lot of times you can't see the audience and you can't hear them that well, you just have to tell yourself that there's lots of people out there that really appreciate what you do.

Violet, designed by Brian Hagen.

29 • Performance Tips

Once you have mastered the basic performance tenets of the Character Commandments, you may want to build more advanced performance skills. Instead of specific "dos and don'ts," this chapter offers general advice to help develop and broaden your performance skills. Above all, of course, it comes down to practice. Skills are honed by exercise and confronting real world situations. But my hope is that these pointers can get you started in the right direction and give you some areas to focus upon.

As soon as you have your costume finished, or even before, you may want to arrange to record some practice performances. Enlist a friend with a video camera to document your rehearsals or sample shows. Watch and evaluate your performances, keeping a keen watch on your technique. Use these videos as tools to help you improve your skills, integrating the techniques below to really help bring your character to life. Remember, the character is more than just a costume. It's the combination of your spirit, acting skills, and personality that brings the character to life.

Don't Panic!

If this is your first performance, don't panic! About fifteen minutes into it, you're likely to realize that you're hot, the costume is very heavy, and it's difficult to breathe. Try to relax and slow down your performance. Focus and react to the people around you. However, if you feel you really are in trouble, signal your escort that you need to be taken offstage.

In general, try to know your skill level and pick performance venues that you can handle. Even experienced performers can sometimes get in over their costumed heads.

Exaggerated Actions

Make physical actions and gestures larger than life. The sheer bulk of fur and padding will obscure subtle movements. With most critter costumes, the character is scaled up to be larger than a human and consequently, needs to similarly scale up all of its movements. Gestures involving small hand movements or slight shifts in body position may be unnoticeable to onlookers.

I recommend practicing in front of a mirror or video camera with a new costume. Try out common actions such as walking, waving, or shaking your head. Experiment with different movements and levels of exaggeration to see what looks best in your costume. The trick, of course, is to remember these movements and then use them when you're performing. As you tire, it's very easy to slip back to your normal range of motion. During a performance, you may notice you've done this. Don't immediately overcorrect; that draws attention to the mistake. Instead, concentrate on gradually building back up to the high-energy, exaggerated actions of the character.

Take the time to practice in your costume. This will help you build the stamina to face long performances. Practicing will give you an opportunity to discover your limitations and gauge how long you can effectively perform in your costume.

Chapter 29

Continuous Movement

Some critter costumes look beautiful when they're standing still but these are a very small minority. Every costume benefits from an active presentation. While in the public eye be sure to always keep the character animated and moving, even if you think you're not being watched. Continuous movement doesn't mean you're constantly doing back flips or some other high-energy activity. It's fine to walk around or even sit for a minute. Just remember to remain active, even if it's only a minor motion such as an arm wave or head bob. This makes your character more interesting and leaves the audience with a favorable and lasting impression.

Practice Your Pantomime

Pantomime skills are your most effective means of communicating with an audience. As a performer, it's important to develop a repertoire of large, easy-to-see hand gestures. If you're pantomiming a specific object, try to make it convincing and consistent. Think about different ways to use the object in order to clarify what it is to your audience.

Practice common gestures such as blowing a kiss, covering your eyes, miming drinking and eating, and sulking. Keep in mind that some simple moves, such as covering your eyes, can be surprisingly tricky while wearing a large costume head. Familiarize yourself with the locations of your character's facial features and learn the exact positions of your eyes, ears and nose so your gestures will be clean and crisp.

Perform at Kid Height

Don't be afraid to squat low or kneel to interact with children. Large fuzzy creatures may intimidate small kids. Can you really blame them? By bringing yourself down to their height, you become much less threatening. The child also gets a better view of the (hopefully) non-threatening facial expression of the character. This will encourage kids to interact with you and improve your general reception with the audience. Remember to get up slowly and carefully after squatting or kneeling.

Remember to Eat and Drink

Pay attention to what you eat and drink before a performance. Each costumer has their own personal preferences for this, so you'll have to learn what's best for your body.

Eat a minimal amount before a performance but drink plenty of fluids. The goal is to find the perfect balance that is right for you. The trick is to drink just enough to stay hydrated, but not so much that you will need a restroom while in character.

Wearing a mascot suit is sweaty business. After a performance drink plenty of fluids. If possible, choose a sports drink or other beverage that will replenish electrolytes lost during performance. Some performers may want to avoid eating immediately after getting out of costume. If you feel dizzy or develop a headache after a performance, you may be low on fluids. Learn to listen to the needs of your body. Dehydration can be dangerous to your health and prevent you from enjoying your performances.

When you're on your hands and knees, you are at eye-level for small children.

Pace Yourself

Pace your performance! Don't use too much energy all at once. Rather than starting out with a bang, and ending with a fizzle, try to spread your energy evenly over your allotted shift. Pacing will help you maintain character consistency and prevent overheating. If you aren't yet experienced at performance, it can be difficult to judge how long your energy will last. The first few times out, I'd recommend taking a cautious approach and moderating your performance.

Keep Cool

Making a costume cool is usually the responsibility of the designer. As the performer, however, there are a couple of things that you can do. When performing outside on sunny days, try to stick to shady areas. If it's hot out, your audience will probably be there anyway. Just remember to that it's better to pose for photos in full sunlight.

Take breaks when you need to. Even five minutes with the costume head removed and a cool drink can revive you. Some performers like to use cool vests to help keep their body temperature down. On the hottest days, a cool vest can be very welcome. Although some performers swear by cool vests, I've not had good luck with them. They seem to lose their cooling ability very quickly and within twenty minutes, they're just an extra weight to carry around. Experiment until you find the right combination of cooling techniques that work best for your body.

Not feeling like yourself? If you are unwell, don't perform.

Don't Perform When Sick

If you are feeling even slightly sick, performing is not a good idea. Being inside of a mascot costume is physically strenuous work. Don't try to do "just a short run" if you're not feeling up to it. Evaluate your body and how it feels and be totally honest with yourself. Let me just say this: sneezing while wearing a costume head is a *Bad Thing*.

Arrange a Changing Area

An essential yet often overlooked part of performance is having a designated changing area. When setting up appearances for your character, try to negotiate a designated changing area. I know many people who've changed in public restroom stalls. A designated area should be a safe space to leave your costume container, travel kit, and clothes. At the very least try to arrange for a secure place to leave your wallet and keys unless you plan to carry them inside your costume. If it's impossible to arrange a changing area, be prepared to make do. Do not complain to your host or liaison. Instead, designate someone in your party to guard your gear or stow it in a vehicle.

Don't get caught without a place to change!

Jimmy Chin

Jimmy Chin has been a professional sports mascot for several different teams, including the San Francisco Giants. He also creates and performs his own costume characters at a variety of different venues.

How did you get started as a mascot?

I've always been interested in performing. I originally started out with a heavy dose of stage fright and this is one way that I got around it. Being a completely anonymous character helps combat the stage fright. One of the first big things was a job at Six Flags, as some of the Warner Bros characters: Wile E. Coyote, Bugs Bunny, and so forth. I found it to be exciting, to get into the role of a well-known character, and gallivant around and act as they would act.

From there, I started branching out and doing occasional sports mascot jobs. I did backup work with a hockey team in Anaheim and a couple appearances at a minor league baseball stadium. I didn't have the schedule to go to all of the seventy season games of a minor league baseball team considering I lived sixty miles away. I still had a day job on top of all this.

Then I moved up to the San Francisco Bay Area. I applied with the Giants and although I didn't get the main position, I was asked to be the backup and escort. It turned out to be a good deal. I got to see a lot of the inner workings of major league baseball and watch someone doing real mascot work. I observed his moves and repertoire of characterizations and saw how he handled particularly sticky situations with hostile fans, drunk people, and so forth. That, in turn, helped me advance as a performer.

What's different about working for a sports team versus doing other character appearances?

With a theme park character you're restricted on what you can do since there are other people portraying those characters, too. You have to "generify" yourself. Develop just the fundamental moves and protocol for dealing with people. You don't want to push the envelope too much because there's usually heavy management; if they hear complaints from park attendees that a particular coyote was a little too mischievous and ran off with someone's food, for example, that wouldn't end well for you.

In a sports environment, you're calling your own shots as far as interactions go. You're more accountable. You know your limits, you know your fans, and many times you find you're seeing the same fans over and over. You can get away with more when you're with a friendly crowd. With a stranger, you can't read them as well and you don't know if they're going to find offense at something you do.

What factor is most important to the quality of a costume, however you might define "quality"?

I like to consider a few things. How good it looks is important. But what's more important is how well it moves. If you've got a wonderful costume that moves like a brick, it's not going to sell itself as a character. For me, part of making this costume into a character, as opposed to a walking sculpture or a guy in a big suit, is seeing it move and perform. If it moves well and looks good, it becomes this other critter, not just a guy in a costume.

What piece of advice would you give to a beginning performer?

I don't want to get in trouble for this, but take chances. You have some free rein as a performer. I know sometimes I play it a little too safe, myself. Within reason, you can go out there and try new things, see if they work. Try different moves or things you wouldn't normally do. You don't want to get yourself in trouble, mind you.

Remember that you are becoming something different. Act differently! If you're working on several characters, emphasize how they differ from each other. Try to get inside the character's head as well as getting inside the costume.

I learned a lot from watching cartoons. I grew up on cartoons, as I'm sure you'd find most mascot performers have. You can learn from the cartoons. I know you can't walk off a cliff or anything, but you learn cartoony moves, character walks, and different physicality. Try to cultivate that as you're performing.

As far as sports appearances, what do you do to prepare for a game?

I don't have a pre-game ritual, per se. I just drink a lot of water and think about what I'm going to do. When I was starting out, I did more to psych myself up for it. With experience, I don't really need that anymore; I find I'm able to slip in and out of character very easily.

Before you go out, something that helps is looking in a mirror. Seeing yourself in a mirror will really help to gel the character in your mind because you look in the mirror and you don't see yourself looking back. There's someone else staring at you!

What does it feel like to be out there as a mascot, getting cheers from the crowd?

It's a pretty big rush. As if you have some wild superpower, you can raise your arms and everyone cheers for you! Well, if you're good, they usually cheer for you. You feed off that big rush of energy coming from the crowd. There are many times when I've been totally wiped out from having a busy game, the sun's beating down, you're completely worn out... but you keep going because of the smiles of the kids and the cheers of the fans.

Blooper, designed by Jimmy Chin

30 • Shticks & Gimmicks

As you gain experience as a performer, you will naturally develop the personality of your character. Along the way, you will perfect scenarios to perform to entertain your audience. In short - shticks and gimmicks. The key to developing your personal repertoire of shticks and gimmicks is observation. Pay attention to what works for experienced character performers. Observe how people respond and relate to them. As you see how their shticks work, consider how those same gigs can work for your character.

This chapter presents a collection of standard performance gimmicks. You can try these out as is or use them as inspiration to develop your own shticks. Keep in mind that these examples are not designed to help you build your character personality. Rather, these are scenarios to help you in performance situations.

Dealing with Scared Children

This is a common situation that you will certainly encounter. In the previous chapter, I recommend kneeling, bringing yourself down to their eye level. Reducing your size can help allay their fears, make your character more appealing, and less scary. However, no matter what strategies you take, some kids will still be scared. Look for body language clues that will alert you to their frame of mind. Some kids try hiding behind their parent's leg. They might even begin crying. If a child looks agitated or scared, do not approach or force interaction.

Instead, try the "scared child" shtick. This gimmick relies on mirroring the child's emotion. If they are obviously frightened of your character, you mimic them, by stepping away and feigning fright. You become as frightened of them as they are of you! If they're crying, cover your eyes and look scared and ashamed. Tentatively move your hand and peek out at them; if they're still scared, shudder and cover your eyes again. If they try to hide behind their parent's leg, try to mimic this as well. Hopefully you will have a friendly accomplice nearby who can lend a leg. If the child has both parents there, try to hide behind the other parent and peek around their leg. The laughter of their parents will help ease the fears of the child.

Children often become inquisitive after they get through their initial reaction. At that point, if they are curious about you, your character can become curious about them. You may be able to approach them and even give them a hug, thus successfully reversing a negative situation.

Chapter 30

Acting Clumsy

Some performers, such as myself, have a natural gift when it comes to acting like a klutz. For those less "fortunate," well, you'll just have to practice! This gimmick is useful when you're on your own and there's no one in the immediate area to interact with. Instead, turn your attention towards an object such as a chair. (Always choose a non-breakable item, for your own sake!)

Fumble with the item. For example, with exaggerated motions, elaborately position a chair. Once you have it in place, make a great show of sitting on the chair - and then miss. Scold the item as if it tricked you deliberately. Try to use the item again and fail but this time act disgusted and leave the object. If someone nearby has begun watching you, approach him or her and shake your head to indicate how unusable the item is. Should they proceed to interact with the abandoned item, for example sitting in the chair, act amazed at their skill!

Looking for Handouts

If you're working in a venue that has vendors, this can be a useful gimmick. It works particularly well with bottled drink vendors. However, don't use this shtick if the vendor is busy, they only sell expensive souvenir items, or there's a line of people waiting.

Go up to the vendor's stand and beg shamelessly for a drink (or whatever they're selling). Drop to your knees, clasp your hands, and make it obvious you're begging. The vendor will probably refuse to give you anything. Begin an exaggerated mime indicating that you're absolutely desperate and about to die of thirst (or hunger or simply desire). If the vendor asks for money, turn out your pockets indicating you're broke yet continue to plead for pity.

If the vendor doesn't look like he's going to play along, give a theatrical sigh and skulk away dejectedly. If the vendor relents and gives you something, act delighted. Then turn around and promptly hand it to the first child you see who is watching you. Wave cheerily at them and walk off as if this was your plan all along. If you do use this gimmick and the vendor is nice enough to play along, it would be good form to return after your performance to thank him and offer to pay for the item. You may be able to develop a working relationship and use this shtick again.

Stealing the Girl

This is a great shtick to use if you see a couple walking together. Size your targets up carefully to determine if they'd appreciate this joke before you dive in. While this works well for male characters and female audience members, if you're portraying a female character, you can turn this into "Stealing the Guy."

Begin the gimmick by holding up your hand in front of the guy, indicating that he should stop. (If they stop, they want to participate. If they keep moving, let them pass and search for a new target.) If the couple is holding hands, separate them with great show and indicate the guy should stand in a particular spot with his arms at his sides. If he plays along, give him a big "okay" sign.

Next, turn your back to him, taking position beside his date. Offer your arm to the girl and jauntily walk away with her! No need to go more than a few paces to convey the joke. If the gimmick works but her beau doesn't want to play along, walk the girl back and hook their arms together.

If they're amused and he's playing along, you can extend the scene in several ways. If he asks for you to return her, you could try to play up to her, indicating your undying love and forcing her to choose. You could act affronted and challenge him to a duel. Play off the reactions of the couple to determine what will work best and when the gimmick has worn out its welcome.

If they are enjoying the shtick, take it one step further and ham it up!

Setting Up a Photo

This gimmick works well if you see someone setting up a photo near you. It also works if you're asked to be in a photo and the cameraman is giving people directions. Instead of taking a passive stance, take control and begin setting up the photo. Go up to a person and adjust his stance slightly. Be gentle. Step back and look at them critically. Rub your chin as if carefully pondering the photo composition.

If they seem to be amused, dive in and start making more elaborate changes to their poses. Have people put their hands in the air or look in random directions. If people are wearing hats, switch them around. (You will be amazed what people will do if they are given instructions by a giant furry critter!) As a final touch, go over to the photographer and turn him so that he is facing away from the group. Then return and strike a pose of your own. Let him finally take the (now quite memorable) photo.

Normal pose: boring!

Take control. Pose the patrons into silly positions.

Have the photo taken.

Part VII

Resources & References

The craft of costuming is quite challenging, drawing on both artistic skill and academic knowledge. In this section we have collected some background information for easy reference. Also included are some sources for obtaining the materials, common and exotic, often used in animal costumes Information is current as of the printing date of this book.

For the most up-to-the minute listings of products, books and resources, visit our website, www.crittercostuming.com.

Material Safety Data Sheets (MSDS) follow this general format. The layout and detail of the information might vary but all of these topics must be included under OSHA regulations.

Product and Company Identification

The top of the form often lists general product, chemical, and manufacturer information. It may also list a company contact or emergency hotline. The header should list the date on which the MSDS was issued and/or revised.

Section I. Material Identification

Product Name: Name of product or chemical covered by this MSDS.
Other Names: Other common names for the product or chemical.
Description: Visual description of chemical, product, or packaging, as appropriate.
Formula: If the MSDS pertains to a single chemical, a chemical formula is often included.

Section II. Ingredients and Hazards

This section lists any dangerous chemicals in a product. Chemicals classified as hazardous are listed if they appear in concentrations above 1%; carcinogenic, above 0.1%. Recommended exposure limits, if known, are listed here.

Ingredient	Amount	CAS#	Exposure
Chemical	Concentration or percentage	Identification number issued by American Chemical Society	Detail on exposure limits, as LD-50* or TLV**

* Exposure limits may be in the form of known lethal doses, labeled LD-50. This represents the does capable of killing 50% of lab animals (animal type and method of exposure is usually listed) as measured in amount of chemical per kilogram of animal body weight.

** TLV refers to the Threshold Limit Value, the concentration of material to which workers may be safely routinely exposed (according to government guidelines).

Section III. Physical Data

Physical data includes chemical information such as boiling point, solubility, viscosity, density, melting point, evaporation rate, molecular weight, etc. It may include practical identification tips, most notably an **Appearance and Odor** entry.

Section IV. Fire and Explosion Data

This section includes information about fire hazards and responses specific to the chemical or product. If the item releases toxic fire byproducts, that will be noted here.

Flash Point: This is the lowest temperature at which a flammable substance releases enough vapor to form a combustible mixture in air. Working with the chemical above this temperature means a fire hazard is definitely present.
Autoignition Temperature: This is the temperature at which the chemical may spontaneously combust or explode.
Extinguishing Material: Specific recommendations are given for putting out fires involving this chemical.

Sample MSDS

Section V. Reactivity Data

Conditions to Avoid: Specific circumstances under which dangerous chemical reactions may occur.

Incompatible Materials: Other common (industrial) materials with which this chemical may react.

Hazardous Byproducts: Results of decomposition, evaporation, or natural dissipation which might be dangerous.

Hazardous Polymerization: If the chemical is capable of changing state through polymerizing, with potentially dangerous results, this heading will be included.

Section VI. Health Hazard Information

This section talks about chemical hazards resulting from exposure through inhalation, ingestion, skin absorption, eye contact and/or injection.

Inhalation: This route represents the most common danger to costumers. Note specific vapor dangers and any symptoms of low-level exposure.

Contact: This category represents absorption of chemicals through skin and membranes (e.g., eyes).

Ingestion: This lists specific hazards associated with swallowing the chemical or product.

Emergency and First Aid Procedures: Emergency treatment information is provided should someone be exposed to dangerous levels of the chemical. Be familiar with this information but don't expect it to be a substitute for proper medical treatment. Use these procedures as first aid while seeking medical care.

Section VII. Spill, Leak, and Disposal Procedures

Spill Procedure: Any unusual procedures for dealing with spilled chemicals are covered. This may include neutralizing agents which are specifically effective.

Disposal: Any requirements for safe and legal disposal are noted. Additional local requirements may apply.

Section VIII. Special Protection Information

Respiratory: Respiratory gear required for safety around this chemical.

Ventilation: Level of workplace ventilation required.

Protective Gear: Clothes, gloves, goggles, and other protective items to be worn. Note that companies do not usually determine these recommendations. They are based on government studies of the constituent chemicals. These protection guidelines are the government requirements, although companies may add extra precautions if they feel it prudent.

Section IX. Special Precautions and Comments

Storage: Special container, temperature, humidity, or other storage requirements.

Handling: Shipping and labeling notes.

This section may also provide any other general precautions or recommendations from the manufacturer.

Aljo Mfg. Co.
(866) 293–8913
www.aljodye.com

Bob's Foam Factory
(510) 657 - 2420
www.bobsfoam.com
Various foam rubbers and packing materials.

Burman Industries
(818) 782–9833
www.burmanfoam.com
Makeup, casting, and prosthetics materials.

CR's Crafts
(641) 567–3652
www.crscrafts.com
General craft supplier including fake fur.

Dharma Trading Company
(800) 542–5227
www.dharmatrading.com
Dye products, dyeable spandex, fabric paints.

Digi-Key
www.digikey.com
Electronic parts and supplies.

Douglas & Sturgess
(888) ART-STUF (278–7883)
www.artstuf.com
Variety of sculpting, casting, molding, and makeup supplies.

Lyonshel Studios
(716) 675–3364
www.lyonshel.com
Readymade animal prosthetics.

Mendel's Far Out Fabrics
(415) 621–1287
www.mendels.com
Fur and fabric retailer, accepts fur mail orders.

Manhattan Wardrobe Supply
(212) 268–9993
www.wardrobesupplies.com
Specialty cleaning supplies, adhesives, sewing notions.

Monster Makers
(216) 651–SPFX
www.monstermakers.com
Mask and casting materials, latex mask instructional books and videos.

Monterey Mills
(800) 432–9959
Fake fur manufacturer selling by the bolt.

National Fiber Technologies
(800) 842–2751
www.nftech.com
Custom and high-quality fur manufacturer.

Radio Shack
www.radioshack.com
Electronic parts and supplies.

Richard the Thread
(800) 473–4997
www.richardthethread.com
Sewing supplies, material, and notions by mail order.

Tandy Leather Company
(888) 890–1611
www.tandyleather.com
Leather, leatherworking tools, and spirit dyes.

Glossary

Accelerant - A chemical used to speed up the **curing** of an **adhesive**; unlike most adhesive **catalysts**, the **accelerant** is not required for the **adhesive** to **set**.

Acid Brush - A type of small disposable brush with a metal handle and stiff nylon bristles.

Acrylic - Acrylonitrile plastic. Used to make thread, fabrics, fake fur, and clear plastics. Lucite™ and Plexiglas™ are trade names for specific types of acrylic plastic.

Adherent - Term for a material or object being **glued** to something else. Synonym for **substrate**.

Adhesive - A bonding agent used to join two separate **substrates** so that they function as one object. Usually synonymous with **glue**.

Bias - A fancy fabric term for diagonal. A "true" bias is a diagonal direction 45 degrees from both the lengthwise and crosswise grains.

Bleach - A chemical used to "whiten" fabrics by removing unwanted colors. We commonly think of chlorine bleach, though many household "color-safe" bleaches no longer contain chlorine.

Bleeding - If color is lost into a water bath when finished material is rinsed, it is said to **bleed**. Rinses during the dye process itself do not constitute bleeding. Compare **migration**.

Bolt - Term for a full roll of fabric, as it arrives from the mill.

Carpet Needle - Another name for an upholstery needle, a specialized semi-circular needle.

CA - Abbreviation for **cyanoacrylate**.

Cast - As a noun, it refers to an item that is produced from a **mold**. The term is also commonly used to refer to the process of creating a **mold**, though this is not technically correct.

Casting - The process of creating an item inside a **mold**, or the resultant item itself. If referring to an item, the term **cast** is usually preferred.

Cartridge - Used to describe a **respirator** that uses replaceable filter **cartridges** such as **OVAG**. (Remember to check expiration dates!) Also sometimes used as a term for glue containers, especially tubes of mixable components.

Catalyst - A chemical that triggers a reaction with another chemical(s). The **catalyst** may or may not be consumed in this process.

Coloration - In this book, generally refers to the broad color patterning in an animal's fur. Smaller color details would be **markings**.

Colorfastness - A measure of how well a color treatment endures over time. Colorfastness is often separated into **lightfastness**, resistance to fading in sunlight, and **washfastness**, resistance to loss of color due to washing.

Costume - An outfit or style of dress evocative of a particular character, animal, period, or culture.

Crazing - A web of fine cracks that sometimes appear in rigid **glues** or **castings**. **Crazing** may indicate a poor chemical mix when the item was made or damage from unusual thermal expansion.

Crosswise - Perpendicular to **lengthwise**.

Curing - The chemical process (sometimes **polymerization**) by which an adhesive **sets**.

Cyanoacrylate (CA) - The technical name for superglue.

Diluent - An inert solid substance used to dilute dye and other dry weight powders.

Dilutant - A liquid in which another substance is dissolved, thereby diluting it.

Dorsal - The back side of the body; opposite of **ventral**.

Dressmaker Shears - Besides being a profession, the term **dressmaker** refers to a particular variety of scissors where the handles are offset from the blades. (This type is also called drop handle scissors.) This allows you to cut fabric while it is lying flat on a table without lifting it.

Dry - Much as you would expect, a **glue** dries when it sets via evaporative action. Usually a synonym for **set**. When referring to fabric, it may mean either air drying or drying in a machine.

Dye - A coloring agent that bonds to fibers. Dyes work by absorbing light in part(s) of the spectrum, meaning the underlying fabric reflects only other portions of the spectrum. Since dyes are *subtracting* color from white light, you cannot dye something to a lighter shade. Compare **pigment**.

Dye Bath - The large volume of water and chemicals in which dyeing occurs.

Emulsion Adhesive - A **glue** where water is used to deliver small **adhesive** particles. As the water evaporates or is absorbed, the particles leave the water dispersion and condense on the **substrate**, where a bond is formed.

Fixative - A chemical used to improve **colorfastness** that is applied *after* dyeing is completed. Compare **mordant**.

Framework Head - My term for a costume head constructed on an **underskull** that is built rather than **cast**.

Fur - As used in this book, "fur" means "synthetic fur". Any of a variety of deep-pile plush fabrics made from natural or synthetic fibers.

Fursuit - Slang for an animal costume, especially a mascot-style costume. Contraction of "fur suit".

Gel - Many adhesives pass through a **gel** phase as they transition from liquid to solid. A gel is solid enough to be unworkable. See also **pot life**.

Glover - A type of lightweight leatherworking needle. Glovers often have angular tips to help penetrate the leather without tearing.

Glue - A liquid **adhesive** that dries and hardens, traditionally one derived from animal hides. Usually used synonymously with **adhesive**.

Guard Hairs - Natural fur has longer stiffer hairs that protrude above the majority of the pelt. Some, often more expensive, synthetic furs mimic this. Guard hairs are often a different color than the regular hairs, providing variegation in the animal's coat.

Hand - With fabrics, refers to the weight, body, and feel of a fabric. Sometimes also used to describe the feel of paints applied to fabric and how they modify the texture.

HDPE - Abbreviation for High-Density Polyethylene. See **polyethylene**.

Kicker - Slang term for an **accelerant**, especially with **CA**.

LDPE - Abbreviation for Low-Density Polyethylene. See **polyethylene**.

Lengthwise - In fabrics, refers to the grain of the fabric parallel to the **selvage edge**. Otherwise refers to distance along the long dimension of the body.

Lifecast - A **cast** reproduction of a person. **Lifecasts** are usually made of the head (down to the shoulders) or just the face. It is possible, though, to make **lifecasts** of any part or the entire body.

Lightfastness - Resistance of a color to fading when exposed to sunlight, particularly ultraviolet.

Lycra™ - The trade name DuPont uses for their blended **spandex** fabrics. It's often mistakenly used as a synonym for **spandex**.

Markings - As used in this book, refers to localized fur color effects. This is in contrast to the larger scale color changes which are the **coloration** of the animal.

Material Safety Data Sheet (MSDS) - Government-regulated summary sheet for dangerous chemicals and products. All manufacturers provide an **MSDS** for their products containing toxic or hazardous chemicals; sometimes they're available at the point of sale. Many companies make their **MSDS**s available online. The sheet summarizes import information such as health risks, handling precautions, and safety equipment.

Migration - The spread of colors to adjacent pieces of fabric. Usually this happens as a result of an improperly bonded dye or pigment seeping within a material. Compare **bleeding**.

Modacrylic - A synthetic plastic that is between 35% and 85% acrylic (*acrylonitrile*). Used to make thread, fabrics, and fake fur.

Mold - A concave hollow in which objects may be **cast**. Usually created by covering an object to be reproduced with a liquid that hardens (e.g. cement, plaster, rubber, plastic), such that the inside of the **mold** exactly matches the surface details of the original object. **Molding** is a term sometimes used to mean the creation of molds, but also the **casting** of objects in a **mold**.

Monomer - A small molecule (or solution of such molecules) that can hook together to form a **polymer**. For example, **cyanoacrylate** is a monomer that reacts to make **acrylic**.

Mordant - Some dyes, especially natural dyes, do not create strong bonds with fibers. A mordant is added during the dyeing process to help the dye bond more effectively, increasing intensity and **colorfastness**. Most mordants are metallic salts (chromium is commonly used in the form of *potassium dichromate*) and can be quite toxic. Fortunately, very few modern dyes require separate mordants. Compare **fixative**.

MSDS - Abbreviation for **Material Safety Data Sheet**.

Nap - A fuzzy or short-pile fabric surface. Also, the direction fibers in the pile of a material tend to naturally flow. In this book, I tend to use **nap** to indicate direction and **pile** to indicate surface texture.

Neoprene - The first synthetic rubber to be discovered, **neoprene** (chemically speaking, **polychloroprene**) is famed for its use in wetsuits. You may occasionally run into it in costuming materials and as a basis for adhesives.

Nylon - A family of plastics used to make thread, fiber, and fabric. Sometimes use to make **fur**.

OVAG - Abbreviation for "Organic Vapor/Acid Gas". One of the common **respirator cartridges** used in costuming to protect against things such as thinner and adhesive fumes.

PETE - Abbreviation for polyethylene terephthalate. See **polyethylene**.

Pigment - A colored particulate substance that is water insoluble. Pigments do not bond directly to fibers; instead, they must be adhered by another agent. Paints are examples of pigment systems. Synthetic fibers are often colored by adding pigments during the fiber's manufacture, trapping pigment within an otherwise clear fiber. Compare **dye**.

Pile - Fibers extending above the surface of a fabric to create a furry or fuzzy effect.

Glossary

Plush- A fabric with a distinct **nap** on its surface. Often used as a term for fur with a short (quarter-inch) nap. Sometimes refers to the stuffed animals (i.e. "plush toy") which are often made from this sort of fur.

Polychloroprene - The rubber polymer used to make **neoprene**.

Polyester - Synthetic fiber used to create an era of really bad clothing. One of the hardest materials to dye post-production. **Polyester** is made from a member of the **polyethylene** family of plastics.

Polyethylene - A variety of plastic often used to make containers and a variety of molded plastic objects. Polyethylene comes in many forms, including low-density (LDPE), high-density (HDPE), and polyethylene terephthalate (PETE, which is actually the plastic used to make **polyester** fibers). **Polyethylene** is also used to make a variety of foam products.

Polymer - A long molecule made from a repeating series of small units; the small units, **monomers**, hook together to form a giant chain, the **polymer**. By extension, a material composed of such molecules. Plastics are examples of polymers. Many adhesives use **polymerization** to create bonds.

Polymerization - The chemical reaction whereby **monomers** join together to form a **polymer**.

Polypropylene - A tough and flexible variety of plastic often used in containers. Identified by a number 5 in the plastics recycling symbol.

Polystyrene - The variety of plastic used to make **Styrofoam**, identified by the number 6 in the plastics recycling symbol.

Polyurethane - A flexible polymer used to manufacture a wide variety of items. Almost every padded chair in the world contains **polyurethane** foam cushions. Many paints contain polyurethane to increase their durability. **Spandex** fabric is a polyurethane derivative.

Polyvinyl Chloride - A tough and durable plastic known for its use in pipes and plumbing fittings. Occasionally useful in costuming, especially as framing elements. **PVC** can be identified by the number 3 in the plastics recycling symbol.

Pot Life - The working time for a glue, measured from when the glue is poured or mixed to when it gets too thick to apply.

PP - Abbreviation for **polypropylene**.

PVC - Abbreviation for **polyvinyl chloride**.

Raglan - A type of sleeve (or sewing pattern featuring such a sleeve) where the arm pieces go all the way up to the neck. This is in contrast to modern shirt patterns (featuring "set-in sleeves") where the sleeve ends in a circular seam at the shoulder.

Respirator - Filtering mask completely enclosing nose and mouth, similar to a gas mask. Most industrial **respirators** use **cartridges** rated for different inhalation hazards.

Room Temperature - If instructions use this term, they generally mean 65-70° F with low to moderate humidity.

Room Temperature Vulcanization - The ability of a rubber compound to **vulcanize** without external heating (**thermosetting**).

RTV - Abbreviation for **Room Temperature Vulcanization**.

Sizing - A treatment applied to fabric or thread to affect its **hand** or stain-resistance. **Sizing** is usually in the form of a chemical which coats the fibers; this will interfere with **dye** absorption.

Soaping - Immediately after dyeing and rinsing, fabrics should be washed with a mild detergent and then rinsed again. This process, **soaping**, helps to remove unbonded dye from the material and thus prevent **bleeding** and **migration** of colors. This term is also occasionally heard in **casting** to mean the application of a mold release agent or sealer, which might or might not actually be soap-based.

Seam Allowance - In a sewing pattern, it's assumed that the seam will be inset a short distance from the edge of the fabric. When machine sewing, this gives the feed mechanism a chance to grip the fabric evenly. The distance between the edge of a pattern piece and the actual seam centerline is known as the **seam allowance**. Commercial patterns should list what **seam allowance** they are factoring into their designs.

Selvage Edge - The finished edges of the fabric made as part of the knitting process. The selvage in fur is usually a double thickness of backing running parallel to the nap and should not be included in any pattern cuts, even as **seam allowance**.

Set - In glue terms, when an adhesive has become solid, even if not yet at full strength.

Shag - Term sometimes applied to fur with a deep pile. Can also mean a decorative fringe. Costumers rarely use it to mean a style of carpeting.

Sharp - A needle with a sharply-pointed tip is sometimes just called a sharp.

Spandex -A stretchy fiber used to make the fabric of the same name. Technically known as "elastane", this synthetic material is a close cousin of the **polyurethane** used in foam rubber. Most "**spandex**" fabrics are actually a blend of spandex and cotton fibers. **Spandex** is often incorrectly called **Lycra**™, which is a specific brand name.

Spirit Dye -Any alcohol-based dye. Commonly used to stain leather.

Solid Grin - My term for a cartoon-style smile composed of two rows of solid teeth. It can be built from a single curved plastic surface with black dividing lines added.

Solvent - A chemical able to dissolve, liquefy, or loosen another substance. Compare **dilutant**.

Stretch -In fabrics, the ability to elongate and then return to shape. Measured as a percentage increase in length when fully stretched. **Stretch** on fabrics is usually different **lengthwise** than **crosswise**.

Styrofoam™ - A lightweight and rigid material made from foamed **polystyrene** plastic. Because it's not very strong and reacts to many glues and paints, it's not an ideal material for costuming. **Styrofoam**™ is the brand name owned by Dow Chemical.

Substrate - Term for a material or object being **glued** to something else. Synonym for **adherent**.

Tacky - In costuming, it can mean either sticky to the touch or gaudy and tasteless. Or, if you're good at subtle insults, it can mean both at once.

Thermoset - Describes an **adhesive** that requires heat in order to **set** or the process of applying that heat.

Underskull - Refers specifically to the shell or structure upon which a costume head is built. Heads containing articulated or animated pieces almost always have a rigid underskull to which the mechanics may be anchored.

Urethane - Often a shorthand name for **polyurethane**, a common synthetic rubber. The term **urethane** is also commonly used in **casting** circles where it refers to the **RTV urethane** monomer mixes used to create rubberized **molds**.

Ventral - Antonym of **dorsal**, the **ventral** side of the body contains the abdominal and chest area. From our costuming standpoint, animals often have lighter fur on the ventral surface as part of their coloration. This lighter contrasting color is sometimes reduced to just a "belly patch."

Volatile - Can describe inflammables, substances that evaporate (e.g. "volatile organic compounds"), or a costumer facing a looming deadline.

Vulcanize - The process of **vulcanizing** rubber involves the application of heat in conjunction with sulfur and chemical accelerants. This changes the chemical structure of the rubber to make it harder, stiffer, and much more durable. Rubbers treated in this way are referred to as **vulcanized**. The **vulcanization** process can also happen during a regular **curing** process if the components have been pre-treated. This is called **Room Temperature Vulcanization (RTV)**.

Washfastness - A color's resistance to fading from washing.

Selected Bibliography

Adams, Norman and Joe Singer. *Drawing Animals.* Watson-Guptill Publications, 1989.

Allison, Drew and Donald Devet. **The Foam Book: An Easy Guide to Building Polyfoam Puppets.** Grey Seal Puppets Inc., 1997.

Armstrong, Helen Joseph. *Patternmaking for Fashion Design.* Prentice Hall, 1999.

Betzina, Sandra. *Fabric Savvy: The Essential guide for Every Sewer.* Taunton Press, 2002.

Dalby, Gill and Liz Christmas. *Spinning and Dyeing: An Introductory Manual.* David & Charles, 1985.

Dryden, Deborah. *Fabric Painting and Dyeing for the Theater.* Heinemann, 1993.

Ellenberger, Wllhelm. *An Atlas of Animal Anatomy for Artists.* Dover Publications, 1956.

Francois, Ber and Guineau Delamare. *Colors: The Story of Dyes and Pigments.* Harry N. Abrams, 2000.

Hamm, Jack. *How to Draw Animals.* Perigee Books, 1982.

Hultgren, Ken. *The Art of animal Drawing: Construction, Action Analysis, Caricature.* Dover Publications, 1993.

Ingham, Rosemary and Liz Covey. *The Costume Technician's Handbook: A Complete Guide for Amateur and Professional Costume Technicians.* Heinemann, 1992.

James, Thurston. *The Prop Builder's Mask-Making Handbook.* F&W Publications, 1990.

James, Thurston. *The Prop Builder's Molding & Casting Handbook.* Betterway Publications, 1990.

Kehoe, Vincent J-R. *Special Make-Up Effects.* Focal Press, 1991.

Laury, Jean Ray. *Imagery On Fabric.* Watson-Guptill, 1993.

Moss, Sylvia. *Costumes and Chemistry: A Comprehensive Guide to Materials and Applications.* Quite Specific Media Group Ltd., 2001.

The Reader's Digest Association, Inc. *Reader's Digest Complete Guide to Sewing.* Reader's Digest Publishing, 2001.

Rogers, Barb. *Costuming Made Easy: How to Make Theatrical Costumes from Cast-Off Clothing.* Meriweather Publishing, Ltd., 1999.

Rosen, Sylvia. *Patternmaking: A Comprehensive Reference for Fashion Design.* Prentice Hall, 2003.

Sartor, David and John Pivovarnick. **Theatrical FX Makeup.** Heinemann, 2001.

Strand-Evans, Katherine. **Costume Construction.** Waveland Press, Inc., 1999.

Walter, Cindy and Jennifer Priestley. *The Basic Guide to Dyeing & Painting Fabric.* Krause Publications, 2002.